OBSCENE IN THE EXTREME

OBSCENE
IN THE
EXTREME

———◆———

The Burning and Banning
of John Steinbeck's
The Grapes of Wrath

RICK WARTZMAN

PublicAffairs
New York

Published in the United States by PublicAffairs™,
a member of the Perseus Books Group.

The author gratefully acknowledges permission to quote from the following:
"Some Random and Randy Thoughts on Books," from *America and Americans and Selected Nonfiction* by John Steinbeck, edited by Susan Shillinglaw & J. Benson, copyright © 2002 by Elaine Steinbeck and Thomas Steinbeck. Used by permission of Viking Penguin, a division of Penguin Group (USA) Inc.
The Grapes of Wrath by John Steinbeck, copyright 1939, renewed © by John Steinbeck. Used by permission of Viking Penguin, a division of Penguin Group (USA) Inc.
"Salinas 1939," from *Dustbowl Okie Exodus* by Dorothy Rose, copyright © 1987. Used by permission of Seven Buffaloes Press.

PublicAffairs books are available at special discounts for bulk purchases in the U.S. by corporations, institutions, and other organizations. For more information, please contact the Special Markets Department at the Perseus Books Group, 2300 Chestnut Street, Suite 200, Philadelphia, PA 19103, call (800) 810-4145, ext. 5000, or e-mail special.markets@perseusbooks.com.

Designed by Brent Wilcox
Text set in 11.25 point Adobe Caslon

Library of Congress Cataloging-in-Publication Data
Wartzman, Rick.
    Obscene in the extreme : the burning and banning of John Steinbeck's The grapes of wrath / Rick Wartzman. — 1st ed.
        p.   cm.
    Includes bibliographical references and index.
    ISBN 978-1-58648-331-9
    1. Steinbeck, John, 1902-1968. Grapes of wrath.   2. Steinbeck, John, 1902-1968—Censorship.   3. Challenged books.   4. Prohibited books.
5. Censorship.   I. Title.
    PS3537.T3234G895 2008
    813'.52—dc22

                                                                    2008014948

First Edition

10 9 8 7 6 5 4 3 2 1

*For Randye, because I love you madly.
And for Emma and Nathaniel,
who make each day better and brighter.*

A book is somehow sacred. A dictator can kill and maim people, can sink to any kind of tyranny and only be hated, but when books are burned, the ultimate in tyranny has happened. This we cannot forgive.

—JOHN STEINBECK

Contents

CHAPTER ONE

Dark Days

"I 'member you. You're one of these here trouble-makers."

"Damn right," said Tom. "I'm bolshevisky."

T HE LIGHTS DIMMED and dimmed some more, and darkness fell upon the Big Room. No one talked or even dared to breathe too loudly. The children had been shushed, whispers stifled, and cigarettes snuffed. The only sound to be heard was the *thwack-thwack-thwack* of limestone water dripping onto rock. It is impossible to know, of course, what those in the crowd felt as this black blanket swallowed them completely, engulfing the afterglow and playing tricks on their eyes. They had come here, to Carlsbad Caverns, to vacation and take their minds off their workaday concerns; and for some, sitting 750 feet below the surface of the earth, surveying a gargantuan stalagmite known as the Rock of Ages, this undoubtedly was the high point of their trip. Before the lights had gone out, the tourists had soaked in the spectacle: several million years old, wrinkled and tinted with orange, rising up nearly forty feet, as huge as a house. The Rock of Ages was such a wonder that Robert Ripley, Mr. Believe It or Not, had visited this spot just weeks earlier to make a radio broadcast, his voice carried upward by telephone cables and then out across the country by CBS. And yet one can imagine that for others, descending deep into the ground and watching the last trace of light vanish would have brought feelings not of joy and adventure, but of angst and foreboding. It wouldn't have taken much of a leap, in those thirty seconds when all was quiet and still, to see that darkness was settling upon the world as well.

It was an uneasy time, late summer 1939. Hitler's troops were amassed along the fifteen-hundred-mile German-Polish border. The Soviets and Japanese clashed along Mongolia's Khalka River. And Franco was ruthlessly consolidating his power in Spain. At home, America teetered on the edge of war. The worst of the Depression was over, but the economy was still sick. The Roosevelt Recession—in which industrial production had tumbled by 40 percent, unemployment had jumped by four million, and stock prices had plunged by nearly 50 percent—was barely more than a year past. The jobless rate hovered above 17 percent, and personal income and total economic output were no higher than they had been a decade before. Even the national pastime had taken on a melancholy cast: in June, Yankees slugger Lou Gehrig had been diagnosed with amyotrophic lateral sclerosis, cutting short his extraordinary career. He may have just described himself as "the luckiest man on the face of this earth," but it seemed like an awfully tough break for a thirty-six-year-old dubbed "the Iron Horse." As for politics, things were as crazy as ever. President Roosevelt's popularity had ebbed in the last few years, and a volatile mixture of -isms was boiling and bubbling all over the place—Communism, Socialism, Fascism, Coughlinism, Longism, Townsendism. It was hard to tell sometimes which one might slosh out of the pot and stick.

Of all the eyes staring into the cave, among the weariest must have been Gretchen Knief's. She had trekked to New Mexico by way of the South and was on her way back home, to California's San Joaquin Valley, where she was the chief librarian for Kern County. She was a tall woman, impeccably dressed, her smile warm. No one would have called the thirty-seven-year-old a beauty, and she could be a little awkward at times. But it was an endearing awkwardness, and everybody admired her smarts. Knief had spent a portion of her trip examining libraries in Florida and Louisiana, and she had walked away feeling pleased with how Kern County's far-flung network of seventy-one branches, many of which she had single-handedly expanded, stacked up by comparison. But pressures were mounting too. Kern's main library was housed in the basement of the county courthouse in Bakersfield, in quarters so cramped that some of its materials were buried beneath old lighting fixtures, furniture, and other bric-a-brac. A proposed $300,000 bond issue to finance a new facility was scheduled to go before the voters in the fall. But who knew what they'd decide, given the budget squeeze afflicting the county? The situation showed no signs of easing, either, the way people were still streaming in to California's heartland, taxing public services of all kinds. "Authorities Predict Increase in Migrant Flow to Kern Soon," read the headline in the August 7 edition of the *Bakersfield Californian*.

The exodus had been underway for nearly a decade, with as many as four hundred thousand folks from Oklahoma, Arkansas, Texas, Missouri, and other states flocking to California in search of a better life. They were by no means exclusively poor. But many were. And the plight of these human tumbleweeds, as one observer had labeled them, had by now worked its way into the national consciousness. Leading periodicals had sent their correspondents to rural outposts up and down Highway 99 to chronicle the suffering. "Uncle Sam Has His Own Refugee Problem," the *Providence Journal* declared during the spring. "Lured to the West, They Find Misery, Squalor, Disease." *Collier's* magazine put it this way: "Perhaps the native and adopted sons of California pitched their voices a note or two too high when they warbled praises of the Golden State. Anyway, they got the idea across, and now they're sorry. An army is marching into California—an army made up of penniless unemployed, desperately seeking Utopia. 'Here we are,' say the invaders, 'what're you going to do about us?' And nobody knows the answer."

Children on their way to California in the 1930s, part of the great exodus made during the decade by as many as four hundred thousand migrants from Oklahoma, Arkansas, Texas, and elsewhere. (Photo by Dorothea Lange, Library of Congress)

That may have been a tad hyperbolic, but coming up with answers was in no way simple. Kern County, for one, had seen its population swell by more than 60 percent in the last five years, and although health officers had cleaned up the squatter camps that once plagued the area, many migrants were still living in slums with inadequate sewers and drains, ramshackle houses, and litter-strewn dirt roads that would turn to mud after a hard winter rain. Who, though, was culpable for such conditions? Were they the fault of a grudging local government? Or were the newcomers themselves guilty somehow? Many suggested as much. The migrant community in Kern was branded as being full of "drunks, chiselers, exploiters and social leeches"—and that was in an official county report that had just been released. The language used on the street was even more blunt; in the lobby of a Bakersfield movie theater, a sign was posted: "Negroes and Okies Upstairs."

An alternative view, however, had also found its voice. This one laid the blame for the migrants' deprivation at the door of California agriculture, an industry that since the late nineteenth century had been defined by one main thing: its enormity. The state's giant landowners had made a travesty of the Jeffersonian ideal of 160 acres, assembling dominions that ballooned to one thousand times or more that size. "We no longer raise wheat here," said one grower. "We manufacture it." This wasn't family farming; it was agribusiness. And with it came a caste system in which relatively few got rich while many remained mired in the worst sort of poverty: Chinese in the 1870s, Japanese two decades later, Hindustanis early in the new century, Mexicans and Filipinos during and after World War I. Joining this ethnic parade were Armenians and Portuguese, Italians and Swiss—wave after wave of low-priced labor. Among the leviathan landholders were those who took care of their workers, some patronizingly, others with a genuine measure of respect. But many big farmers regarded their hands as expendable—"beasts of the field," in the words of an 1888 edition of the *Kern County Californian*. In many ways, things hadn't changed much in the fifty years since that description had been written, and with the Okies and Arkies now faring so terribly, social critics were pointing their fingers at California's agricultural elite.

The most articulate and powerful of the finger-pointers was author John Steinbeck, whose book *The Grapes of Wrath* had not only leapt onto the best-seller list after its publication in April but was also well on its way to becoming seared into the public's imagination forever. Darryl Zanuck was already busy with the film version of the story, starring Henry Fonda, and Woody Guthrie would soon record his ode to Steinbeck's protagonist, Tom Joad: *Wherever little children are hungry and cry / Wherever people ain't free. / Wherever men are fightin' for their rights, / That's where I'm gonna be, Ma. / That's where I'm a gonna be.* First Lady Eleanor Roosevelt had called her reading of *The Grapes of Wrath* "an unforgettable experience." And in the coming months, the president would tell the nation that he, too, had read of the Joads' journey from the bone-dry plains of Oklahoma to the bountiful lands of California, where they and others toiled away for a pittance and found themselves wishing "them big farmers wouldn' plague us so." "There are 500,000 Americans," the president said, "that live in the covers of that book." By 1940, *The Grapes of Wrath* would be invoked so often that it almost seemed to cheapen the novel. Good Samaritans, looking to raise money to aid the migrants, would hold "Grapes of Wrath" parties. The union seeking to organize California's farm fields—the United Cannery, Agricultural, Packing and Allied Workers of America—recruited five young Broadway actors to tour the West and Southwest, with ticket sales going into UCAPAWA's coffers. The troupe's name: The Grapes of Wrath Players. Meanwhile, pundits of all stripes would reference the Joads in articles and speeches, as if they were real: "Meet the Joad Family," "The Joad Family in Kern County," "What's Being Done About the Joads?" "The Joads on Strike." Men began to wear a hat called the "Joad Cap."

Knief peered into the inky cavern, and slowly the lights came up, like a sunrise in the distance. Then a ranger's voice washed over the Big Room:

> *Rock of Ages, cleft for me,*
> *Let me hide myself in Thee;*
> *Let the water and the blood,*
> *From Thy wounded side which flowed,*
> *Be of sin the double cure;*
> *Save from wrath and make me pure.*

In that very instant, it is conceivable that Knief and all the others assembled in the Big Room let their worries—the weight resting on "our troubled and confused generation," as she once expressed it—melt away. Whether that sense of tranquility lasted very long is another matter. As Knief headed back to Bakersfield, her vacation done, she motored along Route 66, the same stretch of highway on which the migrants "scuttled like bugs to the westward," as Steinbeck wrote. The Mother Road, as she was known, was the path to California's promise. Knief counted herself a Steinbeck devotee, having briefly met him during one of his research outings to the area. And on the eve of the publication of *The Grapes of Wrath*, she had lauded him as "one of our major creative writers in America today," a literary force on par with Faulkner, Hemingway, Saroyan, and Dos Passos. In "The Reading Hour," a column that she wrote for the Bakersfield paper, Knief had also noted that this tale of migratory labor was bound to be "of more than passing interest" to local readers.

As she'd soon discover, that would prove to be quite an understatement.

The classical revival courthouse in downtown Bakersfield, which held the chambers of the Kern County Board of Supervisors, was a stately structure, with freestanding Corinthian columns rising skyward, the parapet over the main pavilion decorated with bas-relief figures, and the exterior clad in white Manti stone. It gave the entire edifice a benign glow. Inside room 213, however, the affairs conducted by the five members of the board—bellies pressed against three-piece suits, dour faces cast downward over sheaves of paperwork—were decidedly drab. Regardless of the level of government, it's axiomatic: the public's business is tedious business. This was particularly true in a place such as Kern County, where the board had a special gift for making the head throb and the eyes glaze. The meeting of Monday, August 21, 1939, gaveled into session at 10:15 a.m., gave little hint of defying this dreary routine. The supervisors began by approving the minutes from the previous week's meeting and swiftly dispensed with a few other perfunctory tasks. After that came a motion from Supervisor Charles Wimmer, seconded by Supervisor C. W. Harty, to authorize a series of payments to those who had fortified the Kern River levee: $4.50 to Baker Machine Company for welding; $66.19 to Fred L. Gribble for miscellaneous expenses; $7.31 to Pioneer Mercantile Company for materials. "Ayes?" A small chorus of "ayes" filled the room. "Noes?" Silence. Next up: more payments to vendors, followed by the formal filing of a county insurance policy, no. B0 2729010, with American Surety of New York. And so it went, on and on, through forty-six agenda items—all of them equally humdrum, all of them unanimously accepted without debate—until, suddenly, without any fanfare, it happened.

Supervisor Stanley Abel—gruff, stubborn, thick-necked Stanley Abel—broke the monotony by blindsiding his colleagues. The resolution he introduced went like this:

WHEREAS, John Steinbeck's work of fiction, *The Grapes of Wrath*, has offended our citizenry by falsely implying that many of our fine people are a low, ignorant, profane and blasphemous type living in a vicious and filthy manner, and

WHEREAS, Steinbeck presents our public officials, law enforcement officers and civil administrators, businessmen, farmers and ordinary citizens as inhumane vigilantes, breathing class hatred and divested of sympathy or human decency or understanding toward a great, and to us unwelcome, economic problem brought about by an astounding influx of refugees, indigent farmers, who were dusted or tractored or foreclosed out of Oklahoma, Kansas, Nebraska, Arkansas, Missouri, Texas and others of our sister states, and

WHEREAS, Steinbeck chose to ignore the education, recreation, hospitalization, welfare and relief services, unexcelled by any other political subdivision in the United States, made available by Kern County to every person resident in Kern County, and

WHEREAS, *Grapes of Wrath* is filled with profanity, lewd, foul and obscene language unfit for use in American homes, therefore, be it

RESOLVED, that we, the BOARD OF SUPERVISORS, in defense of our free enterprise and of people who have been unduly wronged, request that production of the motion picture film, *Grapes of Wrath*, adapted from the Steinbeck novel, not be completed by Twentieth Century-Fox Film Corporation and request that use and posses-

Stanley Abel blindsided his colleagues on the Kern County Board of Supervisors when he introduced the resolution to keep *The Grapes of Wrath* out of schools and libraries. (Kern County Museum)

sion and circulation of the novel, *Grapes of Wrath*, be banned from our library and schools.

There is no record that Abel's proposal was discussed at all. Seconded by Harty, it was promptly put to a vote and passed, four to one. The lone dissenter was Ralph Lavin, the most liberal member of the board. Without pause, the supervisors then returned to their regular regime—"On motion of Supervisor Abel, seconded by Supervisor Harty, it is ordered that Requisition nos. 13838–13846 . . . are hereby approved"—which lent a surreal quality to the whole episode. With no fuss made, it was almost as if nothing extraordinary had happened, as if these five men—an erstwhile building contractor, bank teller, grocer, newspaper publisher, and pharmacist—hadn't just censored the most popular book in the country. Were they being cavalier? Or had Abel caught them so off-guard, they never had time to react, to think? At five past noon, after ripping through fourteen more items, Board Chairman Roy Woollomes adjourned the meeting. The supervisors stood up from their hard-backed chairs, an American flag behind them, and ambled out.

Several floors below, in the courthouse basement, Gretchen Knief was busy at work, trying to navigate reentry. Returning from vacation is never pleasant, and one wonders if Knief even found time to read the newspaper that day. Had she, she may well have noticed a front-page article in the *Californian* that detailed local reaction to the banning of *The Grapes of Wrath* the week before in the libraries of Kansas City. Annette Moore, one of four members of the Board of Education in Missouri voting to repress the novel, had condemned its vulgarity, saying that "it portrays life in such a bestial way." Moore was far from alone in her judgment. Earlier in the month, the public librarian in Buffalo, New York, had refused to acquire *The Grapes of Wrath* on the grounds that "once in a while some book comes along at which we have to draw the line." Other libraries, including those in Trenton, New Jersey; San Francisco; and Detroit confined *The Grapes of Wrath* to "closed shelves." In East St. Louis, Illinois, the library board would soon vote to burn the three copies of the book it had in its collection. Aboard the U.S.S. *Tennessee*, the chaplain removed *The Grapes of Wrath* from the ship's library, even though more than fifty men were on the waiting list to read it. And for at least a time, the U.S. Postal Service barred the novel from the mails.

The story out of Bakersfield that morning noted that the Associated Farmers of California, a group representing the interests of the state's biggest growers, had wired Kansas City with thanks and congratulations. "We hope their action will be the forerunner of a widespread denouncement against the book before schools open and our boys and girls find such filthy material on the shelves of our public libraries," said Bill Camp, president of the Associated Farmers chapter in Kern County.

Whether Knief had paid attention to Camp's comments or not, she was totally taken aback when, around 3:00 p.m., the secretary of the Board of Supervisors showed up at her spare office and handed her a copy of the resolution ordering that *The Grapes of Wrath* be removed from her own library system. "We had not had a single complaint on the book from any patron," she pointed out later. Until that moment, "No one had even suggested that we restrict circulation" of Steinbeck's work, much less ban it outright. Knief gathered herself and shot upstairs. There, she found one supervisor still lingering in chambers—Stanley Abel. She pressed him on who was behind the resolution and, after some hesitation, he explained that he had asked Emory Gay Hoffman, head of the Kern County Chamber of Commerce, to craft the ban. "Won't Kern County get a lot of publicity out of this?" Abel said, adding that the hullabaloo might even encourage the federal government to focus on the migrants' dire condition and chip in more for relief; Washington had been cutting back on aid for several years now. Abel also fretted about some of the language that Steinbeck had used, but Knief didn't take this too seriously. Although he "stressed the immorality of the book," she'd recall, "the true reason for the ban was economic."

It was difficult to argue with Knief's appraisal. *The Grapes of Wrath* had helped to put the valley's entire wage structure in jeopardy—once again—by emboldening organized labor. The United Cannery, Agricultural, Packing and Allied Workers of America "is turning the Joads' struggle for a decent living into a successful struggle," the union's president, Donald Henderson, declared. "Every community which is alive to the need for agricultural organization, which has been impressed by Steinbeck's *Grapes of Wrath* . . . must give their active support." Hoffman, meanwhile, griped that tourist travel along Highway 99 had fallen off markedly since Steinbeck had sullied Kern's reputation. And Bill Camp questioned how long the county, with its limited finances and a population that had already reached 135,000, could continue to swallow a tide of down-and-out souls that seemed to have no end. "It stands to reason," he said, "that unless steps are taken to halt this migration at its source we cannot hope to cope with the increasing burden of the problem."

On some level, Knief could understand the frustration. It was just five years earlier, before anybody had heard of the Joads, that Abel and his fellow supervisors were being lauded for reaching out to help the migrants—one thousand of whom had congregated on the outskirts of Bakersfield in tattered tents and shacks of tin and paper. "The Kern County Board of Supervisors, one of the best I've seen, has tried to do something about these colonies," Lorena Hickok, sent on a fact-finding mission by Harry Hopkins, chief of FDR's Federal Emergency Relief Administration, reported back to Washington in August 1934. "The townspeople object to the camps being cleaned up because they think a clean camp will attract more of these people. However, near one town, the supervisors leased a piece of land, piped in some water, built some community toilets, and have let the people move in."

Knief herself had made sure that the county stocked the libraries at the migratory farm-worker camps near the towns of Arvin and Shafter. And, most notably, Kern continued to be the only county in the state providing free medical care to migrants, footing the bill for three-quarters of all Okie babies delivered at the general hospital in 1939. One historian would come to call the county's health policy "the most enlightened" in rural California. But, despite such efforts, the crisis had gotten worse and worse, and now, Steinbeck had poisoned everything, painting a "mental image of Kern County," as one journalist put it, "as a land of squalor, starvation and despair."

Still, censorship? Wasn't that how the Nazis behaved? Wasn't that a tactic of Fascists?

That night—with the news of the Kern County vote having knocked the Kansas City story off the front page in the paper's final edition—Knief wrote a letter and sent it to Abel and the three other board members who had backed the ban. "I was extremely sorry, both as librarian of our proud and free Kern County Library and as an intelligent adult reader," she began, to have been presented notice of "the first instance of . . . censorship in the entire history" of the institution. Knief knew that Abel was a bully—"He enjoys nothing better than a good fight," she once said—and she was always cognizant of her standing as an employee of the county, appointed by the supervisors and serving at their pleasure. But as the daughter of a German newspaper editor from Milwaukee, she was also spirited—a "combination of an idealist and a realist," as one of her former staffers remembered her. Casting aside any sense of propriety or fear she may have felt, Knief let her passion pour onto the page:

Kern County librarian Gretchen Knief, pictured here with a group of school children, was taken aback by the censoring of *The Grapes of Wrath*. "If that book is banned today, what will be banned tomorrow?" she asked. (Kern County Museum)

I realize only too well that this resolution may have been "sprung on the board," that all kinds of pressure may have been brought to bear on you, that any number of things may have happened to make it seem advisable to pass such a resolution. But the thing that worries me is that "it could happen here." If that book is banned today, what will be banned tomorrow? And what group will want a book banned the day after that? It's such a vicious and dangerous thing to begin and may in the end lead to exactly the same thing we see in Europe today.

Besides, banning books is so utterly hopeless and futile. Ideas don't die because a book is forbidden reading. If Steinbeck has written the truth, that truth will survive. If he is merely being sensational and lascivious, if all the 'little words' are really more than fly specks on a large painting, then the book will soon go the way of all other modern novels and be forgotten.

Furthermore, Kern County does not need to follow Kansas City or any other group. Kern County needs no defense, because we can honestly look the world in the face and say that we have done more for the migrants than all the rest. And for that reason all adults in Kern County should have the privilege of reading The Grapes of Wrath if they want to so that they can go out and tell the world where Steinbeck has erred. Will you not, therefore, in the interest of a healthy and vigorous democracy, where everyone can speak his mind freely and without fear, and for the sake of the . . . readers in Kern County who still wish to read the book, please rescind today's motion when you meet next Monday?

If only it had been that simple.

———•———

California's San Joaquin Valley offers no shortage of interminable views—field after field of grain and cotton and vegetables that unfurl clear to the horizon. The Sierra and the Coast Range sit along the eastern and western flanks, some fifty miles apart, but you have to be close enough to one, on a blue-sky day, to see its rock walls rising. Ride out into the long valley's big middle, away from the nearest town, and you're apt to find a vista unbroken by so much as a hummock. William H. Brewer, an early explorer, beheld "a tedious plain . . . as boundless as the sea." The Spanish, too, knew the vast region as *llano*—the flatland. A certain beauty can be found in this endlessness; ennui has been known to summon mirages. But for others, the effect is exactly the opposite. One son of the San Joaquin has painted the landscape this way: "so empty, so consuming of human imagination."

Kern County, though, has always been different. By dint of being located at the valley's southern end, it stands in the shadow of another mountain range, the Tehachapis, and as such it is both the gateway to the San Joaquin and, coming from the other direction, its exit door.

You can't help but look up at the tawny hills, stretching to more than four thousand feet, and dream of what's on the other side; here, the imagination stirs anew. The reverie works in reverse, as well. From atop the mountain, or clambering down its backside, Kern spreads out before you like an oversized quilt. It's a dazzling sight, bursting with possibilities. Steinbeck's Joads rumbled toward this panorama by way of the Mojave Desert—a bleak environment "that supports no man," as Mary Austin remarked in *The Land of Little Rain*—and then, all at once, they saw it: a place of such abundance that it helped support the entire nation.

THEY drove through Tehachapi in the morning glow, and the sun came up behind them . . . Al jammed on the brake and stopped in the middle of the road, and, "Jesus Christ! Look!" he said. The vineyards, the orchards, the great flat valley, green and beautiful, the trees set in rows, and the farm houses.

And Pa said, "God Almighty!" The distant cities, the little towns in the orchard land, and the morning sun, golden on the valley. A car honked behind them. Al pulled to the side of the road and parked.

"I want to look at her." The grain fields golden in the morning, and the willow lines, the eucalyptus trees in rows.

Pa sighed, "I never knowed they was anything like her." The peach trees and the walnut groves, and the dark green patches of oranges. And red roofs among the trees, and barns—rich barns. Al got out and stretched his legs.

He called, "Ma—come look. We're there!"

Ruthie and Winfield scrambled down from the car, and then they stood, silent and awestruck, embarrassed before the great valley. The distance was thinned with haze, and the land grew softer and softer in the distance. A windmill flashed in the sun, and its turning blades were like a heliograph, far away. Ruthie and Winfield looked at it, and Ruthie whispered, "It's California."

This agricultural paradise had not materialized by accident or, for that matter, from the hand of God. Had the Joads gazed down on the valley just a few generations earlier, they would have seen little more than forbidding swampland, home primarily to antelope, elk, quail, and Yokut Indians. It was a terrain caught in a cycle of severity, lurching from flood to drought and back again. "No place can be imagined more forlorn or desolate," U.S. Army Lieutenant George H. Derby wrote in 1850 of the expanse around Buena Vista Lake. "Clouds of the most venomous mosquitoes tormented us during the day and goaded us to madness during the night; and we found here scorpions, centipedes and a small but extremely poisonous rattlesnake . . . which, with the gophers and ground rats, are the only denizens of the unpleasant and uninhabitable spot."

It required man's corralling of the Kern River; his tilling of a soil thick with tule reeds and forested with willows, cottonwoods, and sycamores; his irrigating of what would otherwise be a moonscape to make these acres bloom. Just thirteen years after Derby's assessment, Colonel Thomas Baker settled on the site of what would become the city named for him: Bakersfield. A purposeful man with penetrating eyes, he hired thirty Indians to assemble a head gate on the south fork of the river and put up a levee, and he erected a dam across the northern end of Buena Vista Lake. It was only the start. By 1878, local developers were crowing that more than $1 million had been invested to construct a series of irrigation canals in Kern County; it was said to be enough plumbing to make 350,000 acres flourish.

At least one man had his heart set on all those acres, plus a lot more. James Ben Ali Haggin, the "Grand Khan of the Kern," was a Kentucky native who had come West during the Gold Rush and, with his brother-in-law, Lloyd Tevis, helped to shape San Francisco. One old portrait of Haggin shows him sitting in a chair of arabesque design, dressed in a dark shirt and coat, a fob dangling over his ample frame. With his neatly cropped white hair and full beard, and wearing an expression that bespeaks an easy confidence, Haggin looks nothing less than regal. And in a real sense, he was. His interests ran, literally, from fire to ice—San

James Ben Ali Haggin, known as the "Grand Khan of the Kern," amassed hundreds of thousands of acres during the nineteenth century and helped define the region's dependence on corporate agriculture. (Bancroft Library, University of California at Berkeley)

Francisco's Risdon Iron Works and Pacific Ice Company were among his many assets—and they included mining, banking, transportation, and champion thoroughbreds. Now, Haggin was intent on establishing what one enthusiast called "the greatest farm in the world."

To get there, he worked his Republican political connections and shamelessly manipulated the provisions of the Desert Land Act. By 1890, his Kern County Land Company laid claim to more than four hundred thousand acres sluiced by an intricate irrigation system. Haggin didn't aspire to keep all that land for himself, though. He was a developer as well as a farmer, and in both cases he understood the importance of planting the right seeds. So the Land Company hired Carleton E. Watkins, the celebrated photographer, to capture scenes of a quickly maturing region—schools, churches, and property enhanced in various ways. It was all part of an effort to persuade prospective settlers that Kern "does not partake of the wild and woolly west," as one advertisement proclaimed. Lured by such depictions, people packed special excursion trains and poured into Bakersfield, where Haggin's hucksters served up heaps of barbecue and gave them the hard sell.

Haggin, however, wasn't the only rapacious character in the county. Henry Miller, a German immigrant who had started out in San Francisco as a butcher and later moved into cattle and grazing land, began snapping up acres in Kern in the late 1860s. Within ten years he and his partner, Charles Lux, owned nearly eighty thousand of them along Buena Vista Slough, and in another ten years they had collected eighty thousand additional acres there. It was but a tiny piece of Miller & Lux's domain, which had been largely built, with the aid of well-compensated lobbyists and government insiders, on the shrewd acquisition of public land. Before the company was finished, its holdings would encompass 1.25 million acres in three Western states; 122,000 head of cattle stamped with Miller & Lux's distinctive Double-H brand; and a labor force of more than 1,200 segregated by race and ethnicity—an arrangement intended, in part, to make it more difficult for the workers to organize and strike. It was an empire, to be sure, and Miller would become known as "the Cattle King." But unlike Haggin, he didn't seem regal in the least. A late-nineteenth-century picture of Miller finds him clad in a suit and tie, but the outfit is rumpled, and he doesn't appear very happy being all dressed up. By all accounts, he probably wasn't. While Lux hobnobbed with bankers and politicos in San Francisco, Miller favored riding through the valley with his cattle and *vaqueros,* dusty expeditions filled with smoking and swearing and spitting tobacco.

The winter of 1877 saw Miller surveying the west side of the valley for grassland to feed his livestock. He found none. "The whole country is burned up," Miller warned Lux, predicting—correctly, as it turned out—that much of their herd would starve. Drought was partly responsible. The other culprit was James Ben Ali Haggin, who had been diverting water upstream for his own ends. The fracas that followed helped lead to a courtroom battle that lasted nearly a decade and became the seminal case in California water law. On the books, it's known as *Lux v. Haggin.* It might as well have been called *Goliath v. Goliath.* Miller & Lux argued that it had a riparian right to the water because it owned the land along the Kern River's banks. Haggin averred that he had a right to the water under the concept of prior appropriation—that is, he had grabbed it first and put it to good use. Only because "industrious citizens" like Haggin were able to dip their straws into the river, his lawyer contended, could the untamed valley be cultivated "into a garden spot" blossoming with grapes, almonds, alfalfa, and wheat, wheat, wheat. In 1881, a Bakersfield judge sided with Haggin. The California Supreme Court later reversed the decision and sided with Miller & Lux. It would all soon be moot anyway. In 1888, Miller and Haggin cut a deal and became partners on the Kern. They built a reservoir that could supply enough river water to satisfy them both. And they divvied up the downstream flow—two-thirds for Haggin, one-third for Miller. The two sovereigns had opted for peace.

Over the next fifty years, much would change. Miller died in 1916, with his company in decline. Haggin had passed away two years earlier, as his company was being absorbed into a new arena: oil. It had been known since the 1860s that rich deposits of energy lay under the land. One of Henry Miller's old drudges recalled sitting around the chuck wagon at dinnertime, watching the *vaqueros* eat their bacon and beans, when one of them lit a cigarette and casually tossed the match into a squirrel hole. It happened to be brimming with natural gas. The blast, "loud as a cannon," nearly triggered a stampede. But it wasn't until 1899, when a hand-dug hole exposed the massive Kern River oilfield, that the area's petroleum boom began in earnest. The Kern County Land Company unearthed some oil on its property in the coming years, and eventually it struck a bona fide gusher: the Ten Section Field, which would yield more than eighty million barrels of crude. Through the 1930s, geologists continued to tap numerous other oilfields in Kern so that by the time Steinbeck rendered the Joads looking over the valley, the county boasted nine thousand wells, which pumped out 20 percent of the world's petroleum.

Beyond black gold, the valley also had been transformed by the introduction of white gold—cotton. The Kern County Land Company had played a role in the explosion of this industry as well, furnishing the federal government with a forty-acre plot in 1921 so that it could set up a testing station and gauge the suitability of the local soil for growing the crop. The results showed it suitable—and then some. Only Egypt's Nile Delta could rival the valley's fecundity, and by the 1930s California stood as a power in the global cotton trade, shipping bale after bale to Japanese spinning mills. With two international commodities flowing from the fields of Kern, the place began to take on a more sophisticated air, and boosters touted the county's "industrial cavalcade" as well as its recreational outlets—tennis, golf, and, for a gilded touch, polo. That was certainly a far cry from what passed for entertainment less than a lifetime earlier: watching five horse thieves get dragged from their jail cells, strung up, and hanged. Still, even in the best light, nobody was about to confuse Bakersfield with New York or Paris, and residents continued to display the traits that they had since Henry Miller's era: a fierce independence and more than a few rough edges. Even when the place got gussied up, it could never really shake its cowboy past, as this poem penned in 1925 made plain:

> *Bakersfield,*
> *I can see you*
> *As if you were embodied.*
> *. . .*
> *You have discarded your overalls*
> *For a hand-me-down suit of clothes.*
> *Clean face,*
> *White shirt,*
> *Store teeth,*
> *Red tie,*
> *Silk sox*
> *And yellow shoes.*

Your faded hair is stringy,
And one thin lock sprawls across
Your bony forehead.
Watery pale-blue eye,
Nose leaning to the left,
Mustache gone—
Corners of mouth pulled down
And leaking tobacco juice
From your chaw.

In June 1939, a couple of months before Gretchen Knief embarked on her summer vacation, John Steinbeck had set out on a holiday of his own, traveling from his home above Los Gatos in the Santa Cruz Mountains. He was ready for a break. *The Grapes of Wrath* was already into its fifth printing, and the swirl of publicity was getting to him. "I have always wondered why no author has survived a best-seller," he said. "Now I know."

His destination was the Golden Gate International Exposition on Treasure Island in San Francisco Bay. Steinbeck was "nuts about fairs, even county fairs," as he told a friend, and this was no mere bearded-lady-and-cotton-candy affair. Here, you could eyeball archeological specimens from Ecuador, ogle native dancers from New Zealand, and marvel over an authentic feudal castle from Old Japan. You could watch yourself being broadcast on a television with the latest cathode-ray technology, make a demonstration long-distance phone call to any point in the United States, and enjoy the antics of "Willie Vocalite," an electric robot who smoked and yakked. Treasure Island, Steinbeck said approvingly, "was all one big toy."

The exposition provided a chance, as well, to revel in the history and culture of the West. There were covered wagons, square dancing, a reenactment of the discovery of gold in 1849, and the running of two steam locomotives, which converged at the center of a stage to represent the completion of the transcontinental railroad. All parts of California sang their virtues. Among them was the San Joaquin Valley, which occupied a building featuring a twenty-by-forty-foot relief map of the region. On one side was placed an elaborate diorama of Yosemite; on the other, a large mural of Friant Dam, construction of which was about to begin, choking the San Joaquin River. In all, four of the valley's eight counties put together presentations: Merced, Madera, Fresno, and Kern, which had paid $25,000 for the privilege. There's no indication that Steinbeck stopped by to see any of these exhibits but, as he was already keenly aware, it was Kern's reputation that needed the most burnishing, thanks to him.

When *The Grapes of Wrath* first hit—with the Joads making the area around "Bakersfiel,'" as Tom pronounced it, their new home—county leaders felt ambushed. But as was their bent, they had come back swinging. In mid-July, in something of a prelude to the resolution banning the novel, Bill Camp and another prominent Kern County farmer, Joseph Di Giorgio, had rattled over the mountains to Los Angeles to speak on radio station KFI. "The growers object to the whole book as being based on falsehoods, in the main, from beginning to end," Camp told listeners. Steinbeck, he added, was wrong to put forward "that growers are exploiting this labor and hiring them for a few cents per day . . . California farmers pay their labor more than twice as much as most of these migrants received back home.

"The book clearly shows that Steinbeck picked out some isolated cases, such as can be found in any state or large city," Camp went on, "and twisted such cases to fit into the picture he wanted to paint. He could have easily obtained the true facts had he wanted to do so." Indeed, Di Giorgio had earned plaudits just a few years earlier for his fairness with his workers. "Our men who have been employed by Di Giorgio speak in praise" of his operations, the manager of a government farm-labor camp in the area reported in March 1936. "Di Giorgio has set the pace for a farm wage."

Camp didn't just defend the growers, though. He professed to be speaking out for the valley's laborers too. "These migrants as a class are the finest kind of people," he said, "yet this book pictures them as being very mean and of the lowest class of humanity." For his part, Di Giorgio chimed in with another line that would be uttered again and again in the weeks to come: "I think the book is indecent."

Di Giorgio and Camp weren't taking up the cause only for themselves. Di Giorgio, the biggest fresh fruit grower in the United States, was a major fund-raiser for the Associated Farmers, a group that attracted controversy the way a feeding trough does flies. And Camp, in addition to leading the Kern County arm of the organization, also served as its state treasurer. The Associated Farmers—Steinbeck had referred to it by the thinly veiled name "the Farmers' Association" in *The Grapes of Wrath*—had emerged after a series of labor strikes swept through the fields of California in 1933. One crop after another was affected: peas, lettuce, cherries, berries, apricots, peaches, pears, beets, tomatoes, hops, grapes, cantaloupes, prunes, and cotton. Especially cotton. In October of that year, fifteen thousand pickers walked off the job, cutting into the profits of growers, ginners, and financiers. Six days into the work stoppage, violence erupted. Vigilantes took up guns and shot at strikers in the Kern County town of Arvin and the Tulare County town of Pixley. Three were killed. In the end, the pickers won a pay raise—seventy-five cents for every hundred pounds of fluff stuffed into their sacks, up from the sixty cents the growers had offered initially. But the cost was high. The union leaders who had spearheaded the cotton strike were shipped off to prison; unabashed Communists, they were charged under the state's criminal syndicalism law with agitating to overthrow the government. The big farmers, meantime, swore that they'd never be caught flat-footed again. If the workers could organize, so could they—only better.

Unlike what was churned out at an industrial site, the farmers maintained, their products quickly rotted in the fields when workers took to the picket lines, threatening an entire year's investment. This was unacceptable. "A farmer has a right to grow his crops, to harvest them and to move them to market," thundered Colonel Walter E. Garrison, the Associated Farmers' president, "and no person nor groups of persons shall deny him that right." This edict applied to the Committee for Industrial Organization—deemed a hothouse for "known radicals"—as well as to the more moderate American Federation of Labor, which one Associated Farmers official said was "led by racketeers." Most of the Associated Farmers' name-calling, in fact, was reserved for labor leaders of any kind, along with anybody else considered "anti-God," "anti-Christ," or otherwise part of "the Red curse."

The Associated Farmers backed anti-picketing ordinances throughout California and worked with local police and sheriffs to crack down on union activities—in other words, to run the bastards out of town. It encouraged the prosecution of labor organizers under the criminal syndicalism statutes. And it lobbied furiously in Sacramento, trying to compel strikers to return to their jobs by ensuring that they couldn't obtain public relief, a policy summed up by the brusque catchphrase: "No work—No eat." But Associated Farmers' members didn't just wield influence; they wielded axe handles too. When four thousand Sonoma County apple workers went out on strike in 1935, the Associated Farmers incited a mob that tarred and feathered union organizers. In 1936, the Associated Farmers was trying to help crush a citrus strike in Orange County when night riders attacked 150 workers with tear-gas bombs. During a strike at the Stockton canneries in 1937, the organization armed more than one thousand growers with clubs, rifles, and shotguns. The local sheriff then deputized the mob and turned them over to Colonel Garrison to deploy as he saw fit. More than fifty people were injured during the melee that ensued.

In time, the Associated Farmers sought to soften its image. "Like every other organization, we have had some bad boys," one higher-up in the group acknowledged in late 1938. "Some of their past actions have not done the association any good"—at least in terms of public relations. The bare-knuckled Garrison stepped down as president and

Holmes Bishop, an ex-choir singer, took the top spot. "A silk glove has been drawn over the A.F. iron fist," *Business Week* reported. The fist was still clenched, but now the preferred option, according to the magazine, was "smooth strategy, political pressure and 'campaigns of education.'"

It was in this spirit that Wofford B. "Bill" Camp prepared to take on John Steinbeck. Camp, a bespectacled forty-five-year-old with thinning hair and jug ears, wasn't the slickest guy around. But he was tremendously well regarded, having come to Kern County during World War I as a government agronomist on a vital mission: to turn California into a cotton kingdom. The military needed more fiber to spin into the cloth that covered the wings of its warplanes, and it was up to Camp, fresh out of Clemson College, to see if the irrigated fields of California were up to the job. In one year alone, he put more than fifty thousand miles on his Model T, skittering across the West, making experimental plantings. Eventually, he oversaw the federal research station near the town of Shafter, about fifteen miles north of Bakersfield, on a plot of sandy loam provided by the Kern County Land Company. From there, with pluck and perseverance, he spread the gospel of planting a particular variety of cotton, known as Acala, throughout the San Joaquin Valley. Before long, Bill Camp was the proud father of a thriving industry.

Beyond being highly thought of, Camp knew how to get his point across. He could be pleasant enough if you shared his worldview. But if he disagreed with you—or, worse, if you openly disagreed with him—he didn't have much patience. He was a teetotaler and a prig, once going so far as to admonish his daughter-in-law for wearing a skirt while she whooshed back and forth on a swing, revealing a bit of leg. "You stop that!" he told her. "That's not nice." Many years later, Camp's youngest son, Don, would recall his father's prescription for winning an argument: "Stand up close to them, look them in the eye—and talk loud." Anybody who knew Bill Camp would have added one more thing to the formula: never waver so much as an inch. "With Dad, everything was black or white," said Don's older brother, Bill Jr. "There was no gray ground with my father. None."

It's tough to say just what made Camp such a rigid man. But there is no question that he was hardened during a stint in FDR's agriculture department in Washington, where he tussled over the direction of farm policy with a young lawyer (later accused of being a Soviet spy) named Alger Hiss. By the time Camp returned to Kern County in late 1936 to take up farming for himself, he was convinced that America was engaged in a grave struggle for survival: the Communist menace was real, and its agents had burrowed into the gut of California. "I have faith in my country," Camp said, "and want it to remain as it is and not go Communistic as these people who come in here want it to go." In this way, Steinbeck's book was part of something much bigger: Those who claimed that the migrants were being ill-treated, Camp believed, were simply slanting things so that the unions, controlled by a bunch of Marxists and their fellow travelers, could gain a foothold.

Besides, he was taking good care of his workers, at least in his own mind. Growing up in Gaffney, South Carolina, Camp had slogged away in the cotton fields just like the Okies were doing now—he'd brag of having bagged 353 pounds in a single day—and he didn't see anything wrong with it. He had raised himself up from nothing and forged his own way, and they could too. "I understand these people," Camp said. "No person ever picked any more cotton than I did." Even though he had made it out of the fields, he and his wife and sons still chose to live in the same type of converted railroad car that some of his laborers did (though they had single cars and he, as lord of the manor, had arranged five into a U-shaped home). He had disposed of their outhouses and brought in flush toilets. "They were . . . fixed up comfortably," Camp said. "There was no discomfort." He threw his workers a big barbecue, the meat slow-cooked in the ground, every year. When it came to those in his employ, Camp said, "They are very happy."

From Camp's black-and-white, no-shades-of-gray perspective, two things escaped him: First, he couldn't grasp—or wouldn't grasp—that other growers might not be watching out for their workers the way he was, and might even be taking advantage of them. "I don't think Dad could see that," Bill Jr. said. "Dad sees, 'I'm doing right. Therefore, Steinbeck and Mrs. Roosevelt are wrong.' Period." Second, it never would have occurred to Camp that his notion of "they are very happy" might not have squared with what at least some of his workers thought. Camp's paternalism was a Southern paternalism, as ingrained in him as his fondness for grits and black-eyed peas or the impulse to give his potatoes brand names such as "Mammy" and "Pickaninny." "When any-body would bring up slavery," Bill Jr. recalled, "Dad would say, 'They weren't mistreated . . . I know on my own family farm back in Gaffney, we played with the Negro children. They looked after us and we looked after them. It was real happy. They weren't unhappy until the Yankees came in.'" (With his avid affection for Dixie, you have to wonder whether Bill Camp took umbrage at the mere title of Steinbeck's book, given that it came from Julia Ward Howe's "Battle Hymn of the Republic"— a song beloved by Union troops during the Civil War. Lest anyone miss the reference [*Mine eyes have seen the glory of the coming of the Lord / He is trampling out the vintage where the grapes of wrath are stored*], as well as to try to root his work in the larger American experience, Steinbeck made sure the lyrics and music were printed on the endpapers at the front and back of the novel.)

In early August, a few weeks after their L.A. radio appearance and a few weeks before the book ban came down, Camp and Di Giorgio took their anti-Steinbeck crusade northward to Treasure Island and the In-ternational Exposition. Di Giorgio sent "extra fancy" grapes—Ribier and Thompson seedless—so that fairgoers would be left with a sweet taste in their mouths. Camp worked on their minds. He directed the Kern County Chamber of Commerce to make a three-reel color film that would showcase just how generous the locals had been toward the migrants in providing food, clothing, schooling, hospitalization, and employment. *Plums of Plenty*, as the movie was called, grew out of a six-thousand-word testimonial that had been written by the chamber's secretary, Emory Gay Hoffman, and it included shots of well-fed, well-scrubbed, well-dressed farm-worker children and down-to-the-penny figures meant to refute Steinbeck's charge of miserliness. (It pointed out, for instance, that Kern spent $6.72 per capita on migrant relief.) The reels of film and Hoffman's script, bound behind a cover showing a prairie schooner and a cornucopia overflowing with fruit, were lost long ago. But one can safely presume that subtlety was not among the picture's hallmarks. Hoffman was a fast talker, often bordering on garrulous, but he was especially effusive when selling the county. At one point, he bought a yellow convertible and mounted two flags—one California's, the other Kern's—on the car's front fender. After *Plums of Plenty* debuted at the exposition, Hoffman posed for the newspapers, flashing a big smile below his pencil-thin mustache while luscious globes of fruit spilled from his hands. "The Okies are a fine people and Kern County is trying to assimilate them," he said. Turning on his inner pitchman, he added: "The torch of civilization burns a little brighter, a little higher in Kern County than in the rest of the world. Things are not what they seem; people are really civilized in Kern County. Mr. Steinbeck was doing fine until he hit the Kern County line. He should have stopped there."

Hoffman liked to characterize *Plums of Plenty* as Kern's "soft answer" to *The Grapes of Wrath*. The hard stuff would come soon enough.

———

It is easy to be cynical about Bill Camp and Joseph Di Giorgio and Stanley Abel and Emory Gay Hoffman and all the others who contended that *The Grapes of Wrath* was lewd and full of lies. Their damnation of Steinbeck, their self-reverential declarations of do-gooding, their propensity to see a Red conspiracy lurking here, there, and everywhere—it can seem like nothing more than an attempt to shift the spotlight off of themselves so that, once back in the shadows, they could continue to subjugate their workers and tamp down their wages. As one farm worker said: "Anyone asking for a nickel raise was a Communist." Still, while such comments contain a considerable amount of truth, they

Emory Gay Hoffman, the voluble secretary of the Kern County Chamber of Commerce, wrote the ban against *The Grapes of Wrath* and also produced a three-reel film called *Plums of Plenty* as an answer to Steinbeck's novel. (Kern County Museum)

don't fully explain the big growers' motives. Bill Camp and the others firmly believed that society was in danger of disintegrating; they honestly were afraid that the fabric of American life could unravel. This is not to excuse their cruelty or callousness or calumny. But it is to recognize that the world was a very different place in August 1939 than it is now. And it is to comprehend that central California, in particular, was a tinderbox and *The Grapes of Wrath* a match.

Looking back, it can be hard to appreciate just how unstable the situation was. After all, while other countries fell under the spell of Karl Marx, we know in hindsight that the United States never really came close to embracing Communism or Socialism or any other offering from the radical left. Scholars cite any number of reasons for this "exceptionalism": America's lack of a feudal, class-conscious tradition; the impregnability of its two-party political system; the nation's preoccupation with race, not class; FDR's skillful hijacking of the rhetoric of the Far Left while dutifully shoring up the pillars of capitalism. But in that moment, in the crucible of the Depression, it wasn't so clear that some form of Marxism wouldn't catch on here—and in a big way.

"All generalizations based on the past about what Americans will or will not do, about . . . the impossibility of political realignments, all the windy phrases about the imperishable traditions of democracy and the immaculate conception of the Constitution, stand suspect and tottering," economist Stuart Chase wrote in 1932, before adding: "Why should Russians have all the fun of remaking a world?" Truth be told, they weren't having *all* the fun. Hotbeds of leftist politics during the teens, '20s, and '30s included Minneapolis; New York; Bridgeport, Connecticut; and Reading, Pennsylvania, with its Socialist Party orchestra, a swath of land known as "Socialist Park," and a downtown cigar factory that produced "Karl Marx" stogies. A Socialist mayor ran Milwaukee in 1939. Between 1918 and 1940, candidates from social democratic movements or their close cousins were able to win statewide elections or major-party primaries in North Dakota, Oklahoma, Minnesota, Wisconsin, Oregon, Washington, and, most dramatically, California.

Exactly five years before the outcry over *The Grapes of Wrath*, in August 1934, Upton Sinclair had jolted the nation and the world by winning California's Democratic primary for governor. The race wasn't even close. Sinclair—"one of the grand American cranks," in the eyes of Saul Bellow; a confirmed Socialist; author of *The Jungle* and other muckraking works; eventual Pulitzer Prize winner; health-food nut; friend of Charlie Chaplain, Albert Einstein, Mark Twain, and myriad other members of the literati and glitterati—had laid out his vision in a pamphlet titled *I, Governor of California And How I Ended Poverty: A True Story of the Future.* Sinclair then narrated the tale as if it were 1938, in the manner of Edward Bellamy's utopian novel *Looking Backward.* The tract, which became a huge best seller, was anything but modest in its ambitions: "This is not just a pamphlet. This is the beginning of a Crusade. A Two-Year Plan to make over a State. To capture the Democratic primaries and use an old party for a new job." Sinclair pledged to turn around California's sagging fortunes by putting private factories under government supervision and allowing the workers to own what they had manufactured. Farmers were asked to then bring their crops to the city, where they'd be "made available to the factory workers in exchange for the products of *their* labor." All of this trade would be conducted with special state-issued scrip and supervised by a new government entity known as the California Authority for Money. To close the state's budget gap, Uppie, as he was called, made no secret of where he'd aim: "We are going to have to tax the great corporations of our state."

Sinclair called his platform EPIC—for End Poverty in California—and with it won more votes than his half-dozen Democratic rivals put together. Jerry Voorhis, who would go on to become a Democratic congressman from California, believed Sinclair's triumph to be "the nearest thing to a mass movement toward Socialism that I have heard of in America." The state's political machinery, which hadn't taken Sinclair very seriously at first, sank into turmoil. Normal loyalties were cast aside. "I am by a strange twist of fate appealing with equal force to Democrats and Republicans to join in the common cause of rescuing our state from the most freakish onslaught that has ever been made upon our long established and revered American institutions of government," said California's GOP chairman, Earl Warren. "The battle is between two conflicting philosophies . . . one that is proud of our flag, our governmental institutions and our honored history, the other that glorifies the Red Flag of Russia and hopes to establish on American soil a despotism based upon class hatred and tyranny." Warren, who was no right-wing extremist, wasn't alone in his panic. Uppie's EPIC landslide set off alarms from the White House to Hollywood to the newspaper baronies of William Randolph Hearst and Harry Chandler. "This old Sinclair has throwed such a scare into these rich folks," Will Rogers told his radio audience, "they won't stop shiverin' till this thing is over."

Ten weeks later, it was. After being subjected to one of the nastiest (and, for its time, innovative) dirty-tricks campaigns in history, Sinclair lost the general election to Republican Frank Merriam, 1.1 million votes to 880,000. Still, the rich folks weren't done shivering. Four years later, a Sinclair ally named Culbert Olson took on Merriam, who hadn't distinguished himself as a very capable leader and whose popularity was so slender, as one analyst put it, he could "scarcely rouse a flicker of enthusiasm . . . in any but the most devout of Republican party workers." (At the same time, Sheridan Downey, Sinclair's old running mate for lieutenant governor—together they had formed the Uppie-Downey ticket—ran for a U.S. Senate seat.)

Although the old Sinclair-inspired EPIC clubs that once mushroomed around the state had vanished quickly after Uppie's loss, his spirit and at least some of his ideas had lived on through those who had ridden his coattails. Olson, a patrician-looking lawyer from Los Angeles, was one of them. He had won a seat in the state senate in '34 with Sinclair's endorsement and, once in office, assumed leadership of the legislature's liberal bloc. Over the next few years, he nearly muscled through a production-for-use bill that contained more than a few shades of the old EPIC plan, left his imprint on tax policy, and stood up to Standard Oil. He kicked off his candidacy for governor in September 1937 by railing against the "privileged interests" that he said controlled the Merriam administration. Merriam fired back with campaign ads that cautioned: "California—Watch Your Step! Keep California out of the 'Red' . . . Vote *Against* Olson and CIO Domination in Our State Government."

The Olson bashing reached a new level in October 1938 by way of Washington. Appearing before the House Committee on Un-American Activities was Harper Knowles, a California American Legion investigator of radicals and subversives, as well as executive secretary of the Associated Farmers. He showed up on Capitol Hill wearing pinstripes and bearing volumes of prepared testimony and denouncing all sorts of people for their alleged Communist ties and sympathies—John Steinbeck, several eminent University of California professors, Sheridan Downey, and Culbert Olson, among them. The committee, led by Texas Democrat Martin Dies, had insisted that it wouldn't tolerate any character assassination. "It is easy to smear someone's name or reputation by unsupported charges . . . but it is difficult to repair the damage that has been done,"

Dies had said when he opened the hearings that August. But the panel didn't play by its own rules, and it became the object of ridicule when Dies' lead investigator, J. B. Matthews, insinuated that ten-year-old movie star Shirley Temple was a Communist dupe. In the wake of that fiasco, Olson had the perfect rejoinder to Knowles's accusation that the Communist Party was guiding his campaign. "I am sorry Comrade Shirley Temple is not here," Olson told a throng gathered at the Los Angeles Philharmonic Auditorium. "She should be here to aid us in plotting to overthrow the government of the United States of America."

Olson cruised to an easy win in the November election, becoming the first Democratic governor in California since 1899. He polled particularly well in Kern County, pulling in nearly 59 percent of the vote there. (Downey won too.) In his victory speech, Olson vowed to fashion an administration "devoted to the services of human needs" instead of one "controlled by forces interested only in human exploitation." The new governor then moved swiftly to tilt California to the left. On January 7, 1939, less than a week after his inauguration, Olson fulfilled one of his campaign promises by pardoning Tom Mooney, the militant labor leader who had been convicted of planting a suitcase bomb that killed ten and injured forty at a San Francisco parade twenty-three years earlier. A number of witnesses in the case had come forward long before and confessed to having been involved in a frame-up, but none of Olson's Republican predecessors would intervene, turning Mooney into one of the nation's great liberal martyrs, along with Sacco and Vanzetti and the Scottsboro Nine. Mooney arrived that morning at the state assembly in manacles from San Quentin, and he left a free man. In between, he spoke to the packed chamber—his message surely unsettling to those on the right. "I am not unmindful of the fact that this case is, in reality, not the case of an individual charged with the crime of murder," Mooney said, his voice choked with emotion. "I know that it symbolizes our whole economic, political and social life and all of the forces that go to make it up. I fully realize that those forces are at work, not alone in California, but throughout the world.

A Kern County labor leader stands in front of a campaign poster for Culbert Olson, who in 1938 became the first Democrat to be elected governor of California in the twentieth century. Olson, who would free the radical Tom Mooney upon being sworn into office, was a symbol of the state's deep schism between the Far Left and Far Right. (Photo by Dorothea Lange, Library of Congress)

"I understand those common elementary laws that govern all life," he continued. "They are simple. In the biological world, they are conception, birth, growth, decay and death, and those rules also govern in the sociological world; and so it is with our present economic system. It was conceived like we were; it was born, it grew to maturity and now it is in a state of decay, not only here but throughout the world, and in its place, just as in our place, it will be replaced by a new and I hope better social order . . . . We must establish a real social order wherein people will live for the benefit of one another and not for the profit of themselves at the expense of the other. . . . I thank you, Governor Olson." Though fully expected, Mooney's pardon left no doubt that Olson was a different kind of leader. "California finally elected a governor who was not terrorized by the state's conservatives," the *New Republic* said, "conservatives who knew Mooney was innocent but wanted him kept in jail anyhow."

After his bold start, however, Olson stumbled. He fell ill at the end of his first week in office and was hospitalized for nervous exhaustion. He didn't resurface for nearly a month, making his first public appearance when he opened the International Exposition on Treasure Island in February. By then, Olson had squandered his momentum. He tried to appoint to the Board of State Harbor Commissioners a close associate of Harry Bridges, the head of the longshoremen's union and a suspected Communist. Olson's pick was shot down in the Senate. Through the spring of 1939, the new governor lost a number of budget and tax fights, and his labor agenda, opposed by the Associated Farmers, stalled. He made things worse by asking his son Richard to serve as his private secretary and spokesman. "Dickie," as he was called—that is, when he wasn't being called the "Crown Prince"—was jovial and imprudent and had the habit of lodging his foot between his gums. Less than two months into his father's tenure, Richard Olson told the San Francisco Junior Chamber of Commerce: "We all know most of the senators are bought and paid for, bound and delivered." The comment ignited a ruckus in the Legislature. By August, things got so sour that Olson's foes tried to orchestrate his recall under the slogan: "We want to throw Tom, Dick and Harry—Tom Mooney, Dick Olson and Harry Bridges—out of California politics."

The effort failed, but for Bill Camp and the other big growers of the Central Valley, it had come too late anyway. Olson had already added to his administration's ranks the one man who was possibly as despicable as Steinbeck himself. His name was Carey McWilliams.

———•———

By the mid-1930s, Carey McWilliams was an acclaimed biographer (of the journalist and satirist Ambrose Bierce), an active Los Angeles attorney, and, increasingly, a strident observer of and participant in California's labor and political scenes. He could look serious and smug behind his wire-rim glasses—like he was the smartest guy in the room and knew it. But he also could kick back on occasion, stealing off with his buddy, the novelist John Fante, to have a drink or two or three or four. H. L. Mencken was McWilliams's mentor. And though he never managed to write with Mencken's style or wit, his prose did share at least two qualities with the Sage of Baltimore's: it was uncommonly smart and fearless.

In 1934, McWilliams began writing a series of articles in the *American Mercury*, the *Nation* (where he would later serve as editor for twenty years), and elsewhere, warning of the Fascism he saw spreading throughout California: in the office of Governor James Rolph, Merriam's predecessor; in the movie business, where Gary Cooper and other stars had taken to donning uniforms and drilling under the banner of the Hollywood Hussars; among the state's newspaper publishers, especially Citizen Hearst. In one sense, McWilliams's throwing around of the F-word was as reckless as those who, like Bill Camp, reflexively stamped "Communist" on everyone and everything they disagreed with. But this was not a case of ideological counterpoise. One side had the bulk of the power, and it wasn't far-fetched to think that it would go to great lengths to cling to it. The *American Citizen*, an organ of the Far Right distributed from San Francisco, all but admitted as much in the motto that it ran on its front page: "Published in order that Fascism may not become necessary to prevent Communism becoming a reality."

Actually, McWilliams was not a Communist. He disagreed with the party on too many points and could never abide by its unquestioning allegiance to Russia. But he valued the spunk of the party's leaders. As he explained to his friend, the writer Louis Adamic, "I have worked fairly closely with them locally because they seemed to be the only people who were doing any work." Practically speaking, though, it made little difference to the Bill Camps of the world whether McWilliams was a card-carrier or not. Some historians have focused on the Far Left's internecine conflicts during the '30s—the Communists versus the old Socialist Party; the Stalinists versus the Trotskyists; the Socialists versus the upstart Social Democratic Federation. But to those on the right, these were all distinctions without a difference. The peril they perceived was not so much from any one of these particular factions, including the relatively few Communist Party faithful in their midst, but from all of them. In 1936, the Associated Farmers cautioned its members that others may even "cause more trouble, and are probably more dangerous, than forthright Communists" as it ticked off a list of these dissidents who technically fell outside the "Communist family tree." Among them: "a Socialist, a parlor pink, a minister who thinks he's working for the brotherhood of man, a college professor who thinks it is an indication of mental courage to teach that our government is old fashioned. . . ." Add to this roll countless others who identified with the broad-based Popular Front— unionists, artists, intellectuals, and all of those who, as Michael Denning has written, "thought of themselves as generic 'communists,' using the term with a small *c*." It was into this more expansive framework that McWilliams (along with Steinbeck) fell.

In the summer of 1935, McWilliams turned his focus to what was fast becoming his favorite target: "farmer Fascism." Hoping to learn more about the strikes that had crippled California's agricultural belt in 1933 and '34, he toured from Bakersfield to Salinas, interviewing growers, labor contractors, workers, and union leaders. "It took little imagination," he said, "to sense the importance of this extraordinary social upheaval," and he returned to Los Angeles "determined to tell the story of migratory farm labor." When he did, he minced no words. In six pieces that appeared in *Pacific Weekly*—a spirited magazine edited out of Carmel by Ella Winter and her husband, the famed Russophile Lincoln Steffens—McWilliams applauded the Industrial Workers of the World for the early gains they had made in California's farm fields. He commended "the analytic methods of Marx and Lenin" to best understand "the real social consequences of capitalistic agriculture." And he promoted a strong union presence to "enable the farm workers of California to terminate slavery, starvation and bloodshed." Much of this thinking would ultimately find its way into McWilliams's book *Factories in the Field,* in which he traced the history of agriculture in the state

from the days of Henry Miller to the Dust Bowl migration. Not sur-
prisingly, many growers took issue with McWilliams's account. Rancher
Roy M. Pike delivered one of the most stinging rebukes in a booklet he
titled (à la *Plums of Plenty*) *Facts from the Fields*. Pike claimed to have
uncovered more than seventy examples of "outright untruths and mis-
statements" in *Factories in the Field*. But it was McWilliams's conclusion
that many found most shocking:

> It is now theoretically possible to solve the farm-labor problem in
> California . . . . The real solution involves the substitution of collective
> agriculture for the present monopolistically owned and controlled sys-
> tem. As a first step in the direction of collectivization, agricultural
> workers must be organized . . . the final solution will come only when
> the present wasteful, vicious, undemocratic and thoroughly antisocial
> system of agricultural ownership in California is abolished.

For the state's agribusiness titans, it was hard to conceive of a more
frightening pronouncement. As union organizers pressed into the cel-
ery fields and citrus orchards and along the waterfront in late '39,
McWilliams's words would continue to echo in the big growers' ears.
"We must draft a program to meet this life-or-death threat . . . in what
must be a concerted drive by Communists to seize control of California
farms as advocated by Carey McWilliams with his doctrine of collective
agriculture," one Associated Farmers official would advise Bill Camp by
telegram. "We do not want to be alarmists, but . . . we urge you to contact all county units to launch a last-minute drive . . . so we can stop this
before it spreads wild over the entire state."

McWilliams wasn't the only one appealing for the collapse of capitalism. Throughout the decade, a host of writers were making a case for
the same thing, and on a far grander scale than in California's farming
sector. Some of them, such as the *New Republic*'s George Soule, were so
matter-of-fact in predicting capitalism's demise that, upon reading of
their logic seventy years later, you might well assume the free enterprise

system had perished and given way to some communal alternative, if you didn't know better. What made McWilliams different was that by the time *Factories in the Field* was published, in July 1939, he was no longer just plying a provocative pen; he was forming government policy. In January, Governor Olson had named McWilliams to be the chief of the Division of Immigration and Housing, effectively putting him in charge of farm labor issues in the state. The agency had long been moribund under Sacramento's succession of Republican regimes. But McWilliams immediately invigorated the office, inserting himself in all sorts of matters, including farm-worker housing, the civil liberties of migrants, even the setting of wages.

There is little doubt that *Factories in the Field* would have made a splash even if McWilliams hadn't been part of Olson's staff. But that he was only added to the hue and cry. "The book is Communistic from cover to cover," J. W. Hawkins, an attorney from the Central Valley city of Modesto, complained to Olson in early August. McWilliams, he said, "is an employee of the state. He is my employee and your employee, and an employee of the people of the state, and is not the employee of any particular group. Holding the position he holds, he has no business to circulate . . . a publication that can and will result in creating class hatred."

Yet it wasn't just the title McWilliams held that stirred things up; it was also his timing. *Factories in the Field* appeared just three months after *The Grapes of Wrath* had been published, greatly heightening the significance of McWilliams's work. Although some on the right figured that the release of the books had been coordinated, it had not. The fact was, Steinbeck and McWilliams barely knew each other, having corresponded a few times over the years but never having actually met in the flesh. Still, the two tomes played beautifully off each other—a seamless marriage of fiction and nonfiction. "Here is the data," book critic Robert Brady wrote of *Factories in the Field*, "that gives the terrible migration of the Joad family historical and economic meaning." He was hardly the only one to lump the two books together. Others, though, did so in less flattering terms. Writing in a biweekly farmer newspaper called the *Pacific Rural Press,* under the headline "Termites Steinbeck and McWilliams," editor John E. Pickett belittled the author of *The Grapes of Wrath* as "a scavenger of filth and a dealer in literary scandal." A close friend of Bill Camp's, Pickett didn't think much of those who enjoyed reading the book, either: "How they eat it up, those emotion-hunters, intelligentsia, pinks, reds and cocktail-cuddlers." Pickett was less florid in his condemnation of McWilliams; rather, he quoted at some length from *Factories in the Field,* letting McWilliams's views speak for themselves, before adding: "Perhaps this is the first time an official of our government, sworn to defend that government, has advocated the destruction of democracy and the substitution of Communism."

Across America in the 1930s, it was not unheard of for people to talk about the possible violent overthrow of the government, just as had happened in Russia. But even more common was the idea that change would come not by toppling the president or Congress or the military, but by toppling the established social order. For the big farmers of central California—old cowboys and Southern cotton men who fancied themselves rugged individualists—August 1939 was a time when such a prospect seemed terrifyingly real. The migrants were straining local resources and testing the boundaries of what constituted a decent wage and working conditions. Union organizers were again swarming the area, making trouble. Culbert Olson was governor, and Carey McWilliams was in a position of authority. And to top it all off, *The Grapes of Wrath* was flying off the shelves: by the time Gretchen Knief arrived home from vacation, the waiting list for the book at the Kern County Library had climbed to six hundred.

The novel's purpose was unmistakable in the growers' minds—and in Steinbeck's too. "This is a rough book," he told his literary agent, "because a revolution is going on."

CHAPTER TWO
Monday

"Come along," said Joad. "Pa'll be glad to see you. He always
said you got too long a pecker for a preacher."

As THE KERN COUNTY Board of Supervisors ended its Monday meeting, a crowd at San Francisco's Palace Hotel, some 280 miles to the
north, was just settling into their seats. That is to say, those who could
find seats were settling in. After six hundred guests filled the tables, one
hundred or so were left to stand, and the Rose Room—so named for its
rose-colored velvet hangings and the silken light shades that bore a soft
rose hue—teemed with a strange blend of elegance and fury.

The luncheon, which attracted the likes of former governor Frank
Merriam and former first lady Lou Henry Hoover, was sponsored by
Pro America, a conservative women's organization that had invited "a
panel of experts to report on every angle" of the migrant situation. In
truth, there was only one angle that those on the panel were keen to address: discrediting John Steinbeck and Carey McWilliams.

One after another, they took to the podium: Harold Pomeroy, State
Relief Administration chief under Merriam and now executive secretary
of the Associated Farmers; Thomas McManus, a Bakersfield insurance

man and secretary of a group called the California Citizens' Association, which was lobbying to cut relief to the migrants and opposed any further resettlement in the Golden State; Dr. Stanley Farnsworth of the State Department of Public Health; H. C. Merritt Jr., manager of the giant Tagus Ranch; Loring Schuler, onetime editor of *Country Gentleman* and *Ladies' Home Journal;* and the wonderfully named Ferne Orchard Mattei, the president of Pro America and wife of an oil tycoon.

Merritt saluted California's relatively high agricultural wages, while Farnsworth and Schuler scoffed at Steinbeck's depiction of the Joads' daughter, Rose of Sharon, giving birth without medical assistance, saying that she must have been purposely hiding from the staff of field nurses deployed throughout Kern County who administered health care to the migrants. Pomeroy decried the "hate and antagonism" in *The Grapes of Wrath* and *Factories in the Field,* and Mattei termed the books "smear literature." But as forceful as these speakers were—and most of them came armed with a battery of facts and figures—the star of the show was Ruth Comfort Mitchell, a well-known novelist in her own right who had hopes of giving the "ranchers' side" of things and thus becoming Steinbeck's intellectual and artistic counterweight.

She would never get there, for her storytelling was far too clunky and syrupy to be any kind of real ballast to Steinbeck's masterful prose. Mitchell was, moreover, all too easy to lampoon with her penchant for wearing green clothes, writing on green stationery, driving green cars, and reeking of green in another sense—the green of money. She grew up in luxury and married rich, once confiding to a reporter, "I know nothing about that stimulating lash of adversity that all of you people who have had to fight for your foothold talk about." But for all that, Mitchell was no joke, at least not to the hundreds thronging the Palace on this Monday, and not to many who would read her novel, *Of Human Kindness,* as an answer to *The Grapes of Wrath.*

Mitchell was born in 1882 in San Francisco and, by the turn of the century, she had decided to become a writer. She sought and received guidance from W. C. Morrow, who had formed the Western Authors

Ruth Comfort Mitchell admitted she knew nothing of the "lash of adversity" that so many suffered under, but she was nevertheless determined to give the "ranchers' side" of things in her book *Of Human Kindness*. (Hooked on Los Gatos, Library and Museum History Project)

Publishing Company and whose own ghost stories were so vivid, they were said to make "the reader feel as if a stream of lizards, fresh from the ice, were streaking it up his back and hiding in his hair." In hindsight, it was an odd relationship: Morrow was a close companion of Ambrose Bierce, whom Carey McWilliams would make the subject of his first book, and it's tough to imagine that Mitchell would be attracted to anybody just a step or two removed from someone McWilliams so admired. It's also difficult to envision what Mitchell—who would become known as a writer who "liked to take the bright view"—would see in a man whose tales ran toward the macabre. Yet Morrow commended Mitchell, then eighteen years old, for her "superior abilities" and advised her that it was time to move on from his tutelage. "The exercises that I give out are for those far behind you in development and skill," he said. "You are now able to work out your own plans." And that she did, going on to write for a slew of women's magazines—*Redbook, Good Housekeeping,* and *McCall's,* among them. Mitchell also composed plays, poems, and novels, including *Old San Francisco* in 1933 (released as part of the same series as Edith Wharton's *Old New York*). By 1935, she was so well known that an editor's note preceding one of her short stories began like this: "Ruth Comfort Mitchell's work needs no introduction to American audiences."

Still, it was her outspokenness about *The Grapes of Wrath* that had given Mitchell even more visibility. She lived, coincidentally, in the very same town that Steinbeck did—Los Gatos—where together they shared a stunning vista of the Santa Clara Valley. "Similarities in perspective," as one Steinbeck expert has said, "end there." In 1914, Mitchell wed Sanborn Young, a Chicago native turned California dairy farmer, and together they built their Oriental-flavored house, Yung See San Fong ("Young's Home in the Heart of the Hills"), where they raised vegetables and poultry. Young, a quiet man, would go on to serve thirteen years in the state senate beginning in 1925. There, he took a leading interest in several issues, including narcotics control, the conservation of wild animals (his bill to abolish sawtooth traps was enacted in 1929), and clamping down on organized labor. Young chaired the committee behind Proposition 1, an ill-fated 1938 ballot measure that endeavored to regulate picketing and strike activities. By the late 1930s, Mitchell herself had become a steady presence on the lecture circuit, speaking out on international politics, and in '39 she assumed the helm of Pro America's California chapter.

In June of that year, Mitchell announced that she was working on a book that would be an alternative to Steinbeck's, and as the months went along she poked at her neighbor with increasing ferocity, saying that "My picture of ranch life and labor is going to be a much more accurate one." Among the details from *The Grapes of Wrath* that Mitchell ridiculed were Steinbeck's repeated references to orange-colored handbills, which the big farmers used to lure the Joads to California with promises of work. Once they got there, according to Steinbeck's story, they discovered that thousands of others had seen the same fliers; the whole thing had been a ploy to secure a surplus of labor

Actress Dorris Bowdon, playing Rose of Sharon in the film version of *The Grapes of Wrath*, holds up a handbill that was said to have lured many migrants to California. (Academy of Motion Picture Arts and Sciences)

and to keep wages low. Mitchell sneered at this scenario, saying that there simply were no such circulars. She noted that Kern County had offered a prize to anybody who could turn one up, but nobody ever did. "I'm still waiting for one of those sinister orange-colored handbills," Mitchell said during a speech, causing much laughter. Like so much else in history, however, what really happened is pretty murky. Some scholars say flatly that Mitchell was right: No handbills existed, and groups such as the Citizens' Association, wary of spiraling taxes to pay for migrant assistance, did all they could to keep more indigents from rolling west. "There are no jobs in California," Tom McManus cautioned radio listeners in Oklahoma City. "Do not go to California in spite of anything you have heard. To do so will only bring hardship on yourself and your family." But Carey McWilliams said he had a bunch of handbills in his files—open "for inspection at any time," in case his word wasn't good enough—and added that the Farm Security Administration did too. Beyond that, an Associated

Farmers official acknowledged that some unscrupulous labor contractors did, from time to time, beckon workers "to come here when we
had plenty of people already" and that attempts to discourage the
practice were spotty at best. In the end, it's fair to say that Steinbeck
exaggerated the use of handbills as bait. But either way, the most fascinating part of the whole dispute was that it was provoked by a piece
of fiction. Steinbeck's book was being scrutinized as if it were documentary history, painstakingly picked apart in a way that few, if any
other, novels have ever been. Schuler, the old *Country Gentleman* editor, was among those who parsed *The Grapes of Wrath* sentence by sentence, looking for anything that he could point to as factually
inaccurate. For instance, where Steinbeck wrote of men working for
fifteen cents an hour, Schuler was happy to report in his nineteen-
page analysis that the lowest wage paid in Kern County was twenty
cents, and the bigger ranches often offered thirty.

Mitchell's own novel would never face such a going-over, though
some on the left would denigrate it as a partisan document, just as those
on the right were doing—albeit more ardently—with Steinbeck's book.
Of Human Kindness, published in 1940, would tell the story of the Banner family, third-generation California farmers proud of their "energy
and thrift and robust Americanism." Over thirty-four chapters, their
lives would be shaken up by a procession of preposterous characters:
Lute Willow, the "lazy, happy-go-lucky, good-looking, guitar-playing-
ballad-singing Oklahoman" who'd elope with the Banners' daughter,
Sally; Pinky Emory, the history teacher who'd inculcate her students—
including the Banners' son, Ashley—with the idea that the migrants
have "been ground down by the big corporations" in Oklahoma and
tricked by California's big growers "so oodles and oodles would come
and they could get cheap labor and pay starvation wages!"; and the
"Black Widow," the arrestingly beautiful labor organizer—"willow slim
in her white slacks and thin white sweater which was drawn down re-
vealingly over her round little breasts"—who'd seduce Ashley and ma-
nipulate Pinky, sending her to her death.

Of Human Kindness would be panned as an inferior work, a book "not to be confused with that kind of higher-bracket fiction one means when one speaks of a novel," *San Francisco Chronicle* book critic Joseph Henry Jackson would say in his review. But it would nonetheless find an audience among those raring to see Steinbeck get his comeuppance, even in the form of second-rate literature. "It should be compulsory reading for all boosters of *The Grapes of Wrath,* for it is a very interesting presentation of the other side of the picture," one fan of the book would tell Mitchell. "It is convincing—perhaps all the more so because we are anxious to be convinced. . . . "

All such praise, though, was still months away. For now, those jamming the Rose Room at the Palace could only anticipate Mitchell's book and take in her oratory, which in many respects was more eloquent than her writing. "Honey-tongued," one adversary called her. *People's World,* the West Coast Communist newspaper, would mock the proceedings, saying that the guests had arrived "in limousines . . . swathed in silver foxes and chic fall costumes," ready "to eat a luncheon containing enough vitamins to keep a hungry man going for a week." Just how faithful this disdainful description was to reality is unclear. But this much is certain: as she rose to speak at the Palace, Mitchell couldn't have been more in her element. Surveying the crowd, her gray head of hair crowned by a huge hat festooned with flowers and flowing lace, she launched right in:

> California neighbors, we have met to discuss the unfortunate publicity given our state in recent publications in fiction and asserted fact.
>
> We make these protests with full respect for the compelling genius of the novelist and for the intensive study and research involved in the alleged history of California agriculture. We realize there have been dark pages in that history—greed, ignorance and hate breeding hate.
>
> This meeting is not boosting ballyhoo for . . . out-size fruits in a fabulous Shangri-La beyond the lost horizon of work and worry. This is a good-humored but a determined protest against destructive propaganda.

We are the grandsons and daughters of the pioneers and Argonauts who crossed the plains in covered wagons and sailed round the Horn, and we deplore the changed thinking, the unsound, inflammatory, revolutionary thinking of great numbers of our people. In the old days California attracted the brave, the ambitious, the forceful, but of late years it has become a sort of Bird Refuge for cuckoos, for scolding jays, even for the sharp-billed butcherbirds—for malcontents, subversive agitators and inciters to violence. It is inevitable that—occasionally—pinkish and even a darker tinge should color our local literature . . . .

We are not bitter. We are not truculent. We are not here to throw mud; we shall try to wipe some off. Not to warble a fulsome "I Love You, California," but to insist that "I Loathe You, California" is an unmerited Hymn of Hate. We ask you to listen with open minds to the other side of the question . . . . The rancher has been painted as wearing horns and carrying a red-hot pitchfork, as a sinister admixture of Old Scrooge and Simon Legree, but you will learn that this is not a true picture.

The crowd at the Palace applauded, but they weren't the only ones. The Mutual Broadcasting System aired Mitchell's talk up and down the coast, and among those listening was Clell Pruett, a laborer at Bill Camp's ranch, just outside Bakersfield. Pruett, who had come to California from his native Missouri in 1937, hadn't read *The Grapes of Wrath*. But he didn't much like what he had heard about the book. As he huddled around the radio, chewing over Mitchell's words, Pruett grew madder and madder. "That woman," he said of Mitchell, "certainly read the riot act straight down the line. She's a cracker-jack talker." By the time Camp and Robert Franklin, an Associated Farmers publicity man, had added their spin, Pruett was so whipped up that he told his boss he'd like to help: How could he give that John Steinbeck a little of what was coming to him?

Just what kind of practical effect Stanley Abel imagined he would have by keeping *The Grapes of Wrath* out of schools and libraries isn't clear. The novel, after all, was still available in bookstores—though in the case of Kern County, that didn't amount to a whole lot.

The phonebook for the big city of Bakersfield listed but one book-seller in 1939: A. W. Davy's shop over on Nineteenth Street, and it had only 130 copies available. (By comparison, Bakersfield claimed 51 barbers, 46 liquor stores, and 47 churches.) At $2.75 each—more than thirty-four times the cost of a loaf of bread—it's also uncertain how many people in Kern County or other parts of the valley could afford *The Grapes of Wrath.* "I want to read the book and decide for myself how bad it is," a missionary from Fresno wrote to Knief after word of the ban had spread. "As you know, charity has little money, so I am begging for one or all the books" that the library can no longer use. (Evidently, Knief didn't send the novel to this particular woman, but she did proffer her inventory of forty-eight to other county libraries, helping them meet heavy demand up and down California. "We were very much thrilled to receive a note . . . that you would lend some of your copies of *Grapes of Wrath*," Knief's counterpart in Santa Cruz wrote back. "That book has caused much heartache in our library—the Trustees disapprove of it very strongly and loudly." Despite the furor, or maybe because of it, the backlog of requests for Steinbeck's text had grown to 125, she reported.)

Whatever the real impact of the supervisors' order, it was imposing enough to arouse the ire of civil libertarians across the country, including representatives from the League of American Writers (an anti-Fascist group where Steinbeck served as a vice president) and the National Council on Freedom from Censorship. And it was powerful enough, as well, to further motivate those eager to muzzle the book's message. Determined to see the ban expand well beyond Kern County, Bill Camp called upon the Associated Farmers to press for similar measures statewide. "We are angry not because we were attacked, but because we were attacked by a book obscene in the extreme sense of the word," Camp

Bill Camp, head of the Associated Farmers chapter in Kern County, said of *The Grapes of Wrath*, "We are angry not because we were attacked, but because we were attacked by a book obscene in the extreme sense of the word." (Kern County Museum)

asserted. "Americans have a right to say what they please, but they do not have the right to attack a community in such words that any red-blooded American man would refuse to allow his daughter to read them."

Actually, Americans were of a mind during the 1930s to let their daughters and sons read more and more—or at least they weren't inclined to bottle up books and make them inaccessible, as they had been only ten or twenty years before. The New York Society for the Suppression of Vice—the organization from which Anthony Comstock, beginning in the nineteenth century, had inveighed against that which "debauches the imagination . . . and damns the soul"—was in full retreat. In 1938, free-speech activists could count only one book in America (Ernest Hemingway's *To Have and Have Not*) that had been banned. "In the past year," the president of the vice society lamented in 1939, "we were abused far more than we have been" in recent times. Indeed, the '30s would ultimately be seen as a period of intellectual openness in the United States, making the supervisors' stance seem all the more backward, all the more fanatical, all the more desperate.

Some trace the history of censorship as far back as 585 BC, when, according to legend, the Greek storyteller Aesop was hurled off the cliffs of Delphi for the blasphemy contained in his fables. Through the centuries, the Chinese, Romans, and other Europeans followed suit, gagging authors and outlawing books for various reasons—espousing religious heresy, making political affronts, and promoting eroticism. Pope Paul IV published the church's first Index of Forbidden Books (*Index Liborum Prohibitorum*) in 1599. America, too, would join in this game, though over the years its censors have been preoccupied with one main thing: sex. For a long time, few protested. When the federal government expanded its obscenity statute in 1873—passing what is commonly known as the Comstock Law—it was right in step within the mores of the day. Twenty-five years later, Harvard professor Francis Peabody saw the "vice societies" that had sprung up around the country—from New York to Boston to Cincinnati to San Francisco—as a social reform movement in the tradition of the Abolitionists. He likened the New England Watch and Ward Society to sanitation pipes, "unobtrusively working underground, guarding us from the pestiferous evil which at any time may come up into our faces, into our homes, into our children's lives." Most of the time, the vice societies' mere presence was sufficient to keep publishers and booksellers in line. (When Comstock and his compatriots did find it necessary to challenge books and periodicals in the courts, they prevailed about 90 percent of the time.) Even librarians cheered. In 1908, Arthur Bostwick, head of the American Library Association, advocated batting down "bad books" with an "immoral tendency." Some authors, such as Mark Twain and Stephen Crain, bumped up against the boundaries, but most stayed happily within the margins of what was acceptable. Out of the Victorian age, through the Progressive Era and into World War I—where U.S. soldiers were held up as paragons of rectitude compared with the "lustful" Huns—little changed. But some were beginning to at least ask the question: Had things gone too far? "There is a borderland," *Publisher's Weekly* opined in 1916, "in which the exact delimitation of the obscene is a very complex matter, and the excessive zeal sometimes displayed by semi-official or unofficial censorship in the suppression of 'borderland' literature has been often ludicrous, generally annoying and sometimes positively unjust."

With the end of the war and the roaring in of the 1920s, such feelings only intensified. Young Americans, once content to abide by puritanical practices, were now being swept away by movies, cars, and pulp magazines. A new generation of writers—Sherwood Anderson, F. Scott Fitzgerald, Sinclair Lewis, Eugene O'Neill—was anxious to make its mark by flouting conventions, by being avant-garde. From the throes of change, tensions proliferated between those intent on keeping the clock from turning and those who, in response, would rally against the censors' "Clean Books" campaign. "A great deal will be heard during the next few months about censorship," *Current Opinion* predicted in late 1922. "Those who believe in it, and those who don't, have for some time been lining themselves up into opposing camps."

The fight soon raged, at one point sucking in none other than Upton Sinclair. The imbroglio unfolded in the spring of 1927 in Boston, where police arrested a young bookstore clerk for selling a copy of Sinclair's *Oil!*, a novel that explored Southern California's petroleum fever— "human nature laid bare!" as Uppie put it—but so much else too: the Teapot Dome scandal, an oilfield strike (based on labor strife in Kern County in 1921), religion, class consciousness, Bolshevism, petting parties, birth control, and abortion. Naturally, it was the last few subjects that grabbed the attention of the Boston authorities. Sinclair hurried east, where he attempted to have his name substituted for the clerk's on the indictment, only to be informed that this was impossible. Next, he tried to get himself arrested, peddling copies of *Oil!* on Boston Common. None of the cops on the beat would play along and buy one, though, and so he moved on to plan C: He made a "fig leaf" edition of the book, removing the nine pages cited as obscene, and tried to sell it while wearing an advertising sandwich board cut in the shape of a fig leaf. The exposure for the novel was more than Sinclair could ever have hoped for. You might think, "Your book is dead, and your wife and kids can't go to the seashore this summer," he deadpanned. "But then some good angel puts into the head of a Boston preacher to read your book and take it to the Boston police. . . . Instantly the press agencies flash the name of your book to every town and village in the United States, and your publisher gets orders by telegraph from Podunk and Kalamazoo." He continued: "If it were necessary to write really obscene books, I wouldn't recommend this plan, because real obscenity is foreign to my interests. But the beauty of the plan is that you don't have to write anything really harmful; all you have to do is to follow the example of the great masters of the world's literature, and deal with the facts of life frankly and honestly." Before leaving Boston, Sinclair arranged to sell a copy of *Oil!* to Lieutenant Daniel J. Hines of the vice squad. But when it was discovered that Sinclair had actually forked over a Bible instead, charges were never brought. "We think you have had enough publicity, Mr. Sinclair," the local magistrate told him. With sales of *Oil!* now skyrocketing, Uppie returned to California, where seven years later he'd create an even bigger sensation as candidate for governor.

By then, the banning of books was all but a thing of the past. Society had moved on to other concerns: the Depression, for one. American authors, publishers, booksellers, and librarians—hitherto ambivalent and divided on the issue of obscenity—were as of the mid-'30s firmly in the anticensorship camp. The Germans had also sparked a storm of disapproval in the United States with their massive book burning of May 10, 1933—in which titles by Sinclair, Einstein, Freud, Hemingway, London, and many more were left to smolder in a Berlin square—and the last thing anybody wanted was to be seen in the company of Hitler's jackboots. Even the New York Vice Society elected, at long last, to remove from the cover of its annual reports its time-honored emblem: a top-hatted gent tossing a pile of books into a blazing fire.

In the view of many, the decade's most significant court ruling on censorship was reached in December 1933, when federal judge Munro Woolsey wiped away a Customs Bureau ban on James Joyce's *Ulysses* and allowed Random House to import the book into the United States. Even Joyce's use of "fuck" didn't faze His Honor: "The words which are

Seven years before he ran for governor of California—and nearly
won—Upton Sinclair was caught up in a fight over censorship.
Here he hawks a special "fig leaf edition" of his book *Oil!* on the
streets of Boston. (Lilly Library, Indiana University)

criticized as dirty are old Saxon words known to almost all men and, I
venture, to many women," Woolsey wrote, laying down a common-
sense standard that a book should be evaluated "in its entirety" and by
how it was likely to affect someone "with average sex instincts"—not an
adolescent. Among those hailing the decision was attorney Morris L.
Ernst, the biggest name in anticensorship law, who had defended
Ulysses during the trial. Thanks to Woolsey, terminology "long banned
from polite conversation and literature" was "no longer taboo," Ernst
said years later. "It cannot be doubted that Judge Woolsey's decision di-

rectly paved the way for the degree of forthrightness to be found in John Steinbeck's masterly *The Grapes of Wrath.*"

But it's that very forthrightness that so rankled those in Kern County. Some of the censorship that did surface in the '30s, it's worth noting, was aimed not at material that was blue but, rather, that was regarded as Red. Diego Rivera's mural at Rockefeller Center, with a portrait of Lenin in the middle, was covered over by tar paper and a wooden screen before he could finish. A mural in Los Angeles by David Alfaro Siqueiros, *Tropical America,* was similarly whitewashed because its allusion to U.S. imperialism didn't sit well with the city's business and political elite. A Federal Theatre production of *The Cradle Will Rock,* a play about union organizing in "Steeltown, U.S.A.," was shut down because it was considered too "dangerous." NBC barred the show *Pins and Needles* from the radio until song lyrics were changed from "Fifty million union members can't be wrong" to "Fifty million happy couples can't be wrong." Leon Trotsky's works were banned in Boston. And several social science textbooks, including those by Harold Rugg, were barred in schools because they were said to teach Communist ideas. For their part, the supervisors in Kern County didn't wrestle with either-or; they covered all the bases, effectively referring to Socialism ("breathing class hatred") as well as sex ("lewd, foul and obscene language") in their banning of *The Grapes of Wrath.* Steinbeck, in the judgment of many, hadn't held back on either front. "Almost every passage in the book would ordinarily be considered violently revolutionary and profane by the majority of those who will read it," one critic suggested not long after *The Grapes of Wrath* was published. "But the author . . . is in vogue now. In America, those in vogue can do little wrong."

Steinbeck's novel brazenly lumped together Paine and Marx, Jefferson and Lenin, while openly taunting those "who hate change and fear revolution." He wrote that business owners—the capitalists—were trapped in the role of "I" while the masses, America's restive "we," mobilized and prepared for action. He stopped short of championing an insurrection, but just short:

 AND the great owners, who must lose their land in an upheaval, the great owners with access to history, with eyes to read history and to know the great fact: when property accumulates in too few hands it is taken away. And that companion fact: when a majority of the people are hungry and cold they will take by force what they need. And the little screaming fact that sounds through all history: repression works only to strengthen and knit the repressed. The great owners ignored the three cries of history. The land fell into fewer hands, the number of dispossessed increased, and every ef- fort of the great owners was directed at repression. The money was spent for arms, for gas to protect the great holdings, and spies were sent to catch the murmuring of revolt so that it might be stamped out. The changing economy was ignored, plans for the change ig- nored; and only means to destroy revolt were considered, while the causes of revolt went on. ▣

Steinbeck was just as bold in his application of expletives. Early on in the novel, the Reverend Jim Casy gives Tom Joad some insight into his proclivity for cussing. "Maybe you wonder about me using bad words," Casy says. "Well, they ain't bad to me no more. They're jus' words folks use, an' they don't mean nothing bad with 'em." Casy could have been speaking for Steinbeck himself, who put not only into the lapsed preacher's mouth but into the mouths of many of his characters a panoply of profanity: *bastard, bitch, shitheel, ass, tit, dong, pecker, nuts,* and *a fingerin' hisself.* He wrote about the Joads and others picking up prostitutes—once, Uncle John bedding three whores at a time and, on another occasion, Tom fondly recollecting a one-legged gal who charged extra for sleeping with her because of the novelty. He told of Casy getting his flock all worked up, "talkin' in tongues, an' glory- shoutin'," until he'd steal off with a girl into the grass for a little "screwin'." *The Grapes of Wrath,* Westbrook Pegler said in his syndicated column, "contains the dirtiest language I have ever seen on paper." It could have been even dirtier. After the manuscript had been completed,

Steinbeck's agent, Elizabeth Otis, came to California to implore him to clean up the novel, at least a bit. Steinbeck's litmus test was whether the words "stopped the reader's mind." Otherwise, he said, those "insulted by normal events or language mean nothing to me." Still, Otis coaxed a few changes out of him and then raced to send them back to New York via Western Union. But the operator was horrified by the crudeness of what she heard and refused to send the telegram. "You are obviously not a Christian, madam!" she exclaimed. Otis eventually won her over.

For many of those who cared about such things, the most outrageous part of the book was the end. That's when Tom's sister, Rose of Sharon, having just lost her baby—blue and stillborn—bares her breast to feed a starving man. The yarn is apparently based on an incident that a hobo had related years earlier to Steinbeck when he was a fledgling writer and had ventured out on the road, offering $2 to anybody with a good story to share. As Steinbeck jotted down notes, Frank Kilkenny sat beside a Northern California campfire and told of the time that he had gotten lost in the country as a fourteen-year-old and was wandering around for days, "starving to death," before he stumbled upon a homestead where a Finnish farmer and his wife took him in. The woman was wet-nursing a newborn, and her husband, fearful that Kilkenny was so weak he might die, sent her into his bed where she suckled him. Many years later, Kilkenny recalled his back-and-forth with Steinbeck that night as the firelight flickered:

"You mean a woman put her breasts in your mouth?" the writer, obviously incredulous, asked.

"Yeah. It's a fact," Kilkenny replied.

"I'm going to keep this," Steinbeck said. "This is going to be my punch point."

"A punch point?"

"Yeah, don't you know: every novel has to have a punch point."

Steinbeck called it "a survival symbol, not a love symbol." But the scene vexed Archbishop Francis Spellman of New York, who heaped scorn on *The Grapes of Wrath* from the pulpit. And one can surmise that

Rep. Lyle Boren was also picturing Rose of Sharon when, the following year, he derided the novel for being "a black, infernal creation of a twisted, distorted mind." "Some have said this book exposes a condition and a character of people," the Oklahoma Democrat remarked, "but the truth is this book exposes nothing but the total depravity, vulgarity and degraded mentality of the author."

It's hard to say who else was bothered by Steinbeck's choice of words. Despite what the supervisors' resolution stated, it's doubtful that the board members were too upset by it; as a group, they weren't known for being terribly prim. Then again, the cursing and explicit references probably did gnaw at Bill Camp. He wasn't a churchgoer, but "I never heard that man ever make a cuss word," said his secretary, Mara Daniel. "He was a man I would pin to be a Christian." Camp's son, Bill Jr., put it a different way: "He was a prude." And where would most Americans have come down on all this in 1939? What did the majority of Kern County residents make of Steinbeck's vocabulary—a taste of the vernacular bound to "bring the blushes to a maiden's cheek," as Heywood Broun said witheringly? It is tempting to say that most people would have deemed the book detestable, given the sensibilities and standards of the day. And surely many did. Even Steinbeck's sister Esther was "half-way apologetic" about her brother's work. "She did wish John wouldn't use such language as he did," recalled Carma Leigh, director of the public library in Watsonville, where Esther lived. According to a tally made by one detractor of the book, "Fornication is the keynote of forty-four passages, and . . . there are 147 instances of blasphemy."

"The fact of the matter is," said literary critic Joseph Henry Jackson, a friend of Steinbeck's, "*The Grapes of Wrath* found tens of thousands of readers who had never come across a book of its kind before—readers who had never been exposed, for example, to the Jameses, Joyce and Farrell." These were readers, Jackson added, "who had grown up through the magazines as far as *Gone With the Wind,* perhaps, or *So Red the Rose,* and who honestly felt themselves betrayed when a best seller turned out to harbor anything from a turtle which frankly wet the hand of the person who held it to a new mother who shockingly gave her breast to a full-grown man."

But given that, how can one account for the book's runaway success? And what were the nation's standards, as 1940 dawned and Americans faced bigger issues of war and peace? Were they the values of the strait-laced and starchy, of those who rushed to the theater to watch relatively tame fare such as *The Wizard of Oz, Stagecoach,* and *Mr. Smith Goes to Washington*—or of someone tickled by the Sally Rand Nude Ranch at the International Exposition on Treasure Island, where the femme fa-tales wore cowboy hats, gun belts, boots, and little else? Society had a way of sending mixed signals.

Scandalized or not, a good many people—hundreds of thousands of them—managed to get past the swearing and the sex and find something more lasting in *The Grapes of Wrath.* Among them was Eleanor Roosevelt. "The book is coarse in spots," she said, "but life is coarse in spots. . . . We do not dwell upon man's lower nature any more than we have to in life, but we know it exists and we pass over it charitably and are surprised how much there is of fineness that comes out of the baser clay.

"Even from life's sorrows some good must come," the First Lady added, before concluding: "What could be a better illustration than the closing chapter of this book?"

———•———

It wouldn't take long for the cries against censorship to reach the Board of Supervisors, with the oil workers' and hod carriers' unions, a Methodist minister, and a group of migrants among those demurring. But of all the letters that came in chastising the supervisors for the book ban, there was one that stood out from the pack. The missive wasn't striking because of what it said: "We respectfully petition you to recon-sider your Resolution and withdraw the ban." It was remarkable because of two of the names embossed on the stationery: L. L. Abel and Ralph

Abel, both members of the Kern County Committee of the American Civil Liberties Union and both brothers of Stanley Abel, the supervisor who had squashed *The Grapes of Wrath*. It's hard to fathom how they grew up in the same household and came out the way they did, these three sons of a California rancher. But their divergent philosophies become even more curious when you factor in another brother, Edson, an accomplished lawyer who had been instrumental in forming the Associated Farmers. It made for perfect symmetry: two Abels on the left and two on the right, two set on fighting for the underdog and two who had spent their lives trying to protect the establishment.

L.L. (his first name was Lindley) was shy and gangly, the slightest of the foursome. For him, defending *The Grapes of Wrath* wasn't just about the ACLU's fealty to the First Amendment. "He thought Steinbeck was right," said his daughter, Linda Franson. A machinist who was forty years old in the summer of '39, "he felt for the migrant workers, for their plight, that they had come from nothing, that they were misused." His big brother Edson's outlook couldn't have been more dissimilar. A Stanford-educated lawyer, the forty-nine-year-old often wore a grin and liked a good joke so much that if he heard one, he'd write it down so he wouldn't forget. But Edson was deadly serious about what he called "the Communist menace to agriculture"—specifically, the unions that he contended were not sincerely interested in seeing farm workers' wages rise but were, instead, trying to foment "civil war" in pursuit of "absolute social and racial equality." Among the organizations that Edson lashed out against was the ACLU, which he said had "played an important part in aiding and abetting the Communistic unions in their strike activities and . . . always rushed to the defense of their leaders when arrested." That his little brother Lindley would be drawn in might have disappointed him, but it wouldn't have astonished him. "The paid propagandists of the doctrines of Communism are . . . masters in the art of parading misery and poverty," Edson said in early 1934, around the time that, as attorney for the California Farm Bureau Federation, he was traveling the state, urging counties to adopt anti-picketing ordinances, and laying the groundwork for the founding of the Associated Farmers. "Their achievements along this line have been a godsend to the sob-sisters, both male and female, who like nothing better than to shed their tears in public."

Edson sounded tough, but at the other end of the ideological spectrum, Ralph could more than hold his own. Set to celebrate his thirty-third birthday six days after the book ban was passed, he was the youngest brother and also the biggest—a six-foot-two, two-hundred-pound oil driller and small farmer with a Clark Gable mustache who boxed competitively across Southern California in the mid-1930s. He could be pugnacious in other ways, too, constantly ready to engage in political debate—often with his very own relatives. "I remember him saying how wonderful Communism was," recalled Barbara Brown, a niece. "My sister was a Bircher. She told him, 'If it's so wonderful, why don't you go over there" to Russia to live? At times, the family friction spilled into the open. About six months before *The Grapes of Wrath* ban, Ralph was angling to become secretary of the Kern County Water Association, a position requiring the blessing of the Board of Supervisors. Ralph was vying for the job against another man and, to bolster his bid, he lined up a show of support from the grange and several labor unions. That elicited a harrumph from his brother Stanley, who said the choice shouldn't be based on who could exert the most pressure on him and the other supervisors. Ralph jumped to his feet before the packed chamber, denying that he had done anything heavy-handed, but the hostility between the two siblings was plain. "Abels Clash," the *Californian* reported the next day. It wouldn't be the last time. Two months later, Stanley Abel cast the decisive vote to abolish the water association, effectively wiping out his brother's job. Ralph insisted that his ouster was orchestrated because he had tried to ensure that the little guy was treated fairly when purchasing water. "The controversy is one of the corporate interests against the interest of the average farmer," he said. With *The Grapes of Wrath* now under siege, it was a theme that he would expound upon again. "Certain so-called farmers in this state are nothing but corporate stooges," Ralph

The Abel family was divided sharply along political lines. Standing from left to right in this photograph are Edson, Stanley, Lindley, and Ralph—the first two diehard conservatives, the second two staunch liberals. (Courtesy of Barbara Brown)

said after his brother censored the novel. "I refer to the Associated Farmers—and the association has a decided influence on the actions of this Board of Supervisors. The real issue here is whether the Associated Farmers are going to dictate to the people."

In fact, there's little question that Bill Camp and the Associated Farmers had a hand in the supervisors' resolution. Stanley Abel, however, didn't need much of a nudge from anybody to go after *The Grapes of Wrath*. Born in 1891, he had worked briefly at the *Los Angeles Examiner* as a young man and then as a roughneck in Fresno County and later on the west side of Kern. Eventually, he published a newspaper called the *Oilfield Dispatch*. Years after he had died, when a relative popped open a suitcase full of family photos, one characteristic of Stanley's jumped right out: he never smiled. Not in a single picture. In most of them, the man with a faint resemblance to Alfred Hitchcock just scowled. His disposition didn't hurt his attractiveness as a politician, though. In 1916, at age twenty-four, Stanley Abel was elected to the Board of Supervisors, becoming the youngest man ever to win such a post in California. His constituents were those in the town of Taft and thereabouts—a hardscrabble area where "beer was cheaper than water" during Prohibition, as one student of the place has observed, and that would long be regarded as a redneck redoubt, where blacks weren't welcome, especially after sundown.

Over the years, Abel would prove himself a dedicated supervisor, concentrating on public health and the surfacing of miles and miles of county roads. A couple of months before *The Grapes of Wrath* contretemps, Pacific Coast University in Santa Monica bestowed upon Abel an honorary doctorate, extolling his "untiring energy and undaunted vision." Family lore has it that he was the one responsible for putting stripes down the center of California's highways to keep oncoming traffic safely apart; if so, it was the only thing middle-of-the-road about him. Away from the board, Abel was a joiner the way many politicians are, signing up with the Elks, the Moose, the Scouts, and the Native Sons of the Golden West. But it was his involvement in another group that roiled—and forever marked—his career.

In 1922, the Ku Klux Klan tore through California, from Los Angeles to Fresno to the Bay Area. But nowhere was the KKK more formidable than in Kern County where, for months, hooded bands of men went after anybody they claimed was a threat to "common decency"—gamblers, johns, dealers of booze and drugs, at least one abortion doctor, newspaper reporters, and assorted "loafers." "Law breakers, you cannot escape us," the Klan announced on the front page of the *Californian* in February. "We know who you are, what you are and where you are. Change your ways this hour lest you be stricken as with lightening from the sky. The good will welcome us; the evil will meet with a swift and stern retribution. We have given fair warning. Beware!" Kern's hundreds of Klansmen meted out punishment as they saw fit—with horsewhips and ropes, oil and feathers, fists and guns. They left their victims beaten and bloodied. Their "reign of terror," as one local official called it, prompted a federal investigation and the empanelling of a grand jury. In April the Los Angeles district attorney raided the offices of William Coburn, the Klan's Grand Goblin, and confiscated membership lists for the KKK throughout California.

The following month, the names hit the papers—and they were salacious to say the least. In Bakersfield, the chief of police, justice of the peace, a police judge, the county sealer of weights and measures, the superintendent of the courthouse, four firemen, three deputy sheriffs, and a policeman were pegged as Ku Kluxers. In Taft, those fingered included the mayor, the postmaster, four of the city's trustees, the city treasurer, the city clerk, the assistant fire chief, and Stanley Abel, then chairman of the Kern County Board of Supervisors. Many of the politicians who had been identified did the natural thing: They ducked and covered, maintaining that they had never been involved with the Klan or, if they had, they hadn't really understood what it was all about. But not Stanley Abel. Ever brash, he issued a statement to the newspaper unlike any other:

> Yes, I belong to the Knights of the Ku Klux Klan, and I am proud to be associated with many of the best citizens of Taft and vicinity in the good work they are doing. I know nothing of the activities of the Klan in other localities, but the Klan at Taft is certainly deserving of praise for the good work it has done in ridding the community of the class of scoundrels who were selling bootleg whiskey and doped candy to high school boys, and others attempting to debauch the young womanhood of the community.
>
> We have tried to cooperate with the proper authorities, but they refused to do any effective work . . . .
>
> Good people cannot and will not stand idly by after repeated efforts to get the law enforced, and see the boys and girls of the community debauched by lawless aliens who curse the Constitution and defy our laws.

I know nothing of any lawless act committed by the Klan or its members. Those who accuse the Klan or its members of lawlessness should place their information in the hands of the proper officials.

I make no apology for the Klan. It needs none.

In August, with its ranks unmasked, the Klan pulled back in Kern County, and in the fall, an embarrassed and fed-up citizenry recalled from office a number of politicians, including several city councilmen, the city clerk, the mayor, and a justice of the peace. Of those placed on the ballot, only one survived: Stanley Abel. If he was at all humbled by the experience, he didn't show it. Over the next fifteen years, Abel continued to consolidate his base of power so that, even when he didn't hold the chairmanship of the Board of Supervisors, it was apparent that he was in charge. Most of those elected to join him on the board were cast in his mold anyway: conservative good ol' boys dressed up in suits and ties, instinctively pro-agribusiness and anti-labor.

In 1938, a tiny crack developed in Abel's machine: forty-five-year-old Ralph Lavin, a self-described "progressive," won a spot as a supervisor. Lavin, who had served as San Joaquin Valley campaign manager for the reform-minded Robert M. La Follette during his 1924 presidential run, had tried once before to get elected to the board but was unsuccessful. This time, with strong backing from the unions, he made it—a local manifestation of the same groundswell that had catapulted Culbert Olson into the governor's office. Rail thin and willing to flash a big grin for the cameras, Lavin was Abel's opposite in every way. But he was no bug-eyed radical. An Army veteran who'd talk up the importance of patriotism, Lavin would later introduce a motion to deny welfare or a government job to "any person who refuses to salute our flag in all sincerity and who cannot subscribe or offer his oath of allegiance to our Constitution." His idea of relaxation was to pore over copies of the Congressional Record. During his run for office in '38, he trumpeted his credentials as a pharmacy owner, saying that his acumen for "sound business administration" was precisely what the county government

Ralph Lavin, the only member of the Board of Supervisors to vote against banning *The Grapes of Wrath*, empathized with those who were less fortunate. (Kern County Museum)

needed. Yet Lavin, more than the other supervisors, had empathy for the less fortunate, in part because he had been there himself.

During the depths of the Depression, Lavin lost his two drugstores. He wound up as a record keeper with the Works Progress Administration, but money was still so tight, his daughter, Hallie Killebrew, would remember the reverberations for the rest of her life: the family having to move out of their house and into a small apartment; her father being forced to give up the country club and golf; their Hudson falling apart, so that her dad had to walk to the WPA, his thumbs stuck in the lower pockets of his vest; a hole appearing on the top of his black shoe that he'd disguise by rubbing polish into his sock. It was during this period that Lavin had his first head-to-head encounter with Stanley Abel and the supervisors. He had gone before the board to bring to light circumstances that he thought were patently unfair: Lavin had learned of a man who operated a thriving drugstore in Bakersfield and also held the contract for the apothecary at the county general hospital. He asked why this guy "had two jobs when some people had none," Killebrew recounted. The supervisors' response, she said, was not what her father wanted to hear. "They laughed at him." At that moment, Killebrew said, Lavin "made up his mind that he was going to get on that board."

When he finally did, having recovered some financially by landing a job with the Southern Pacific, he quickly realized that he'd have to stand his ground or he'd get steamrolled. The old guard, led by Abel, threatened to sack county workers who had voted for Lavin. "You raise one finger to fire that man," the normally soft-spoken Lavin told them, his voice now booming, "and I'll never rest until I get you." After that, they backed off. Most of the board's business was so mundane and bureaucratic that there was far more agreement than disagreement among Lavin and the other supervisors on official matters. But the resentment below the surface was palpable, especially between Lavin and Abel. "There was no love lost there," Killebrew said. "They differed so politically." Abel's ambush of *The Grapes of Wrath* was just the sort of thing that would set her dad off, grumbling as he came home, "That damn Ku Kluxer." Lavin hadn't yet read the book when the ban was put into effect. But he soon would. And where Abel saw a story that was nothing more than "a lie and a libel," Lavin discovered a tale that he knew to be all too true.

"But for the hand of fate or the grace of God," Lavin's wife, Josephine, inscribed in the copy of the novel she bought for him, "the Joad family may have been us . . . ."

CHAPTER THREE

Tuesday

And the rain fell steadily, and the water flowed over the high-ways, for the culverts could not carry the water. Then from the tents, from the crowded barns, groups of sodden men went out, their clothes slopping rags, their shoes muddy pulp. They splashed out through the water, to the towns, to the country stores, to the relief offices, to beg for food, to cringe and beg for food, to beg for relief, to try to steal, to lie. And under the begging, and under the cringing, a hopeless anger began to smolder.

J OHN STEINBECK looked like hell. He felt even worse. He had arrived back home from Hollywood on this day, August 22, 1939, "suffering arthritis and nervous exhaustion," according to one news dispatch. His wife, Carol, told reporters that he'd been overworked in L.A., where he had been conferring with producer Darryl Zanuck on the movie version of *The Grapes of Wrath*. But Steinbeck's weary state was the result of much more than one strenuous business trip. The writing of the "big book," as he called it, had left him completely spent—"I'm almost dead from lack of sleep . . . . My stomach went to pieces yesterday. May have been nerves," he noted in his journal, just before finishing the manuscript ten months earlier, in October 1938—and he hadn't really felt right since the novel's completion. He'd had his tonsils out in July, and his throat ached. An infection in Steinbeck's leg, which would continue to beleaguer him through the rest of the year, caused him to walk with a limp; broad-shouldered and normally proud of his physicality, the thirty-seven-year-old had to be helped down the stairs and into cars, as if he were an old man. "Jesus, how I hurt," Steinbeck informed a friend. "Can't smoke, can't drink." All the while, the requests for his time kept rolling in—a never-ending stream of invitations to lecture or take part in this or that civic organization. Fifty to seventy-five letters a day crowded his mailbox, "all wanting something," he said. The phone rang nonstop, forcing Steinbeck to unlist his number. "Why do they think a writer, just because he can write, will make a good after-dinner speaker or a club committee man—or even a public leader?" he said in a rare newspaper interview, granted earlier in the summer to the *Los Angeles Times*. "Just because Henry Ford made a good car, they wanted him to run for president. That's silly—unless he happened to be equipped for the other job as well.

"I'm no public speaker, and don't want to be," he continued. "I'm not even a finished writer yet. I haven't learned my craft. A writer, anyway, is just one step above a buffoon—an entertainer. If the public makes him think he is really somebody it destroys him. He pontificates, and that's the end of him. They're not going to lionize me .... That's one reason you're not going to get a photograph of me—nobody is going to exploit me. I don't want my face to be known. As soon as I get over this condition, I'll be out on the road again, sleeping in a ditch or somewhere, getting material for another yarn."

The *Los Angeles Times* story described Steinbeck as having adopted a siege mentality, sequestering himself near Los Gatos in his canyon home, "inaccessible to friend and enemy alike." Even inside this citadel, however, peace was elusive. He and Carol had drifted apart, and Steinbeck could sense that the end of their life together was coming nearer.

"The simple fact of the matter is that Carol doesn't like me," he wrote to Elizabeth Otis, his agent, the weekend before his return from L.A., and "she suppresses that feeling until such times as the pressure of her dislike (usually when she has been drinking) breaks free and comes out . . . . I want her to be, if not happy, at least a little contented and it seems that I personally am not able to make that true."

John and Carol had been together since the late '20s, and from the start he saw her as an alter ego of sorts. She is "lovely and clever and passionate," Steinbeck once wrote, while "I am pettish and small and sullen." As an author, Steinbeck depended on Carol to type his handwritten manuscripts, correct his bad spelling and slipshod punctuation, and make editorial suggestions that could be hugely significant. It was she, for example, who had thought up the title for *The Grapes of Wrath*. Even more crucial was that Carol "pulled him up when he was down, revived him when he was out," as Steinbeck's biographer, Jackson Benson, has described it. "As he got older, Steinbeck tended to lose some of his ability to enjoy; occasionally, his sense of humor faded under the strain. Carol brought humor back to his consciousness; she wouldn't let him feel sorry for himself."

For a long time—before John and Carol began boozing it up too much; before she had an affair with Joseph Campbell, the great scholar of mythology; before he started having an affair with a long-legged band singer, eighteen years his junior, in L.A.; before all the hangers-on were intruding into their lives; before the fighting got too bad; before she had gotten pregnant and he insisted she have an abortion; before an abject loneliness had set in for both of them—they were happy. Broke, but happy. During the worst of the Depression, the young couple had found a certain romance in their struggle to get by, stealing fruit after going days without a meal, downing thirty-five-cent jug wine with their friends, and dreaming of success for John as a novelist. "John and Carol were good together when they were poor," his sister Elizabeth said. "It was only when the money started coming in, and when John became more famous, that things really went sour." His first financial breakthrough came in 1935 with *Tortilla Flat*, a national best seller. Then in 1937 he finished *Of Mice and Men*, a Book-of-the-Month-Club selection whose adaptation on Broadway, followed by a cross-country tour of the play, generated a steady flow of royalty income. Suddenly, there was enough money ($10,000 to be exact) to buy the forty-seven-acre Biddle Ranch in the mountains above Los Gatos, where he'd build a brand new house complete with a swimming pool. It was there that he'd correct the galleys for *The Grapes of Wrath*, his days as a destitute artist clearly over.

All of that, though, paled with what was happening now. "What an awful lot of money" *The Grapes of Wrath* was throwing off, Steinbeck remarked in April. "I don't think I ever saw so much in one place before." Other proletarian literature from the '30s—Jack Conroy's *The Disinherited*, Robert Cantwell's *The Land of Plenty*, Erskine Caldwell's *Tobacco Road*, and James Farrell's trilogy, *Studs Lonigan*—would command the attention of the critics, but *The Grapes of Wrath* alone would become a true commercial phenomenon, with Steinbeck on pace to sell 430,000 copies by the end of 1939. He also had sold the film rights for $70,000—equal to nearly $1 million today and, at the time, one of the highest prices the studios had ever paid for a novel.

The riches, however, seemed as much a burden as a boon. Desperate strangers contacted Steinbeck, hoping for a handout. And on some level, he felt guilty over becoming wealthy from a story about the needy. "I simply can't make money on these people," he once said. Earlier, with Hollywood offering to toss him a pile of cash for *Of Mice and Men*—another tale of the down-and-out—Steinbeck hatched a plan to give three thousand migrants $2 each. Pascal Covici, his publisher, talked him out of it. This time, Steinbeck's windfall provided his most rabid challengers with just the target they were looking for. Ruth Comfort Mitchell's group, Pro America, printed this ditty, titled "Migrant to John Steinbeck":

> *You've written a best seller,*
> *That stands on every shelf.*

We hear you've sold the movie rights
With profit to yourself.
Now, just to clear the record,
And this is meant for you,
Most of us don't think or talk
The way you say we do.
But since your pity for us
Has swelled your bank account,
Why don't you give us migrants
A generous amount ? ? ? ? ?

A little doggerel was the least of it. On top of all the unrelenting demands on him, on top of his sickness, on top of his crumbling marriage, Steinbeck faced a kind of get-even from those insulted by *The Grapes of Wrath* that few authors, before or since, have been subjected to. It wasn't just the public carpers, such as Ruth Comfort Mitchell, who were tormenting him. It was the prospect of something far more serious. "The Associated Farmers have begun an hysterical personal attack on me both in the papers and a whispering campaign," he said. "I'm a Jew, I'm a pervert, a drunk, a dope fiend." When Lewis Milestone, who was working on the screenplay for *Of Mice and Men*, came to central California to scout locations for the movie, Steinbeck escorted him. But he'd never stop at any ranches, driving swiftly on and off each property. When Milestone asked why he didn't pull over and get out so they could look around, Steinbeck talked straight: "Because I'd get my ass full of rock salt. They hate me around here." One friend, the undersheriff of Santa Clara County, warned Steinbeck not to stay in a hotel by himself. "Maybe I'm sticking my neck out, but the boys got a rape case set up for you," he told him. "You get alone in a hotel and a dame will come in, tear off her clothes, scratch her face and scream, and you try to talk yourself out of that one. They won't touch your book, but there's easier ways."

If the allegation of a sex crime wasn't to materialize, Steinbeck wrote Elizabeth Otis, "I began to wonder if . . . a drunk driving charge or

John Steinbeck found himself under tremendous stress and strain in August 1939. (Photo by Sonya Noskowiak, Department of Special Collections, Stanford University)

something like that might not be in the offing for me. You must understand that the Associated Farmers absolutely control the sheriff's office in this state. I went to my attorney, and he said there was no way of stopping a charge but advised me to keep a diary containing names of people I saw and when so that I could call an alibi if I had to. I don't think they would dare attack me but they have done as bad . . . . Please keep this letter with the dated envelope. This group is the same that put Mooney . . . in prison for life on trumped up charges. They are capable of anything."

In such an environment—with so many enemies real and imagined—it was hard to know whom to trust. Steinbeck adopted an alias when staying in Los Angeles ("Mr. Brooks" he called himself at one point), used a friend's house for a mail drop, and secreted away records on the mistreatment of migrants in safety deposit boxes. In late June, he alerted a friend that he had "placed certain information in the hands of J. Edgar Hoover in case I take a nose dive." But it was Hoover's FBI that would keep an inch-thick file on Steinbeck. And it was Hoover's FBI that apparently had sent agents into a bookshop in Monterey, where Steinbeck once lived, asking questions of the owner, Miss Smith. "When she asked why," Steinbeck recounted, "they said they were investigating me for Mr. Hoover—that Mr. Hoover considered me the most dangerous subversive influence in the West . . . . Miss Smith didn't think it was a joke."

Yet of all the stresses and strains, one rumor may well have gotten to Steinbeck the most: the migrants themselves, it was said, hated him and had threatened to kill him for lying about them. When the *Los Angeles Times* reporter visiting his ranch raised this issue, Steinbeck couldn't hide his exasperation. "Show you the letters from my friends, the Okies? No, I won't do that," he roared. "But I've got them—lots of them! Here—I'll show you what some of the Okies think of me." And with that, he had Carol take out a stuffed dog made from scraps of colored cloth. A group of valley laborers had sent it to him as a gift. Around the critter's neck, a little tag hung down. "Migrant John," it said.

———•———

"Migrant John" was a hard-earned sobriquet—an appellation that came from years of traveling among the valley's farm workers, earning their trust, taking in their stories, and, eventually, feeling their anger and making it his own. But Steinbeck wasn't always angry. At the beginning, he was mostly just curious.

In large part through Carol, Steinbeck had in the mid-1930s started to socialize with a group openly supportive of the Cannery and Agricultural Workers Industrial Union (CAWIU) and active in the John Reed Club in Carmel—an organization named for the American Communist leader who had imparted the drama of the Bolshevik Revolution in his firsthand account, *Ten Days That Shook the World*. Steinbeck didn't share the group's devotion to Marxist dogma or obeisance to the Comintern in Russia. Steinbeck possessed a relentlessly probing mind, and the strict discipline demanded by the Communist Party—"Discussion of

questions over which there have been differences must not continue
after the decision has been made"—was anathema to him. Still, Steinbeck found the Red crowd stimulating, and he was happy to be around
them, listening more than he talked, sometimes even taking notes. "We
were just human background reference material," joked Francis
Whitaker, a blacksmith and John Reed Club participant who was close
to Steinbeck during this period.

Besides, there was no shortage of others willing to take up the slack
and pontificate. Several of the most famous names from the radical
Left—Lincoln Steffens, Ella Winter, Langston Hughes, Anna Louise
Strong, Mike Gold, Marie de L. Welch—were part of the scene. Some
regarded Steinbeck as a bit of an oddity because, in an era of political
and ideological extremes, he seemed intent on occupying the middle
ground. "He did not want to be connected with any one side," Winter
said, "lest people thought he was writing propaganda." Whitaker had a
less flattering take on Steinbeck's attempt at neutrality: "He was very
naïve of politics" in those early days.

Whatever the case, in the spring of 1934 Steinbeck received one of
his first intimate lessons on the labor unrest that was gripping the Central Valley. Winter and others associated with the John Reed Club had
been passionate advocates for the embattled pickers in the just-ended
cotton strike, supporting the union and visiting the workers' tent city in
the Kings County town of Corcoran, where more than three thousand
"nomad harvesters," as the poet de L. Welch called them, were holed up,
demanding higher wages. Now, two of the strike organizers—having
watched some of their comrades jailed for their activism—were on the
run and hiding in an attic in Seaside, about ten miles from Carmel.
Steinbeck and Whitaker went to see the fugitives, and Steinbeck spent
hours chatting with one of them in particular: Cecil McKiddy, who had
functioned as a section secretary for Pat Chambers, one of the leaders of
the CAWIU. Nobody knows precisely what McKiddy told Steinbeck,
but the union man was in a great position to relate the nitty-gritty of
how the cotton strike was put together, as he was the one who typed up

instructions to the CAWIU leadership. What's more, McKiddy himself loved to read, so his eye for the telling little nugget that could enliven a story was probably better than most.

Steinbeck would ultimately pour many of these particulars into his novel *In Dubious Battle,* which was based on the cotton strike but set, fictitiously, in California's apple orchards. Published in January 1936, the book included some of the same kind of rough language that so many would protest a few years later in *The Grapes of Wrath.* And, as he would do then, Steinbeck defended his choice of words without hesitation. "A working man bereft of his profanity is a silent man," he told Mavis McIntosh, Elizabeth Otis's partner. "To try to reproduce the speech of these people and to clean it up is to make it sound stiff, unnatural and emasculated."

Unlike with *The Grapes of Wrath,* however, Steinbeck did his utmost to make this story completely apolitical. He was, he said, more interested in using *In Dubious Battle* to delve into the dynamics of group action than to take a stand for labor. And, in fact, the union leaders in the book, Mac and John, are not very likable. Neither are the big growers. Mostly, Steinbeck wanted his story to be believable. "I'm not interested," he said in January 1935, a few weeks before he sent off the manuscript, "in ranting about justice and oppression." Perhaps because of that, the book wasn't attacked with any real fervor from the right. Nor, though, did most of the left pillory the novel. *In Dubious Battle* "is a stunning, straight correct narrative about things as they happen," Lincoln Steffens told Sam Darcy, the district organizer for the Communist Party in California. "I think it is the best report of a labor struggle that has come out of this valley . . . . It may not be sympathetic with labor, but it is realistic about the vigilantes."

Most important for Steinbeck, the depth with which *In Dubious Battle* had been written turned him into an instant authority on farm workers and set him up for an assignment in the summer of '36 that would lay the foundation—in regard to facts and feelings—for *The Grapes of Wrath.* George West, the editorial page editor of the *San*

Francisco News, had been arguing in the paper for the federal government to erect more farm-labor camps in California to accommodate the migrants who were overwhelming the resources of the state. The Associated Farmers hated these facilities—"Communistic" was how Bill Camp referred to them—because its leaders feared, often accurately, that they were loci of union organizing. And West worried, rightfully, that "powerful influences" might be on the verge of stopping the camp-building effort "dead in its tracks." So he decided to go on the offensive. Impressed by *In Dubious Battle,* West recruited Steinbeck, whom he had met at Lincoln Steffens and Ella Winter's place, to explore the migrant situation and to write about the camp program for the newspaper. It's not clear why, or even whether, Steinbeck may have suddenly felt comfortable aligning himself with an ardent left-winger like West, who was married to Marie de L. Welch. But he didn't pull back when West had him begin his reporting by meeting with several federal officials who weren't exactly known for the kind of cold detachment that Steinbeck had maintained in *In Dubious Battle.*

Among his first stops was Frederick Soule, who oversaw the Resettlement Administration's information division out of Berkeley. The RA, which ran the labor camps (and a year later would be transformed into the Farm Security Administration), was the invention of Roosevelt "Brain-Truster" Rexford G. Tugwell. Its mandate was wide-ranging, its geographic reach widespread: Operating through the South and the drought-stricken plains states, the RA relocated impoverished families from farm and city alike, taught proper land use techniques, fought soil erosion and promoted forestation, and created "greenbelt communities"—suburban housing developments—outside Washington, Cincinnati, and Milwaukee. It extended its mission into rural California and the lives of the Dust Bowl migrants largely at the urging of economics professor Paul Taylor, with the help of his bride-to-be, photographer Dorothea Lange. "The trek of drought and depression refugees to California is the result of a national catastrophe," Taylor said. "The succor of its victims is a national responsibility."

As sensible and straightforward as that may have sounded, the RA was among the most polarizing of New Deal agencies. Those on the left saw it as a heroic and humanistic institution that was helping to deliver a needed measure of social justice for the downtrodden. Those on the right viewed it as a dreadful and dangerous experiment by socialist dreamers. Fred Soule, a former Hearst newspaperman, was nothing if not a dreamer—a Jeffersonian Democrat who was helping to administer a farm-worker housing program in a state where the giants of agribusiness had made Jefferson's notion of the yeoman a joke. Tall and scrawny, Soule looked "like Abe Lincoln's ghost," recalled Helen Hosmer, who worked for him. "He used to clean his fingernails with a big paring knife and suck his teeth, *slurp, slurp.*" When Hosmer first went in to apply for her job, she found Soule with his shoes up on his desk—"one foot on the *New Republic* and one foot on the *Nation.*"

"The chickens are home to roost," he told her. "The land is stripped. The people are here."

When Steinbeck came through, Soule and Hosmer opened up to him their extensive files on the history of California agriculture—a trove that evidently included lots of information not just on the extent of the state's staggering bounty but also on the vanquishing of its field hands. The archive left a profound impression on him—though, for quite some time, Steinbeck would remain "scared to death of all these left-wingers swarming around," Hosmer later recalled.

From Berkeley, Steinbeck headed into the valley. His mode of transportation was an old bakery truck that he had purchased for the occasion. This "pie wagon," as he called it, was outfitted with a cot, an icebox, a chest in which to keep his clothes, and other accessories for living on the road. Accompanying Steinbeck was Eric Thomsen, an RA official who had recently been put in charge of the migrant camps in California. Thomsen had started out in his native Denmark as a prosperous businessman, becoming president of his own steamship company in his early twenties. But he always had a soft spot for the workingman. During World War I, when the sailors' and stokers' unions requested a special bonus in the form of double pay, Thomsen brushed aside the hard-line stance of the Ship Owners Association and agreed to what he regarded as their "reasonable demands." "Why not?" he asked. "We are making plenty of money." By the early 1920s, Thomsen had tired of commerce altogether and set out to teach himself about philosophy, sociology, psychology, and science by studying in the libraries of London, New York, and Chicago. A bit later, he enrolled in the Union Theological Seminary in New York City, intending to become a minister. By the 1930s, Thomsen had moved into government work, serving for a spell as religious and educational director of the Tennessee Valley Authority. Driven by a strong conscience, Thomsen believed "that the burdens of migratory laborers" were "inexcusable and unnecessary in the modern world"—and he did his best to convince Steinbeck of those things.

First, he presented the inexcusable. As Thomsen guided Steinbeck through the valley, he made sure to stop at various squatters' camps and ditch-bank settlements, exposing the writer to a level of poverty that was truly startling: families scrunched in cardboard boxes and large drain pipes, some of them so famished that they were eating rats and dogs. Next, Thomsen attempted to show his companion why such hardship was all so unnecessary. Their final stop was the RA's Kern Migratory Labor Camp outside Arvin, just south of Bakersfield on a piece of land that Bill Camp had once owned. It was a simple complex of tents laid out over a twenty-acre tract, but an absolute sanctuary compared with the Hoovervilles they had seen on their way. For one thing, the Arvin camp was clean despite the name that many knew it by: Weedpatch. For another, its residents were treated with a kind of respect that they hungered for nearly as much as a square meal; they were allowed to make their own rules and govern the camp as a democracy.

The architect of this arrangement was Thomas Collins, who had led something of an itinerant life himself before finding his way to the RA.

Born out of wedlock near Baltimore in the mid-1890s, Collins grew up in a Catholic orphanage, went off to boarding school, and, from there, attended a Maryland seminary to train for the priesthood. He quit after two years, though, got married and then, after the birth of his second child, ran off with the sixteen-year-old daughter of a blue-blood family. They met at a train station, eloped, and hightailed it to Puerto Rico, with private detectives hired by the bride's father in pursuit. The couple soon fled to Venezuela and then to Guam. In 1929, they returned to the United States, where Collins established a school for delinquent boys near San Diego. But the school went bankrupt after a couple of years, leaving Collins deeply in debt. He again abandoned his family and later was divorced by his second wife. After that, he found a job running government soup kitchens in San Diego, and in 1935 joined the RA.

Kind, gentle, witty—and a hard drinker—Collins empathized with the migrants' grim situation, perhaps because of his own topsy-turvy past. Whatever it was, he proved to be the ideal camp administrator: sensitive of the residents' feelings, mindful of their rights—and a keen observer of their ways. In the weekly (and sometimes biweekly) reports he sent back to RA headquarters, Collins compiled copious information on camp life: the migrants' comings and goings; the wages they managed to scrape together in the nearby farm fields; their diets ("Menu: beans, baking powder biscuits, jam, coffee"); their health status ("Number cases illness—one, tonsillitis"); their baseball scores; their song lyrics; their religious practices; whether they were driving Model As or Ts; even their unvarnished voices, in a regular section he called "Bits of Migrant Wisdom":

In Texas, a falla kin git fer wurkin all he wants, cept a littl money. In Cliforny he kin git a littl money but nuffin he wants.

Gawd is good to us farm lab'rs. When we aint got wuk and everything luks blue he sends us a new baby ter keep us happy.

Us farm workers starv ter def ter raise our kids. When the kids grows up we all starves.

Tom Collins, who ran the federal government's migrant labor camp in Arvin, just outside Bakersfield, compiled copious information that Steinbeck put to good use in his novel. (Photo by Dorothea Lange, Library of Congress)

The details and dialect that Steinbeck gleaned from Collins's reports would become invaluable as he crafted his series of stories for the *San Francisco News* and, later, *The Grapes of Wrath*. Indeed, whole scenes in the book appear to have been formed from Collins's sketches of the Arvin camp. That the Joads found the indoor plumbing at the government camp where they settled to be some exotic contrivance, for example, echoes Collins's entry about a migrant who mixed up the toilet and the shower, while his wife confused the crapper with a laundry tub. The regulation of the camp where the Joads stayed mirrored the self-governing setup in Arvin. And Collins's compassion certainly infused the government-camp manager in the novel, Jim Rawley. Some believe, as well, that the chairman of the Camp Central Committee at Arvin, an Oklahoma transplant named Sherm Eastom, was the basis—or at least a basis—for Tom Joad. (Likely a composite character, Joad may well have had a little Cecil McKiddy in him too.) In his reports, Collins also kept tabs on the non-government lodging available to migrant laborers in the area—in many cases unclean, unsanitary housing provided by local farmers. Once again, the contrast with the RA's encampment was glaring, giving Steinbeck another thread to weave into *The Grapes of Wrath*.

During the period that Thomsen and Steinbeck were guests at the Arvin camp, more than four hundred people were living there. Of the 150 men, Collins noted, 135 were employed—many of them picking, packing, and loading grapes—all of them at thirty cents an hour (or less than half the nation's average manufacturing wage). Grape season was just about to give way to cotton, and tensions were running high. Wrote Collins:

> From a very reliable source . . . we were informed that the Associated Farmers had a secret meeting in one of the rooms of the Kern County Court House, Bakersfield. Most of the large growers were represented there. We were also informed that the sheriff of Kern County attended the meeting.
>
> The topic of the meeting seems to have been "Are we law abiding and liberty loving citizens ready and prepared for a strike? Have we sufficient arms and ammunition?" . . . .
>
> A contributing factor to the fright of the Associated Farmers is their knowledge of attempts of the workers to form a union . . . .
>
> To those of us interested in the welfare of the worker we believe these fears to be unfounded . . . .
>
> This meeting, with its prenatal secrecy . . . is a damnable attempt to besmirch . . . hard-working men and women. In their search for a haven—the opportunity to start anew—they have arrived from their scorched homesteads, hearts alive with hope, souls overflowing with faith, demanding work, seeking work, praying for work. Little do they know that about them stalks the ghostly dirge of the machine gun in the hands of . . . selfishness and greed.

Collins's imagery may have been overwrought, but the allusion to "arms and ammunition" was no mere rhetorical flourish. Steinbeck would soon find that out firsthand, as he left Arvin and headed to the central California coast and his hometown of Salinas.

Salinas was not a place that engendered warm feelings in John Steinbeck, even though his turn-of-the-century childhood there seemed almost idyllic in some respects. The region was beautiful, with its
redwoods and rolling hills and the salt spray of the Pacific nearby. His
family was well known, and generally well liked, in town (population:
about 2,500 at the time). Before he died in 1935, Steinbeck's father, also
named John (though Jr. and Sr. weren't used), had worked as a book-
keeper in the local Spreckels Sugar plant and later became treasurer of
Monterey County. His mother, Olive, who passed away in 1934, had
been active on the Salinas social circuit. Steinbeck and his three sisters
grew up in a solidly middle-class home, not as well-heeled as the town's
lawyers, bankers, and industrialists but never wanting for much. The
Steinbecks lived in a two-story, Victorian-frame house, complete with a
white picket fence. But as comfortable as his upbringing was, Steinbeck
had gone off to Stanford University in 1919 full of resentment toward
Salinas and what he perceived as its prejudices and small-mindedness.
If he had any hope of changing that opinion on his trip home now, with
a reporter's notebook in hand, the timing couldn't have been worse.

California's lettuce belt was on edge during the early days of September 1936. The Fruit and Vegetable Workers' Union, looking to re-
negotiate its contract with the Grower-Shipper Vegetable Association,
was insisting on a preferential hiring clause for its members—a stipulation that would make them the first employed and last fired. The union
had a sound reason to seek such a proviso: it had made strong wage
gains, with those in the Salinas Valley's packing sheds earning up to
seventy-five cents an hour. But now, migrants were descending upon
Monterey County, just as they were in Kern, threatening to work on the
cheap and undermine those good union jobs.

The grower-shipper association refused to accede to the Fruit and
Vegetable Workers' demand, however, saying that to give in would be to
surrender control of their business to the union. On September 4, about
thirty-five hundred union members walked off the job, putting $11 mil-
lion worth of fresh produce at risk. Ten days later, lettuce trucks carry-

ing strikebreakers were seen on the outskirts of Salinas, which by now resembled a war zone. The sheriff had called upon all males between eighteen and forty-five to help him deal with the strikers, arming them with blue armbands, shotguns, and hickory clubs that, according to some reports, had been fashioned at the local high school. The sheriff's brigade was only one part of the army that had been arrayed; the Salinas police and state highway patrol were also marshaling officers, making for an antistrike force of about fifteen hundred in all. In the meantime, the local Citizens' Association had recruited Colonel Henry Sanborn to help coordinate this show of police power. Sanborn was an officer in the Army Reserve, a proud vigilante and publisher of the *American Citizen,* the San Francisco paper dedicated to stopping Communism from "becoming a reality."

Just how much the Communists had to do with supporting the union in Salinas is difficult to know. Fruit and Vegetable Workers Local 18211 was part of the American Federation of Labor, which had long had an uncomfortable relationship, at best, with the Communist Party. And the union went out of its way to distance itself from anything and anyone that could be construed as Red, decrying all attempts to paint it as a "non-democratic organization." It's also safe to say that most, if not all, of the rank and file were simply looking for economic protection, not a revolution. Yet it was during this stretch—between the demise of the Communist-led union that had carried out the cotton strike of '33 and the rise of the Communist-led union that would take to the fields of California in the last few years of the decade—that the party was eager to have its members infiltrate the AFL, "boring from within." The Communist newspaper, the *Western Worker,* praised the Salinas strike for giving the workers a "real political education."

Of course, whether the Communists were genuinely involved probably didn't matter much anyway. Sanborn and his "general staff" were bound to stick a Red label on the union, regardless of the facts. At one stage, the highway patrol chief seized hundreds of red flags along the road near town and held them out as proof of a Communist cabal in the area.

As it turned out, the flags were part of a routine traffic check being made by state officials. At another point, the town's fire sirens rang out with four sharp blasts as word spread that hundreds of Red longshoremen from San Francisco were headed for Salinas. None ever appeared.

Sanborn and his cronies were spoiling for a fight, plain and simple, and on September 15 they got what they wanted. Fruit and Vegetable Workers members shouting "Rats! Rats! Rats!" hoisted themselves onto trucks being driven by the strikebreakers as they made their way to the packing operation at the Salinas Valley Ice Company. George Griffin, the Salinas police chief, gave the union men ten minutes to disperse. When they didn't, he ordered his officers to fire their tear-gas grenades. "They stood there and kept firing the gas guns, and we ran into people's homes and anyplace we could find," recalled Otto Ables, one of the union men caught up in the combat. "They surrounded the block. Then the Highway Patrolmen came down six abreast, and they started using nauseating gas, shooting it everywhere." The violence crescendoed the next day when pickets pulled crates of lettuce off a convoy of trucks and threw them into Gabilan Street. The police response was more furious than ever—a salvo of tear-gas bombs that continued through the afternoon and into the evening. In many cases, groups of two and three were fired upon, with no apparent justification. When workers retreated to the Labor Temple, bombs were lobbed inside. Appearing at the head of a group of gun-toting sheriff's deputies was Hank Strobel, county chief of the Associated Farmers.

Brazen as ever, the Associated Farmers would maintain in the days to follow that most of the bloodshed in Salinas had come at the expense of the farmers, not the strikers. Strobel, for one, claimed that a mob of workers attacked him, slipped a rope around his neck, and prepared to hang him. He'd recall, as well, how razor blades were embedded in potatoes and apples and hurled at truck drivers. Some strikers, he added, tried to pour acid on the produce. But the National Labor Relations Board, while acknowledging violence on both sides, would later conclude it was the response by law enforcement and its citizen surrogates that had been completely out of line. What transpired in Salinas, the board found, was "inexcusable police brutality, in many instances bordering upon sadism."

John Steinbeck certainly saw it that way. He passed through Salinas at the beginning of the lettuce strike and would return toward the end of the month. What he witnessed and heard about broke his heart. "There are riots in Salinas . . . that dear little town where I was born," he told a friend. In early October, Steinbeck published a piece on the conflict in the *Literary Digest,* a popular newsweekly (that a couple of years later would fold into *Time* magazine). "The story is not laid in war-torn Spain, nor in Nazi Germany—but in the Untied States, in the once peaceful Salinas valley, Monterey County, California," he wrote. "It is the story of . . . a type of Fascist psychology of which Sinclair Lewis opined that 'It Can't Happen Here.'" But, Steinbeck quickly added, "It did happen."

The events in Salinas were pivotal for Steinbeck in a couple of ways. For one, what had started out at the John Reed Club in Carmel as honest curiosity was now turning into unbridled anger—anger over farm workers being "badgered, tormented and hurt," as he put it. For another, Steinbeck was beginning to make a connection between the poverty he had seen on his way to Arvin and the level of aggression that the big growers were willing to let loose to maintain their income. It was this nexus—linking one man's profit to another's privation—that would become a primary theme in *The Grapes of Wrath.*

First, though, there came his journalism, published in the *San Francisco News* in early October 1936. The writing in the seven-part newspaper series wasn't especially stylish. But it was full of pique and, in describing the migrants' wretched living conditions, Steinbeck left little to the imagination:

The tent is full of flies clinging to the apple box that is the dinner table, buzzing about the foul clothes of the children, particularly the baby, who has not been bathed nor cleaned for several days . . . . There is no toilet here, but there is a clump of willows nearby where human feces lie exposed to the flies—the same flies that are now in the tent.

Two weeks ago there was another child, a four-year-old boy. For a few weeks they had noticed that he was kind of lackadaisical, that his eyes had been feverish. They had given him the best place in the bed, between father and mother. But one night he went into convulsions and died, and the next morning the coroner's wagon took him away . . . .

They know pretty well that it was a diet of fresh fruit, beans and little else that caused his death. He had no milk for months. With this death there came a change of mind in his family. The father and mother now feel that paralyzed dullness with which the mind protects itself against too much sorrow and too much pain.

Steinbeck went on to denounce "the large grower and absentee speculative farmer in California." And he painted a stark contrast between the squatters' camps, with their disease and death, and the federal government camps, where people entered "beaten, sullen and destitute" but before long found "a steadiness of gaze and a self-confidence that can only come of restored dignity." At the end of the series, Steinbeck served up a number of policy prescriptions, characterizing them as "a partial solution of the problem": he urged that federal lands be set aside as subsistence farms for migrants. And when seasonal demand for migratory labor pulled people away from these farms, he suggested that only the men take to the road, leaving the women behind to manage the homestead and the children to be schooled in one place. "The cost of such ventures," Steinbeck wrote, "would not be much greater than the amount which is now spent for tear gas, machine guns and ammunition, and deputy sheriffs."

He also recommended the regular publishing of reliable information about wage rates and labor requirements "so that the harvest does not become a great, disorganized gold rush with twice and three times as much labor applying as is needed." He called for the unionization of agricultural workers. And he pushed for turning the state's criminal syn-

The 1936 Salinas Lettuce Strike helped fuel Steinbeck's anger toward California's big agricultural interests. He said the violence in his hometown was the result of "a type of Fascist psychology." (Photo by Otto Hagel, Dorothea Lange Collection, Oakland Museum of California)

dicalism laws on their head, so that they'd be brought not against Communists and Socialists accused of trying to topple the capitalist system but against practitioners of "vigilante terrorism, which is the disgrace of California."

Not that all of Steinbeck's sentiments were necessarily the most progressive. Running through his *News* stories was an undercurrent of racism, showing that even someone as broadminded as Steinbeck was still, in many ways, a product of his time. Specifically, he contrasted the Okies with the Mexicans, Chinese, and other "foreign migrants" who had "invariably been drawn from a peon class" to work in the fields of California. "It should be understood that with this new race the old methods of starvation wages, of jailing, beating and intimidation are not going to work; these are American people," Steinbeck wrote. "Consequently we must meet them with understanding and attempt to work out the problem to their benefit as well as ours." Given this mindset, it was ironic that the name of the newspaper series—"The Harvest Gypsies"—would come back to bite the author. "I have heard that a number of migrant workers have resented the title," Steinbeck said in a letter that the *News* published October 20. "Certainly I had no intention of insulting a people who are already insulted beyond endurance."

Whatever hard feelings there may have been, they didn't last long, at least among those living at the labor camp in Arvin. There, the Camp Central Committee composed the following:

Dear Mr. Steinbeck

We saw your letter to the Editor of the San Francisco news . . . .

We all understand just Why you found it important to use that word, we know there are lots of People who know from seeing just how Gypsies live, but we also Know that there are more people that don't Know how farm workers live, and never would know if it had not been for your trying to exPlain and Show them.

We think you did a fine job for us and we thankyou. this is a big battle which cannot be won by ourselves, we kneed friends like you . . . .

And he needed them, as well—their voices and, for his own peace of mind, their validation. For, by this point, Steinbeck was bent on telling the migrants' story not just as a journalist but as a novelist, and doing so in a way that, in terms of ambition and artistry, would eclipse anything he had ever attempted. "Down the country," he told the writer Louis Paul in 1936, "I discovered a book like nothing in the world." It would, though, take quite a bit of time before Steinbeck could put his opening words onto the page—at least in a form that he felt good about. First he took a long trip abroad with Carol. They stopped in Copenhagen, Stockholm, Helsinki, Leningrad, and Moscow, a sojourn made possible by all the money Steinbeck had made off *Of Mice and Men*. Though this caused a many-months delay in tackling the new novel, the migrants and their problems never seemed to have left his thoughts, and the hiatus from the project may have even been by design. "The subject is so huge that it scares me to death," Steinbeck confided to Elizabeth Otis in early 1937. "And I'm not going to rush it. It must be worked out with great care."

Upon his return from Europe that summer, Steinbeck visited Farm Security Administration (FSA) headquarters in Washington and then, in the fall, hooked up once again with Tom Collins, who was now managing the government's labor camp in Gridley, about 360 miles north of Arvin in Butte County. Steinbeck's aim was to live among the migrants for a brief period, sleeping in their tumbledown colonies, and following them southward in his pie wagon along the fruit-and-cotton trail. He and Collins covered the length of the San Joaquin Valley, and Steinbeck came back home with enough material to embark on a book that he called "The Oklahomans." But that incarnation of the migrants' saga didn't get very far, and the manuscript would never be found.

In early 1938, Steinbeck took to the field one more time. Only now, things had taken a terrible turn. The rains that pelted the valley that winter were among the harshest on record, and Steinbeck felt obligated this time not only to observe but to help. "I must go to Visalia," Steinbeck wrote his agent. "Four thousand families, drowned out of their tents are really starving to death . . . . The newspapers won't touch the stuff but they will under my byline. The locals are fighting the government bringing in food and medicine. I'm going to try to break the story hard enough so that food and drugs can get moving." Collins, meanwhile, had joined other FSA personnel in the deluged region. Again, he and Steinbeck would join up—though Steinbeck was determined to remain as invisible as possible. Ever since the *San Francisco News* ran its series, he felt like a marked man. "Tom—please don't tell anyone I am coming," Steinbeck directed. "My old feud with the ass[ociated] farmers is stirring again and I don't want my movements traced."

In mid-February, Steinbeck and Collins spent about ten days together, doing what they could to assist those in need. "When we reached the flooded areas we found John's old pie truck useless, so we set out on foot," Collins would later recall. "For forty-eight hours, and without food or sleep, we worked among the sick and the half-starved people, dragging some from under trees to a different sort of shelter, dragging others from torn and ragged tents, floored with inches of water, stagnant water." The two men—Steinbeck "a mass of mud and slime"—found one family that had no food, leaving two kids to preside over their mother, who was so hungry she couldn't move. Steinbeck slipped out into the night, returning the next morning with some provisions. "John and I sat on the dirt floor," Collins said. "We sat there and the five of us ate the food which John had obtained from the little store some muddy distance away. We sat there and ate a bite—a bite that was a banquet . . . . Then names and ages of our new-found friends for delivery to the government agency which would succor the isolated family, and we were off again to find other mothers and children out there in that vast wilderness of mud and deep water."

The floods made Steinbeck even angrier than before—"I want to put a tag of shame on the greedy bastards who are responsible for this"—and he channeled his rage into a couple of pieces, including one in the *Monterey Trader* called "Starvation Under the Orange Trees" and another headlined "'Okies'—New Word and New Hate in California," which appeared in the Communist publication *People's World*. The magazines *Fortune* and *Life* also asked him to do articles on the migrants in early '38. He turned down the former, explaining "I don't like the audience," but he did agree to go on assignment for the latter, and was accompanied to Visalia by photographer Horace Bristol. Though Bristol's pictures ran, Steinbeck's story didn't, seemingly because the language was too bitter—and too far left—for the *Life* editors to bear.

That they reacted that way wasn't surprising. Steinbeck was by now so mad—apoplectic, really—that he couldn't get out of his own way. His long-simmering novel, which he titled "The Great Pig Sticking" and then "L'Affaire Lettuceberg," was as ham-fisted as anything he'd ever written. By May 1938, Steinbeck was on his way to a seventy-thousand-word draft, which he described as "a vicious book, a mean book." "I feel so ferocious about the thing," he confessed, "that I won't have much critical insight." Actually, he had just enough to know that it was time to stop and start over. Within days, he destroyed "L'Affaire." "It is a bad book and I must get rid of it," he told Otis. "It can't be printed. It is bad because it isn't honest. Oh! these incidents all happened but—I'm not telling as much of the truth about them as I know. In satire you have to restrict the picture and I just can't do satire . . . . My father would have called it a smart-alec book. It was full of tricks to make people ridiculous. If I can't do better I have slipped badly. And that I won't admit, yet."

The shedding of "L'Affaire" was a catharsis. It was now the last day of May 1938, and Steinbeck was finally ready to write the book he was meaning to write. And so he began: "To the red country and part of the gray country of Oklahoma, the last rains came gently, and they did not cut the scarred earth." For the next five months, he would diligently plug away, draining himself mentally, physically, and emotionally, until on October 26, 1938, he declared, "Finished this day—and I hope to God it's good."

It would take another six months until *The Grapes of Wrath* was published, leading to the firestorm in Kern County. And yet all that time, even as Steinbeck disappeared into his writing and then waited for his masterwork to come out, his name remained synonymous with the migrants and efforts to relieve their woe. The result was that by the time the big book hit, the Associated Farmers already considered Steinbeck a hazard to the existing order—a pest more perilous than any bug in the fields. Nor were they entirely off the mark. After witnessing the devastation of the winter floods, Steinbeck wrote to his friend, the filmmaker Pare Loretz, whose Dust Bowl documentary, *The Plow That Broke the Plains,* had helped inspire the novelist. "It might interest you to know but not to repeat just now," Steinbeck told him, "that a nice revolutionary feeling is the concomitant of this suffering. I mean it is something that I had hoped but was not sure of, that a certain amount of suffering is deadening, but a quick increase such as this storm shakes off the apathy.

"The thing," Steinbeck added expectantly, "is very dangerous now."

———•———

John Steinbeck was no glory hound. After *Of Mice and Men* was published, he told his agents that he'd gotten "sick to my stomach" when recognized on the streets of San Francisco. In general, he found fame "a pain in the ass." And so it was no small thing that he would allow himself to become a spokesman for those who wanted to help the migrants and vilify the big growers. They, in turn, clung to Steinbeck's emerging identity as a defender of the common man like mud to a field hand's boots. Before long, "Steinbeck" wasn't just a name on a dust jacket anymore; it was a symbol, a shibboleth, for something much, much greater.

In the spring of 1938, as the author prepared to immerse himself in his new novel, a group known as the Simon J. Lubin Society began selling for twenty-five cents apiece a reprinting of "The Harvest Gypsies" series from the *San Francisco News,* supplemented by a handful of Dorothea Lange photographs. Helen Hosmer, whom Steinbeck had first met when she worked for the government's migrant resettlement program, was the firecracker who ran the Lubin Society, and she planned on using the money she raised from selling the pamphlet "to help the cause." Steinbeck, for his part, "didn't ask for a dime," Hosmer said. "He gave us every penny." She called the booklet *Their Blood Is Strong* after a line from one of Steinbeck's *News* articles on the migrants' fortitude in the face of affliction: "They have weathered the thing, and they can weather much more for their blood is strong." The title caused a little confusion, as officials in Nazi Germany mistakenly thought it had something to do with the purity of blood and ordered several copies. But the real effect of the Lubin Society publication was unambiguous: it allied Steinbeck closer than ever with the Far Left.

Hosmer was a member of the Communist Party who had left the FSA in 1937 because, as much as she wanted to help establish more migrant labor camps around California, it wasn't acceptable for her to flaunt her beliefs while in the government's employ. Even in the Roosevelt administration, she had to watch herself. "Helen, they're out to get you," the FSA's regional director, Jonathan Garst, cautioned. "Now it's not going to help when you . . . come running around here with your hair loose and a copy of *New Masses* sticking out of your purse. I can't protect you if you do things like that." Frustrated that she couldn't explicitly support the unionization of farm workers and the organization of small dirt farmers—and advance the idea that "unless they got together, they were doomed" to both be victims of the big growers— Hosmer struck out on her own. She solicited a bunch of donations (most of them quite modest), bought a mimeograph machine, rented an office in downtown San Francisco, and christened her group in honor of one of her heroes.

Simon Lubin, a Sacramento native who had worked with the poor in Boston's South End and on New York's East Side after graduating magna cum laude from Harvard, had served as the first president of the California Immigration and Housing Commission in 1913. In that post, he became known as a devoted guardian of farm workers' rights. He remained active in matters involving agricultural labor for the next twenty years, and before he died in 1936, he arrived at some strong conclusions about who was responsible for all the turmoil in California's farm fields. Lubin—who after his death would be falsely accused before the Dies Committee of having been a member of the Industrial Workers of the World—did not deny that there were lots of "radicals" and "agitators" running around the countryside. But what allowed them to make inroads there, he argued, were the "social, economic and political evils" being perpetrated by some of the state's largest farming interests. "Can the radicals capture the farms of California?" Lubin asked. "If unfairness, inhumanity, injustice and illegality are permitted to persist, sanctioned by some of our 'best people' and by popular opinion, and if we continue to walk in economic darkness—then shall we have open season for all who would disrupt our society . . . . But if the rotten conditions attendant upon these wicked sentiments are eradicated or sufficiently mitigated . . . then will our society become so sound that no mere 'agitator,' whatever his motive or whatever his method, will be able to make even a dent in our economy . . . . It is a fact that we do need a socio-economic house-cleaning. Are we going to encourage the 'Reds,' the 'radicals,' the 'Communists,' the 'outside agitators' to do the job for us? Or are we ourselves going to do it?"

As hard-hitting as Lubin was, the organization that carried on his name was even tougher. It distributed used clothing and blankets to the migrants. And it lobbied for legislation that would improve the lives of agricultural laborers. But above all, the Lubin Society loved to needle the big growers through a little newsletter called the *Rural Observer,* written and edited by the intrepid Hosmer with the help of volunteers. In issue after issue, she excoriated the Associated Farmers, exposing the industrial interests behind the group—utilities, banks, and railroads— and rapping its leaders for lying and hypocrisy. She called them "the big boys," contrasting their wealth and power with that of the small farmer, who was straining "to maintain a decent, debtless standard of living."

Hosmer had an extraordinary knack for hitting a nerve. After she reported on the interlocking farm and business holdings of Bill Camp's buddy, Joseph Di Giorgio, he reacted just the way she'd hoped he would: he was fuming. "Well, I read this article by Simon J. Lubin," Di Giorgio said. "Anything that is in there that refers to me is an absolute lie . . . I don't like it. I am not used to having people lie about me. If somebody wants a punch in the nose, he is going to get it, and it is too bad if I know anything about it. I pay these people good salaries and I give the best of everything, and then they allow something like that to be printed."

In a file that Camp kept of alleged Communist front groups, the Lubin Society was described as "the channel through which the . . . party conducts its bitter fight against the farming industry." Actually,

Hosmer griped that the Reds never did enough to support her organization, despite her Communist membership. "The party just neglected us," she said. "I finally got so I just ignored them all the time because they were not being helpful." Plenty of others, though, did step up. The Lubin Society's Sponsor Committee and Advisory Committee read like a Who's Who of the California Left, with Culbert Olson, Carey McWilliams, George West, Marie de L. Welch, and Kern County's own Ralph Abel taking part. Steinbeck wasn't on the roster, but Hosmer was more than happy to cite his work as well. "In between the business of smoking out the Associated Farmers, John Steinbeck's *Their Blood Is Strong* appeared, published and distributed by the Lubin Society," the *Rural Observer* boasted. "This pamphlet . . . showed that the same forces which oppressed the working farmers were oppressing the migrants" and "emphasized again that the migrants had once been working farmers and had been pushed out by big money."

Hosmer wasn't the only one making good use of Steinbeck's celebrity. He agreed to add his imprimatur, even more patently, to another group whose stated purpose was "to provide the necessary support, financial and moral, to help agricultural workers in California build a strong union." Its name: the John Steinbeck Committee to Aid Agricultural Organization, with the author himself serving in the (largely ceremonial) role of state chairman. Others—including Carey McWilliams and the actress (and, later, congresswoman and political prey of Richard Nixon) Helen Gahagan Douglas—did more of the actual spadework. But having Steinbeck out front was a clear plus. "Will You Join My Committee . . . ?" he asked in one mailer, seeking $10 contributions.

In December 1938, the Steinbeck Committee and other groups worked with the FSA to hold a Christmas Eve party at the federal farm labor camp in Shafter. Helen Gahagan's husband, actor Melvyn Douglas, chaired the nationally broadcast event, which brought a constellation of Hollywood stars to Kern County: Edward G. Robinson, Gene Autry, Edie Cantor, Henry Fonda, Virginia Bruce, Miriam

Hopkins, and others. Steinbeck endorsed the gala—but warned what would happen if this was a one-shot deal. "Candy and food today—and starvation tomorrow," he wrote in *People's World*. "The children will be unhappy tomorrow. The gifts will only serve to emphasize the poverty of the recipients.

"This can make for hatred," he added, "unless one thing—if the gifts can be a symbol of support, not of charity, if the meaning of this party can be, 'We are working with you, not for you, to the end that the good life which is your right will not be longer withheld. These gifts and food are a promise that you are not alone.'"

The Steinbeck Committee's real goal, needless to say, was influencing policy—not planning parties. A few months before the soiree in Shafter and three days after the last words of *The Grapes of Wrath* had been put to paper—"She looked up and across the barn, and her lips came together and smiled mysteriously"—the organization convened a conference on health, housing, and relief in Bakersfield. Steinbeck didn't attend, but a legion of others looked upon with fear and hatred by Bill Camp and the rest of the town's power brokers participated in the October meeting. On the list were McWilliams, Ella Winter, and a cadre of organizers from UCAPAWA, the agricultural workers' union. The program the conferees advocated was hardly startling considering their view of the world: They pressed for thirty new FSA camps in California, on top of the nine already up and running; more inspectors to enforce health and sanitation standards at growers' camps; and additional funding to erect schools for migrant children. They also demanded the state liberalize its welfare program to put more money into migrants' pockets, and they called on the government to intervene in the marketplace and set agricultural wages.

All in all, it was pretty pie-in-the-sky stuff given that Frank Merriam was still the governor and the big growers clearly had the upper hand. If anybody had any doubt about that, they needed only to consider the swiftness with which, just a few days earlier, a cotton strike in Kern County had been stamped out. The kerfuffle had been brewing since late September, ever since three hundred workers at a ranch belonging to Bill Camp's brother, Sol, walked off the job demanding ninety cents for every hundred pounds of cotton they'd scoop into their threadbare sacks. The farmers were paying seventy-five cents, and they argued they couldn't afford more, what with cotton prices in the dumps.

By early October, the number of strikers had grown to seven hundred, and UCAPAWA rushed in an organizer from San Francisco to help the workers further their agenda—as well as the union's own. UCAPAWA set up a strike committee, which upped the workers' formal demand by a dime, to one dollar per hundred pounds picked. In addition, it insisted on having drinking water made available in the fields, the testing of all cotton scales to ensure that pickers weren't being bilked, and an arbitrator at every ranch to help settle any disputes that might arise. The union also dispatched "flying squadrons"—automobile caravans filled with pickets—across the county.

The growers fought back by closing off roads, while the Associated Farmers collected license-plate numbers and compiled a blacklist of strikers. The employers' strongest weapon, though, was pure intransigence. Associated Farmers officials refused to negotiate with UCAPAWA representatives, reiterating over and over that they couldn't meet the union's demand on wages. End of story. Still more maddening to the union, the Associated Farmers wouldn't even acknowledge that a walkout was underway. Part of this was an effort to control public perception. And in this regard, the growers had an advantage: Although as many as three thousand pickers took part in the strike, the labor market in Kern County was so swamped with people willing to work, gins in the area were receiving close to the same quantities of cotton that they always did. When the farmers said that things were just about "normal," they weren't totally blowing smoke.

Yet there was another reason, as well, for the farmers to deny that a strike was actually occurring. If those staying off the job were deemed not to be on strike—and were thus simply refusing to accept work that was being offered them—they wouldn't be eligible for government handouts. That, obviously, would ratchet up the pressure to return to the fields. After a review, the State Relief Administration (SRA) agreed with the growers that no strike was happening, and it removed from its rolls those involved in the labor conflict. Union supporters were aghast at the decision by SRA chief Harold Pomeroy, saying that it left farm workers with an appalling choice: scab or starve. Nonetheless, he stuck to his position.

The federal government, however, had a different policy. The Works Progress Administration provided cash assistance and the FSA offered food—$4.41 worth of flour, shortening, evaporated milk, beans, cornmeal, sugar, and coffee—to any farmhand who said he was in need. "All we ask is, 'Are you an agricultural worker and are you hungry?'" the FSA's Jonathan Garst explained, much to the consternation of Bill Camp.

Camp told Garst that his agency was, knowingly or not, feeding union organizers—"paid agents of the Communist Party"—and without Uncle Sam's sustenance, they would have surely packed up and left the county. "They were ready to go away if not for the FSA," Camp said. "They go up and down the road and beat their tom-toms, scare people out of the fields because of this pork and beans that you give them."

Garst's own temper then flared. "I think it's better the issue be settled without cutting people off and making them go hungry," he replied. "You cannot settle it by saying that you either starve or go to work. That is worse than war."

To the degree the cotton strike of '38 was anything like a war, it turned out to be a rout for one side. On October 25, four days before the Steinbeck Committee conference in Bakersfield, more than one hundred pickets in a thirty-car caravan were arrested. The Kern County Sheriff said that the horde had entered a ranch near Arvin and assaulted those working the rows with stones and clubs. Eighty-four wound up being arraigned and charged with, among other things, inciting a riot. By early November, nearly all of them had been released through a dismissal of the charges or guilty pleas followed by the granting of suspended sentences—but not before the judge in the case had delivered a good chewing out.

"You have been mixed up in something you don't know anything about," Justice Oral Parish said from the courthouse in Weedpatch—that splendidly named spot to which Steinbeck would refer in his novel. "The farmers pay all they are able to pay; this has been proven. You people were just used as tools for something that did you no good at all but just got you into a lot of trouble." Parish added that "this union business is all bunk," leaving no doubt about whose side of the fight he was on. "I want you to get this distinctly," he lectured the workers. "There is no cotton strike!" The union attorney, Raymond Henderson, tried to keep the pickets' spirits up, telling them that Parish's comments were his personal views—not a legal opinion. But about a week later, with wages still stuck at seventy-five cents, the workers folded. The walkout was over with nothing to show for it.

That, though, was 1938. Nearly a year had passed since then, and in many ways it felt as if the world had turned upside down in the months in between. With a new cotton harvest approaching, the union and the growers were in the same place they always were—at odds over wages. But now, there was a book that had given voice to the workers' concerns in a way that nothing had before it—not the Lubin Society's newsletters, not the star-studded party in Shafter, not the well-intentioned conference in Bakersfield. There was, in addition, a new governor in Sacramento and a forceful new head of the Division of Immigration and Housing who thought of the big farmers as "fascists." Seventy-five cents for picking a hundred pounds of cotton may have been acceptable in 1938. But this was 1939, the year of Culbert Olson, the year of Carey McWilliams, the year of *The Grapes of Wrath*.

—•—

As John Steinbeck hunkered down in his home outside Los Gatos on this Tuesday in August, sick and tired of being famous, the apparatus of

Carey McWilliams, who had called for the Soviet-style collectivization of agriculture in California before becoming a state official, held hearings in 1939 to set a "fair wage" for farm workers. (Photo by Will Connell, Will Connell Collection, UCR/California Museum of Photography, University of California at Riverside)

the state pushed forward—an activist, interventionist, New Deal attitude come to California at long last. Over at the governor's office, an aide typed a letter to Carey McWilliams informing him that yet another petition from a group of agricultural workers had been received, this one from Kern County, asking Governor Olson to hold a hearing and help set a proper wage for picking cotton.

"We believe that a wage hearing will avert many struggles and will allow both sides to present their views," the workers had written, attaching to their entreaty hundreds of supporting signatures. Such an incursion by the state into the marketplace would have been unimaginable a year earlier. But under Olson and McWilliams, the rulebook was being rewritten. The first such hearing had been held in May in Madera County, under McWilliams's direction. His primary charge was to draw up a new policy for the State Relief Administration, overturning its past practice of kicking people off welfare as long as there was work available—no matter the pay they'd been offered. McWilliams's belief was that, rather than force workers to be beholden to an industry's "prevailing wage," the government should set a "fair wage" and not force anybody off relief for refusing to work for less than this amount.

In this case, valley farmers had decided that they'd shell out twenty cents an hour for chopping cotton—a task that involved thinning the small plants and clearing away weeds. The rate was established by the Agricultural Labor Bureau (ALB) of the San Joaquin Valley, a group representing the state's largest growers, which had gathered every season since 1926 to determine compensation for the region's field workers. Farmers who weren't part of the ALB could theoretically pay more, but many of them were scared to buck the system because they often depended on ALB members to provide their financing. McWilliams found the whole arrangement detestable, as well as two-faced. The big growers, he noted, kicked and screamed whenever their workers wanted to organize and bargain collectively. But they had no problem coming together collectively on their side of the table, colluding to keep wages down. "Because of the one-sidedness of the bargaining and the very considerable economic and social power represented" by the ALB, McWilliams said, "it is apparent that the prime purpose in fixing . . . rates in this manner is to prevent competition between employers, which might have the effect of raising" workers' pay.

For Madera's laborers, the hearing at the local Memorial Hall was a rare opportunity to openly express the anger that was burning inside them, having worked so hard for so little for so long. One man, Archie Hughes, testified that at twenty cents an hour he could barely afford to eat, despite dragging a hoe all day long, especially when he had to supply his own transportation to and from the fields. Nobody can "drive eight or ten miles out to work and back and make anything on $2 a day," he said. "Everything you eat, even a loaf of bread, is 12 cents." Then he added, "A working man can eat a loaf of bread by himself." At that, the audience broke into applause.

The wage committee acknowledged that the growers' ability to pay was not unlimited. But the notion that twenty cents an hour was all they could afford was roundly rejected. "That does not even represent a subsistence wage," McWilliams concluded, before recommending a rate of twenty-seven and a half cents an hour. McWilliams couldn't force any farmer to pay this much. Yet unless this sum was met, the SRA would no longer drop people from relief—a change in state regulations that would carry over from chopping cotton to picking it, leaving workers jubilant and also a little slack-jawed. "Has anyone ever heard tell of such a thing?" asked the *Tow-Sack Tattler,* the newspaper published by residents of the FSA's Arvin labor camp. "Always before the Growers have set the price and the Pickers never had a chance to get in their two-bits worth. They either picked it, or else. If they were on Relief, they were cut off. . . . But this year, the man who has to pick the cotton has been heard." McWilliams noted that casting a spotlight on what the farmers paid had another effect, as well: it kept them from trimming rates any further. "The growers were afraid," he told the governor, "that if they did make wage cuts, another hearing would be held."

The fair-wage policy was immediately condemned by the Associated Farmers, whose new leader had just come whirling through the revolving door: Harold Pomeroy, the man who'd run the SRA under Governor Merriam, was now executive secretary of the big growers' group. In the coming months, the Associated Farmers tried its best to keep McWilliams's policy from spreading, as it argued that every wage hearing did nothing more than offer a "Roman holiday for people loafing on relief" and a way for labor organizers to disrupt agricultural production. But such protests didn't register nearly as much anymore. For the first time ever, the balance of power was shifting toward the side of the workers—and to those trying to unionize them. "We used to say that when Culbert Olson was elected governor, socialism came to California," Elizabeth Eudey, a UCAPAWA official, recalled later. "It was a joke, of course, but it did make a big difference." Even though the wage levels that McWilliams blessed weren't binding, "we found we could use them" to help carry out a strike, "and we'd settle with individual growers if they'd put this wage into effect. It was a very different atmosphere from before. It was a Culbert Olson atmosphere. It was a Carey McWilliams atmosphere."

UCAPAWA operated under the auspices of the CIO, which in 1938 had splintered completely from the AFL. The new labor alliance, led by John L. Lewis, was eager to barrel past the old federation's focus on representing skilled craftsmen and organize the nation's legions of unskilled and semiskilled workers. Whereas the AFL seemed slow-footed and top down in its organization, the CIO embraced a bottom-up brand of activism that reached out to minorities and wasn't afraid to sweep into its fold Communists, Socialists, and other radicals.

Even in this context, it was an unusually militant band that led UCAPAWA. The agricultural workers' godfather was Harry Bridges, the head of the longshoremen's union who also served as the CIO's leader on the Pacific Coast. An Australian native with a cockney accent, long face, hawk nose, piercing blue eyes, and a head of black hair brushed into a pompadour, Bridges saw America in unbending us-versus-them terms. "We take the stand that we as workers have nothing in common with the employers," he asserted. "We are in a class struggle." Having led the dockworkers through the Great Maritime Strike of 1934, Bridges had been smack in the middle of some of the decade's most unforgettable—and disturbing—events: the "Bloody Thursday" clash between unionists and San Francisco police that left scores injured and two workers dead; the funeral cortege that trudged along to the strains of Beethoven and helped build support for a general strike, leading to a virtual shutdown of the entire city; the deployment of nearly five thousand heavily armed National Guardsmen who helped bring the tempest to an end, but not before the longshoremen had achieved most of the gains they were seeking.

Bridges's vision was to take his success on the waterfront and broaden it through a "march inland," organizing mainly warehouse workers at first but, over time, others too. He considered agricultural laborers an essential part of the equation, if for no other reason than their extremely low wages and peripatetic lifestyle made them easy to recruit as strike-breakers in other industries. "It is difficult to recruit scabs among workers who are organized," he said. The longshoremen's union, "if only from a selfish standpoint, is concerned with the drive to bring organization to those who work in the fields." He then took the idea a step further, deciding to bring together farm, cannery, and packing workers into a single union. By using year-round cannery employees as a foundation, Bridges figured, he could then help seasonal workers find jobs through union-controlled hiring halls.

In 1937, UCAPAWA was born, adopting as its battle cry (just as the longshoremen had) the old Industrial Workers of the World slogan "An Injury to One Is an Injury to All." The union's president, Donald Henderson, was a young ideological soul mate of Bridges who had tried previously, without success, to organize agricultural workers for the AFL. Before entering the union movement, Henderson had been booted from his job as an economics professor at Columbia University, where he'd played guru to a budding group of campus Communists, drinking beer and singing revolutionary anthems with them. He swore that he'd since shaken any Communist Party ties, but many even within the councils of labor didn't believe him. "If he's not a card-carrying Communist," said one critic, "he's cheating the party out of his dues."

Henderson's radicalism made UCAPAWA an easy mark for the Associated Farmers, which described the union as "more Communistically controlled than any other." Henderson's response was to take a herring, paint it bright red, and then hold burial services for the little fish. "It's a sign and a guarantee that we're doing our job when they start calling us names," he said.

Bridges was also dogged by charges that he was a Communist. On this August day, as Steinbeck withdrew from the world and McWilliams busied himself with the state's affairs, the longshoreman sat in a San Francisco courtroom, facing possible deportation to Australia. The allegation: that Bridges was affiliated with an organization promoting the violent overthrow of the U.S. government.

A UCAPAWA organizer addresses a crowd in Kern County in 1938. (Photo by Dorothea Lange, Library of Congress)

But whether the union was led by Communists or not, it didn't seem to make much difference. Though UCAPAWA was weighed down by real problems, including finding sufficient funding to organize field workers and a nasty internal fight with the Southern Tenant Farmers' Union, it claimed 125,000 members by 1938. In the San Joaquin Valley, UCAPAWA foot soldiers such as Dorothy Healey didn't even bother to hide their convictions. "The first thing I would do is tell them I was a Communist," she said. "They didn't give a damn. They saw me as their organizer. There was nothing even vaguely threatening about me. They were far more likely to be wary of my gender than my politics. They weren't used to having women as leaders. But they soon got over that too. I was de-sexed."

The important thing for workers—and the frightening thing for the big growers—was that the union was trying to muck up the way business had been conducted in California agriculture for decades. When UCAPAWA came in, "they was mostly drilling us to be good labor people," remembered cotton worker Ollie Lewis, who in the late '30s joined Local 272 at the San Joaquin Compress Company in Bakersfield. "We voted in the union, struck for three days, and won a contract with better wages, overtime, holiday pay, seniority and a grievance system. After that we began to get very particular about the hours, gettin' time and a half and so on. And 100 bales an hour became the production standard. The boss might get 103 or 105 or 97, but he wouldn't be gettin' no 125 bales like he used to. He would get a fair day's work, that's all."

Others were clamoring for more than basic fairness. On this very same day, August 22, another letter was typed to Carey McWilliams. It was composed by a man named J. B. Ely, who had just finished reading *Factories in the Field* and was planning to pick up *The Grapes of Wrath* next—though he had "no idea when I shall be able to purchase it." His reason for contacting McWilliams was to encourage him to write another book as soon as possible, only this time one with less measured prose and more ire on every page. "Under a capitalistic government, such as we have, there is no hope for the poor man," Ely told him. "Like the fishes in the sea, the biggest ones are eating the less bigger ones, and the less bigger ones the next size down . . . . Try again, Mr. McWilliams. Write another book . . . . You can have it ready to follow the wave of popularity created by *The Grapes of Wrath*. And I will stoop along under you with my little butcher knife and cut his tail off while you behead the giant."

CHAPTER FOUR
Wednesday

"I knowed a fella. Brang 'im in while I was in the jail house.
Been tryin' to start a union. Got one started. An' then them
vigilantes bust it up."

F OR THE THIRD day running, complaints about the book ban poured
into the main library in Bakersfield. Some patrons flocked downtown, determined to register their dissatisfaction in person. Others
called, tying up the phone lines. At least a few people, frustrated that
they couldn't borrow a copy of *The Grapes of Wrath*, asked in vain to buy
one. So persistent was the protest, "We were scarcely able to do our regular work," Gretchen Knief would later say. By week's end, the remon-
strance would grow only louder and sharper. From his home up the road
in Fresno, renowned author and playwright William Saroyan would
weigh in, defending the rights of the artist and ridiculing those with the
inclination to gag him. Steinbeck "has not, despite criticism to the contrary, overemphasized profanity and obscenity," said Saroyan, whose
Broadway production, *My Heart's in the Highlands*, made clear the folly
of trying to silence a writer: "Go ahead. Fire your feeble guns. You won't
kill anything. There will always be poets in the world."

"Steinbeck has attempted to tell the need for a remedy" of the migrants' miserable predicament, Saroyan added. "His own background, his research, his talent qualified him for the attempt. Those who would deny the public an opportunity to enjoy *The Grapes of Wrath* have taken a not exactly stupid, but a dull action." It was a mighty fine distinction, dull versus stupid—one probably lost on the Board of Supervisors, whose members were, with each passing day, feeling more and more heat over what they had done.

Still, as harsh as Saroyan's take on the situation was, nobody would assail the Kern County Board with more zest than Raymond Henderson, the Bakersfield attorney who, the previous year, had defended the eighty-four farm workers charged with causing a riot in the cotton fields. The hat he wore on this day, August 23, 1939, was that of counsel to the local branch of the ACLU, which was preparing to lodge a formal protest on Monday at the next supervisors' meeting. "As champions of civil liberties," Henderson proclaimed, "we are not interested in whether the book is right or wrong, but we are deeply concerned that any group of public officials should set themselves up as censors and tell the good people of this county what they should and what they should not read." Citing the First Amendment, Henderson went on: "The supervisors took upon themselves a privilege which the Founding Fathers saw fit to deny the Congress of the United States."

These would prove to be Henderson's most placid comments of the week. Throughout, he would speak out again and again, becoming more trenchant at every turn. "About 10 years ago our industrial machine went haywire," Henderson wrote in a labor journal article that would appear a couple of days later, as he laid out the conditions—"the rains forgot to fall plentifully, and the winds mussed the earth all up"—that led so many from America's Dust Bowl to uproot their families and plant themselves in California's Central Valley.

Sometimes our state relief people were unnecessarily cruel; sometimes they stretched the law to help them.

Our reactionary citizens formed committees to cut down what relief they were receiving. Our liberal people formed a committee to put on a big Christmas show for them.

Then one of our most talented young authors put them in a book. It was not a sweet book. The writer did not pull his punches. He called a spade a spade; and he called things dirtier than spades by their common names.

Was the book true? Most people thought it was about as true as you expect a book to be. Some people thought it was too true; and those people did not like the truth; and they told us that nobody had any business writing books like that . . . .

The book had to be stopped . . . . All and sundry were warned not to read the book. We are a law-abiding folk. If the Board of Supervisors says the book is not fit to read, we will not read; and all will be well in the world. The ostrich will stick his head in the sand. He will see no dirty, unkempt, neglected, degraded migratory workers; and there will be no dirty, unkempt, degraded migratory workers; and the spirit of Polly Anna shall rule the land.

Ray Henderson (no relation to union leader Donald Henderson) was what might be called a little man of history—not a household name when he was alive, and all but forgotten after he died in 1945. But during the '20s and '30s, he stood in the thick of some of the major conflicts of his time: epic fights over the treatment of union workers, freedom of speech, and the rights of the blind. Born in 1881 in the San Joaquin Valley farming town of Livingston, Henderson was partially blind himself. A self-described "country lawyer," he spoke with a bit of a twang and had an avuncular appearance: a balding pate, a brush mustache, a dimpled chin, and irises that floated upward in the whites of his eyes, making him look sweet and sad all at once. He was capable of discerning certain shapes and was enchanted by the trace of the world he could see. "A great big summer moon is moving above the grand old trees which are casting fantastic shadows down on the big porch where

I am sitting at my typewriter," he wrote to a friend earlier in the summer. "Fantastic."

But if Henderson's sight was fuzzy, his insights were razor sharp, having been honed during an early life of struggle. Because there was no aid for the blind at the time, he worked his way through the University of California by taking whatever odd jobs he could find. He spent his summers in the fields, though it "was tough for a half-blind man to pitch hay and pick up sacks of wheat," he'd remember. He also earned some money coaching high-school debaters in San Francisco. (Earlier, he had helped lead the California State School for the Deaf and the Blind to two state debating championships.) In addition, Henderson recounted, "I did a little occasional ghost writing for members of women's clubs who had to prepare 'papers' to display their culture."

After graduating from Berkeley in 1904 with a bachelor of laws degree, Henderson expected to become a teacher. But he found that "the people who employ teachers would not hire me" despite his "good record and excellent credentials" from the university. So he spent a number of years in what he termed "an uninspiring position in a blind school" before he later "crammed up" and, in 1917, passed the bar exam. "I should not be surprised," he later said, "if a good teacher was changed into an indifferent lawyer." This remark, while providing a peek into Henderson's humility, could not have been further from the truth. Indeed, nobody familiar with Henderson's work as a lawyer would have described him as indifferent. Some might have called him indignant or indefatigable or even inspired. But indifferent? Never.

Perhaps because he had been an underdog himself, Henderson by 1939 had spent twenty years defending the little guy. He'd compiled such a valiant record on behalf of those being "persecuted by the employing class," said one union official, he had won "the sincere respect and love of the workers." When Carey McWilliams was researching farm labor in California, he understandably turned to Henderson as a key source of information. Henderson didn't sugarcoat a thing for the

Factories in the Field author. "Every attempt at organization," he told him, "has been met with savage repression."

Early in his law career, Henderson went into partnership in Bakersfield with Wiley C. Dorris, a Democratic Party activist whose flamboyance in the courtroom became the stuff of local legend; in the middle of telling a jury about his client's travails, Dorris was known to cry upon command and then whip out a bandana to wipe away his tears. After a while, Henderson decided to set out on his own and moved to Berkeley, but "the temptation to associate with reds and pinks was so strong," he said, "I found that I did not have time and energy enough left to develop other business connections." As with most people whose idealism doesn't lead to a life of asceticism—"may the pork chops never be wanting," Henderson liked to say—he strived to find the right balance between making waves and making a good living for himself and his family. (He would marry—and later divorce—a single mother whose first husband had been murdered in 1922 by right-wing hooligans in Erie, Pennsylvania. The man was slain after becoming involved with a group called Friends of the Soviet Union and lending his support to striking coal miners and other causes of the Far Left.)

In 1924, Henderson returned to Kern County and took up a wide-ranging civil practice, defending an accused bootlegger one day, handling a tortuous dispute over oil royalties the next. He taught law, as well, doing his best "to keep a number of ambitious young men from snoring while I try to explain the mysteries of commercial paper."

His heart, though, was in representing workers whose affiliation with organized labor had placed them in their employers' crosshairs. "Bakersfield," Henderson once said, "in spite of the drabness of the small city . . . seemed the best place for me. I can hold myself in readiness for any service in class-war cases without living on the labor movement and its friends." And ready he invariably was, bringing to mind Tom Joad's famous coda in *The Grapes of Wrath:* "Wherever they's a fight so hungry people can eat, I'll be there. Whenever they's a cop beatin' up a guy, I'll be there."

As it happened, most of the cops Henderson encountered were beating up union men—specifically, those connected with the Industrial Workers of the World (IWW).

In August 1927, the IWW set its sights on the coalfields of Colorado. The Wobblies, as they were known, were eager to draw unskilled, industrial laborers across America and beyond into "One Big Union." In mining country, they'd arranged for a work stoppage in the aftermath of the electrocutions of Nicola Sacco and Bartolomeo Vanzetti, the anarchists whose questionable convictions on robbery and murder charges near Boston had led to an enormous uproar (and, ultimately, an artistic outpouring: ballads from Woody Guthrie, a wood engraving from Rockwell Kent, a series of paintings from Ben Shahn, poetry from Edna St. Vincent Millay, and prose from Upton Sinclair and John Dos Passos. "If the state of Massachusetts can kill those two innocent men in the face of the protest of the whole world," the labor organizer Mary French says in Dos Passos's 1933 novel, *The Big Money,* "it'll mean that there never will be any justice in America ever again." Mary's pal, a hard-drinking reporter named Jerry Burnham, fills up her glass and replies: "When was there any to begin with? Ever heard of Tom Mooney?"

By the fall, the Sacco and Vanzetti sympathy strike had turned into full-blown demands for higher wages and other concessions, with more than ten thousand coal diggers walking off the job at John D. Rockefeller's Colorado Fuel and Iron Company and other operations. Ray Henderson, who had done legal work for the IWW in California and was now being tapped to help out in Colorado, knew that things could get rough. The state attorney general had declared the strike illegal, a move that made "Mussolini look like a benevolent democrat by comparison," Henderson said. He also suspected that the intention of the mining bosses was "to starve the strikers into submission."

All things considered, that might have been a relatively peaceful way to go. Instead, on November 21, about five hundred colliers headed toward the gates of the Columbine Mine in the town of Serene. The deputy sheriff ordered them to turn back. Led by a Wobbly named Adam Bell, they ignored the order and continued on. The state police met them with rifle butts. The miners stood their ground, throwing sticks and rocks; some wielded knives. The police retreated, regrouped, and then fired shots over the heads of the strikers. But, again, they wouldn't back down. "The whole thing," said Henderson, "was just leading them into a death trap." The cops fired another volley—this time, point-blank into the marchers. Bodies dropped. Six miners were killed and twenty injured, including two women in men's clothing. "The guards followed the strikers," Henderson reported back to IWW headquarters, "cursing and beating them when they attempted to pick up their dead and wounded."

Following this episode—which in later years would be known as the Columbine Mine Massacre to distinguish it from the Columbine High School Massacre of 1999—the level of bloodshed diminished. Nonetheless, things were hardly calm. Henderson feared that Ku Klux Klanners, who loathed the Wobblies, were about to raid the Colorado law office he was using. A company detective, meanwhile, was quartered at his hotel. "I do not keep files of my correspondence and telegrams," he noted. "When I do make copies, I immediately mail them to Bakersfield" for safekeeping.

By early 1928, a large number of strikers had been arrested on vagrancy charges and under anti-picketing ordinances. "Keys to the city and county jail are turned over to the state police," Henderson told Lee Tulin, the general secretary of the IWW, "and whenever one of these gentlemen finds time hanging heavy on his hands, he goes in and beats a prisoner up." Henderson later added that because he went to the district attorney's office and demanded prosecution of these thugs, "the beatings have stopped." Yet the prisoners were then "forced to work with ball and chain."

Attorney Raymond Henderson found himself in the middle of some of the biggest struggles of his time, defending the rights of labor, free speech, and the blind. (National Federation of the Blind)

Of course, this brainy man of letters and the law wasn't above mixing it up himself—at least verbally—and Tulin began calling him "Battling Kid Henderson." One time, Henderson pushed to get out of jail two strike leaders who were being held without charges. As he pressed the matter, "I was threatened with arrest, having my passport revoked, and a beating," he said. "In fact, I had a perfectly beautiful quarrel with the state police, all to myself. It was the best quarrel I have had for many a long day . . . . Between me and these gentlemen, a most cordial hatred has arisen." The next day, with more pressure having been applied on the authorities, Henderson received good news: the two union men had been freed. "I could have danced an Irish jig and sung 'Solidarity,'" he said, "but I didn't. Instead, I just lay in bed and felt good all over."

On another occasion, Henderson petitioned to get a striker named George Speed removed from custody. "Last evening," he informed Tulin, "I had an opportunity to tell the Police Magistrate just what I thought of him, and . . . he is now in a mood to assist in securing Speed's release . . . . The more you abuse these cattle, the more you get out of them. My ability to bawl people out has increased several-fold since arriving here. When I can find nobody else to practice on, I call up the governor long distance and bawl him out."

For all of Henderson's tough talk, the IWW was well past its glory days by the time he got to Colorado. The union had been started in 1905 in Chicago with a goal of fostering "the emancipation of the working class from the slave bondage of capitalism," in the words of Wobbly leader William "Big Bill" Haywood. The IWW—which favored complete racial equality and viewed immigrants as a source of strength, not a danger—had tasted success here and there. It helped steelworkers in McKees Rock, Pennsylvania, make a stand in 1909 and won higher wages for thirty thousand textile workers in Lawrence, Massachusetts, in 1912. It established a presence in Canada, Europe, Latin America, and South Africa in the teens and '20s. And it engaged in more than two dozen major "free speech fights" in the United States between 1907 and 1916, centering on the union's right to recruit members at street rallies.

One of the biggest of these battles took place in March 1911 in Fresno, where police had jailed scores of Wobblies. Model prisoners they were not. The union men lectured their guards on class politics and demonstrated from behind bars. Officials turned high-power hoses on the militants, but still they wouldn't keep quiet; though their cellblocks were knee-deep in water, their spirits weren't dampened in the least. News that thousands more free-speech advocates were on their way to Fresno, its jails already swamped, gave the mayor no choice: he repealed his ban on public speaking on the streets. As the Wobblies were liberated, they added new lyrics to their classic "Hallelujah, I'm a Bum":

Springtime has come and I'm just out of jail
Without any money, without any bail.

For Ray Henderson, the idea of uniting all working people under a single banner was the perfect balm for a battered nation. He didn't have much patience for the Communist faithful in the movement, complaining when he found himself having to "report to the Comrades" as part of a legal case. He also despised the rigidity of the old-line trade unions controlled by the American Federation of Labor, which he regarded as just another "capitalist institution." What he wanted, by contrast, was to build "a revolutionary organization" and to upend the capitalist system—not with violence or under dictates from Moscow but by organizing workers in sector after sector after sector. "Industrial unionism, as really taught by the . . . best thinkers in the best moments of the IWW," Henderson said, "is the most logical doctrine ever conceived by the human brain."

Maybe so. The IWW, however, was never able to sink its roots very deep anywhere. In Colorado, the miners eventually won a dollar-a-day pay increase, due in no small part to Henderson's tireless efforts. But, in what by then had become an all-too-familiar pattern, the Wobblies never gained formal recognition, and they quickly faded from the scene. That the union failed wasn't entirely surprising; the organization had long been besieged from within and without.

Inside the IWW, those who wanted to forgo any involvement with the political system fought with those who thought politics was a viable avenue to shake up society. Those who were convinced that the IWW should be centrally controlled scrapped with those who wanted power to be more diffused. And the union's industrialists squabbled with its Communists who didn't care much for its anarchists. The acrimony got so bad that the union split into rival factions in 1924. By 1928, as Henderson left the Colorado mines, the IWW's ranks had fallen to less than ten thousand overall, down from more than one hundred thousand a decade or so before.

When the IWW wasn't chewing itself up on the inside, it was getting pummeled from the outside. Though the union never actually opposed U.S. involvement in World War I (unlike the Socialist Party), common public perception—fueled by the nation's first Red Scare and fanned by the press—was that the Wobblies were out to damage America's combat effort. IWW members were constantly at risk of being beaten, shot, and lynched by vigilantes. The state's hand was only a tad gentler. In September 1917, 166 IWW leaders were indicted in Illinois for allegedly trying "by force to prevent, hinder and delay the execution" of U.S. war plans. Eventually, 101 stood trial. After five months in court, all were found guilty.

Even when the war ended, the prosecution of the Wobblies did not. Between 1917 and 1920, twenty-one states passed criminal syndicalism laws, which generally prohibited people from encouraging violence as a means to social change. The syndicalists had taken their cue from France's *syndicalisme*, a radical political movement that called for bringing industry and government under the control of labor by the use of direct action, such as general strikes and sabotage. Those who favored the criminal syndicalism statutes portrayed them as bulwarks, standing in the way of revolution. Ray Henderson, though, believed they were designed to thwart something else: the chance for working people to get ahead by organizing collectively. "The real purpose of this criminal syndicalism legislation is to suppress industrial agitation," he said. It is "just another step in the policy of industrial regression," no different than other anti-strike and anti-picketing laws.

Of all the states with criminal syndicalism measures, California was the most aggressive, bringing indictments against 531 people from 1919 to 1924. Of those, 264 were tried and 164 convicted, with sentences ranging from one to fourteen years. Included on that list was a client of Henderson's named William Burns, a construction worker, sailor, and logger who was arrested in April 1923 after allegedly "fomenting trouble" among employees of the Yosemite Lumber Company. Nobody denied that Burns was an IWW member. Picked up by the police while walking along some railroad tracks, he had a bunch of Wobbly literature and credentials on him, including a membership card containing the preamble to the IWW constitution: "It is the historic mission of the working class to do away with capitalism. The army of production must be organized, not only for the everyday struggle with capitalists, but also to carry on production when capitalism shall have been overthrown. By organizing industrially, we are forming the structure of the new society within the shell of the old."

Rather, the Burns case hinged in large part on the meaning of the word *sabotage*. The judge at his federal trial in San Francisco had told the jury, over the objections of the defense, that when the IWW asked workers to dawdle and be inefficient so as to cut into a company's profits, it constituted sabotage under the law. Henderson couldn't believe the judge's logic that "it is just as much of a crime to slow down on the job as to injure machinery," telling a friend that "this is but one sample of what we are up against."

Still, Henderson loved a challenge. "Legal problems are very intriguing," he said. "The harder they make 'em, the better I like 'em." With Burns, he had a doozy on his hands. After his client was sentenced to fifteen months in prison, Henderson continued the fight, taking his appeal all the way to the U.S. Supreme Court, which heard arguments in November 1926.

His co-counsel was no slouch. Walter H. Pollak, a prominent New York attorney who worked with the ACLU, had six months before stood shoulder to shoulder with Clarence Darrow on the appeal of the Scopes Monkey Trial. A few years earlier, Pollak had argued one of the most significant cases ever to come before the high court: *Gitlow v. New York,* which established the precedent that, under the Fourteenth Amendment, states could not deny their citizens freedom of speech or freedom of the press without due process. And a few years hence, Pollak would help defend the Scottsboro Nine, a group of black youths from Alabama falsely accused of raping two white women.

On this day, though, it was Henderson who stole the show. "Blind Lawyer Amazes Court," read the headline in the *Los Angeles Times.* Though Braille had been around for a hundred or so years, it was still enough of a rarity that the Associated Press correspondent covering the case was dazzled by Henderson's dexterity. "The attorney used the latest system by which the totally blind read, his notes and other material all being in raised lettering," said the report from Washington. "There was little, if any, delay between his fingering of the documents and deliverance of his argument."

Addressing the justices, Henderson maintained that the prosecution had failed to prove his client had intended to bring down the government by use of force. Burns, he said, was merely "guilty by association." Then, too, there was the question of whether the trial judge's instructions about slack, or "scamped," work had been in error. California law plainly defined *sabotage* as "willful and malicious physical damage or injury to physical property." In the end, though, the court ruled that plenty of evidence had been introduced to show that the IWW supported tactics that went beyond simply slowing down on the job. One purpose of loading poles improperly on a ship, for instance, "may be to create more work for the men and so to inflict loss on employers," wrote Justice Pierce Butler. But another result is "to endanger the vessels, the cargoes and the lives of those aboard." Burns's conviction was thus upheld.

Henderson was livid. "After reading the Burns decision," he said, "I have come to the conclusion that the phrase 'California Justice' means nothing." This would not, however, be the last time he'd get to tangle with the state's criminal syndicalism law.

———

As the tempest over the banning of *The Grapes of Wrath* gained steam, California attorney general Earl Warren sat in his San Francisco office, shoveling paperwork. Nobody can say for sure if any of it gave him pause, but it wouldn't be surprising if one document, in particular, caused Warren at least a moment's reflection. Included in the stack that he signed on this Wednesday was a formal request to have a cache of material—205 pieces of evidence in all—sent back to a group of defense attorneys involved in a trial that had ended four years earlier. Among them was Ray Henderson.

This had been no ordinary proceeding. Playing out in a Sacramento courtroom beginning in November 1934, the criminal syndicalism case had explored and exposed the depths of California's left-right divide like no other, becoming a national cause celebre. And though the matter had long been settled by an appeal's court, it still resonated to this day, thanks to *The Grapes of Wrath*. Those prosecuted included the chief organizers of the 1933 cotton strike—the bloody conflict that had been so important in Steinbeck's research for the book. Union secretary Cecil McKiddy, whom Steinbeck had interviewed in an attic in Seaside, had been summoned to the witness stand. So, too, had Bill Hamett, another strike leader who, some believe, served as Steinbeck's model for the Reverend Jim Casy in the novel.

The case had grown out of a police raid on Communist Party headquarters in Sacramento in July 1934, followed up by a storming of the Cannery and Agricultural Workers Industrial Union, which was close by. The timing of the sweep was far from random. It was launched just a couple of days after the conclusion of the San Francisco general strike—a cataclysm that had produced one of the era's "most chilling" images in the eyes of historian Kevn Starr: "truck-borne machine guns deployed by American soldiers on American streets for possible use against other Americans." With National Guardsman still patrolling San Francisco's Embarcadero—less than ninety miles to the east—the authorities in Sacramento sprang into action, confiscating a mass of material and arresting twenty-four people. Fourteen would eventually stand trial in the California capital for allegedly advocating "sabotage, violence and unlawful methods of terrorism as a means of accomplishing a change in industrial ownership" and "effecting political changes."

The Sacramento defendants maintained that they were being railroaded—that state officials and their big-business allies were going after them not because they had a predisposition for violence or posed any real risk to people's safety, but because they had been on the front lines of the cotton strike and other efforts to improve the lot of low-income laborers and the unemployed. The defendants' only crime, said one of them, was that "we believe the workers have a right to organize and a right to a living." Added another: "We are being framed . . . because we are a thorn in the side of the capitalists."

Nevertheless, there was no getting around that many of the books, pamphlets, letters, and other papers the cops had scooped up were, if nothing else, inflammatory on their face—a collection bound to rattle a jury from a conservative burgh such as Sacramento. Even the most open-minded of the twelve men and women considering the case (a retired telegraph operator, a pharmacist, an accountant, a music company salesman, a railroad worker, a real-estate broker, a paving contractor, a cigar-stand employee, and four housewives) had to be worried that this was a fragile time for California and the nation as a whole. Who among them wouldn't have been scared that the mayhem Harry Bridges had just wrought in San Francisco might spread elsewhere? Who in the jury box wouldn't have felt at least a twinge of relief that Upton Sinclair, a Socialist at heart if not in name anymore, had only weeks before been rebuffed in his pursuit of the governorship? And who wouldn't have wondered, in turn, what kind of movement might now emerge from Sinclair's long shadow? The most terrifying of all were the Communists, who'd adopted a particularly hard-edged stance at this point in time. This was a period in which the Comintern in Moscow envisioned a world on the brink of "gigantic class battles," and any liberal who didn't accept Communism unconditionally (whether a Socialist or New Dealer or Sinclair admirer) was considered a mere pretender, an impediment to the impending revolution. It was this fear—a fear of radicalism, of unrest, of rebellion—that the prosecution aimed to stoke.

And so the Sacramento Conspiracy Trial, as it came to be called, began simply enough, with the state reading into the record passages from works such as People's Exhibit no. 41. *Negro Workers and Imperialist War* was a Communist guide to what black soldiers in America were supposed to do the next time they were ordered to go out and fight for their country:

The Negroes must line up on the side of the revolutionary front and use the arms which their white oppressors put in their hands not to shoot down their brother workers . . . but to . . . seize the opportunity of turning the imperialist war into a civil war. In other words, instead of Negro workers giving their lives for the capitalists, landlords and bankers as they were misled in doing in 1914, they must put an end to these parasites and over their dead bodies raise the revolutionary banner of freedom for their own working class and the downtrodden and enslaved colonial toilers.

From Exhibit no. 25, there was this: "In order to overthrow the capitalist system . . . the armed uprising of the proletariat is necessary." From Exhibit no. 35: "As the chief power of the state lies in the army, it is necessary, above all things, to undermine and destroy the army." From Exhibit no. 37: "The overthrow of capitalism is impossible without force, without armed uprising and proletarian wars against the bourgeoisie." And from Exhibit no. 4: "The Communists . . . openly declare that their ends can be attained only by forcible overthrow of all existing social conditions. Let the ruling classes tremble at a Communist revolution." Just to make sure that the jurors didn't miss the most seditious-sounding parts of the exhibits should they ask to examine them later, lawyers for the state underlined specific sections. That prompted the lead counsel for the defense, Leo Gallagher, to remind the court that his side "has an equal right to underline any portion it wishes."

"They might do that with another color, if you desire," one of the prosecutors, Chris Johnson, interjected. "Red, for example."

Yet as straightforward as the prosecution's case was on the surface—use the testimony of four undercover agents to show that the defendants were die-hard Communists (not that they denied it), and cite the party's own literature to prove that the Communists called for the forcible overthrow of the government and capitalist system—there was no way that this trial was going to be brief or trouble-free.

A month or so into the case, reports surfaced that some two thousand Communist sympathizers were on their way to Sacramento to show their support for the defense. The city manager swiftly announced that anybody who turned up would be denied permission to carry out demonstrations on public property. The police then mustered at the local fairgrounds and began practicing with tear gas, promising "Red Eyes for the Reds," as the *Sacramento Bee* gleefully put it, if things got out of hand. Meantime, a National Guard colonel was put in charge of law enforcement in the city, and five hundred businessmen were sworn in as deputies.

Inside the courthouse, the atmosphere was just as highly charged. Jury selection alone had dragged on for twenty-seven days, as the defense and the prosecution (led by former Sacramento district attorney Neil McAllister, named a special deputy attorney general for the case) picked through some 260 prospective panel members. Tensions rose when the wife of one of those being considered told authorities that a posse had come to their house and threatened to kill her husband if he served. Just who these toughs may have been was never made clear, but Gallagher argued that the whole story had been fabricated so his clients would look bad.

This alleged tampering was by no means the last of the shenanigans. Gallagher also accused the prosecution of planting people on the jury—a charge that went nowhere. And after both sides had rested, somebody drilled a pair of half-inch holes in the ceiling above the jury room in an apparent attempt to eavesdrop on the deliberations. The plot was foiled when one of the jurors, returning from a lunch break, discovered plaster scattered everywhere.

In between these outlandish episodes, the longest-running criminal trial in California history—a four-month affair that stretched into April 1935—was punctuated by its own share of low blows and high drama. Six of the defendants represented themselves, leading to a constant flurry of objections and miscellaneous outbursts from multiple parties—some of which played right into the state's hands. When a prosecutor picked up a red flag that had been seized in the police raid and started to carry it toward the witness stand, one of the defendants, agricultural union leader Caroline Decker, admonished him to be more respectful.

"If the court please," she said, "I suggest Mr. Johnson not drag the flag on the floor."

The lawyers were far more vituperative. Like elementary school kids, they quarreled incessantly over the littlest things, including the definition of simple words. When Gallagher asked one witness about conditions in the farm fields "worsening," McAllister interrupted the cross-examination.

"What word is that?" McAllister asked.

"Worsening," Gallagher replied. "You never heard of that?"

"No."

"Well, get out your dictionary."

"You get it," said Lloyd Buchler, one of McAllister's co-counsels.

"That must be in the Moscow dictionary," Johnson added.

Presiding over this circus was Judge Dal Lemmon, who demonstrated remarkable patience throughout the case—especially with Gallagher. The attorney, who had studied law at Yale and had a doctorate in philosophy, was nobody's dummy. He had won international acclaim the year before by traveling to Germany to defend a Communist accused by the Nazis of torching the Reichstag—and had been tossed out of the country when he started scoring some points. Still, Gallagher had a tendency in Sacramento to come across as whiny and self-righteous, and his questioning was often needlessly redundant and niggling. His voice got so loud at times that one of the jurors groused to Lemmon, "Your honor, is it necessary for Mr. Gallagher to shout right in the jurors' ears?" At its best, though, Gallagher's nimble mind was too much for the prosecution's lineup of witnesses—a flock of "stool pigeons," as those on the left labeled them.

First up was a tall, flabby undercover investigator named William Hanks. The seventy-year-old had joined several organizations in Sacramento in early '34—the agricultural workers' union, International Labor Defense, and the Unemployed Council—in a calculated attempt to get close to those who'd eventually be arrested. Infiltrating leftist groups was nothing new for him. Hanks had probed the IWW for the

The defendants in the Sacramento Conspiracy Trial pose, with several of them wearing bright smiles, almost as if it were a class picture. Caroline Decker is seated second from the right. (Sacramento Archives and Museum Collection Center)

Justice Department during World War I and had hunted German spies too. "And believe me," he said, "I found plenty of them." Later, he worked his way up and down the West Coast, acting as a snoop for various sheriffs' offices and police departments, as well as for private industry. During the cotton strike of '33, he'd gone to Tulare to gather intelligence for the city attorney there. Hanks, who in Sacramento posed as an old Wobbly, aroused some suspicions when he tried to prod union members into committing vandalism. Yet he was trusted enough that Caroline Decker had him ferry a letter for her to the Bay Area.

Under Gallagher's relentless questioning, Hanks couldn't remember too many specifics about what the defendants had actually said or done. But, in the most extraordinary part of his testimony, he told how he had been menaced by a mysterious man with a pistol and ordered out of town after appearing before the grand jury. (The story wasn't new; earlier, the local paper had played up the supposed "kidnapping," anxious to give the Reds a black eye.) "He shoved a gun in my back, right up against the small of my back," Hanks told the court. "Now whether the Communists put me on the spot, I don't know. I don't know the man. I don't know if he was a Communist or who he was. But I do know that the Communists had known that I went before the grand jury." Concerned for his safety, Hanks said, he went to the bus station, bought a ticket to Omaha, and hightailed it out of Sacramento.

Gallagher did a fine job of picking apart this account. It would have been pretty difficult for anybody to believe, once the attorney was finished with him, that Hanks hadn't made up the whole thing. Gallagher was also skillful in pounding home the idea that during their fiery speeches around Sacramento's parks and union halls, his clients had spoken out for a living wage, equal pay for equal work, the abolition of child labor, a six-hour workday for those under eighteen, and other such principles. By comparison, the prosecution's contention that they wanted to smash the government, a la the Bolsheviks, seemed flimsy and vague.

Gallagher was masterful, as well, in showing that the union organizers in the '33 cotton strike were the victims—not the promoters or perpetrators—of violence. He also made plain that rather than being clandestine documents, as the prosecution intimated, many of the Communists' books were widely available—some of them right on the shelves of the state library nearby. And he elicited from Melville Harris, another undercover operative and star witness for the state, that he was now on the payroll of the Associated Farmers. This admission (coupled with the fact that an Associated Farmers publicity man, Gilbert Parker, was conferring regularly with the attorney general's team; prosecution consultant William Hynes, the former head of the Los Angeles Police Department's infamous Red Squad, was also being paid by the Associated Farmers; and the executive secretary of the Associated Farmers, Guernsey Frazer, had met several times with the prosecutors to discuss strategy) gave considerable credence to the notion that the defendants were being punished purely because of their labor organizing.

But even with all that, the Sacramento trial in some sense boiled down to one question: Just what exactly were the Communists after? Or, to put it another way, just what did all this talk of revolution truly mean?

The answer to that was to be taken up, in large measure, by the most improbable defendant of them all: a twenty-six-year-old former West Point cadet named Norman Mini.

———•———

To study a photograph of Norman Mini from his days at the U.S. Military Academy is to stare into a face full of promise—a handsome visage with bright eyes, a youthful glow, and a slight grin that seems self-assured but not overly cocky. Mini had joined West Point's long gray line not as an accouterment of upper-class privilege but because of his brains and hard work. The only child of a conservative railroad clerk and his wife, Mini grew up in Sacramento, where he attended Sunday school, became an accomplished jazz pianist, and loved to write. He entered West Point in July 1929, and his early days there (at least according to his official transcript) were largely uneventful. He excelled in English and history, and had a bit of a rougher time with mathematics, physics, and French, but he was a perfectly fine student all around. He committed a string of infractions through his early months at the academy, but they were strictly minor—"floor not properly swept," "late falling in after chapel," "shoes not properly shined"—and his conduct was never considered a serious problem.

That is, until the fall of 1931, when Mini was court-martialed and drummed out of the academy. He'd later say that he always "had a suspicion" his dismissal was related to the kind of books he had started to devour while a student at West Point. Among his favorites was Karl Marx's *Das Kapital*. He told his wife that higher-ups had even confiscated some of his reading material; she presumed he was referring to *The Communist Manifesto*. Mini's military file, however, gives another reason for his ouster: marching before the Army-Yale football game,

Mini fell out of formation in a drunken stupor and was hauled off by his superiors. He then puked all over himself and kept falling asleep, except whenever he'd hear a distant roar from the stadium, which led to his own whooping and cheering. "The sordid condition of the accused was so noticeable," said one officer, "that a kindly disposed lady wanted to take him into her home to sober him up."

Whatever the real explanation for his discharge, Mini soon headed to New York, where he figured his West Point credentials would serve him well, despite his ignominious exit and the stranglehold of the Depression. He had $500 in his pocket—the sum given him by the academy upon his sacking—and every confidence he'd soon be employed. "I went around to all the nice shops," he recalled. "I lived in nice hotels. I bought myself nice clothes. I ate good meals . . . I went to shows and generally associated with the people by which one pulls some strings to get a good job in society, to make money." His plan collapsed, however. Broke and alone, Mini wound up on the streets, where his reading of Marx seemed to spring to life.

"There were thousands of men standing around in the soup lines and the bread lines," he said. It had "a profound impression on me." At the same time, he read more Marx and some Lenin, too, "and I saw that what they said about society was true." After a short while, Mini came into a little cash and took the train back home to Sacramento. There, at a mass meeting at the civic auditorium calling for the freeing of Tom Mooney, he observed the Communist Party up close for the first time. "It seemed to be vital and full of life," Mini remembered, and the more he learned about the party's teachings, the more he was persuaded that it was "the only organization in society that was actually going to bring about . . . a betterment of the human race." So in early 1933, he signed on with Sacramento's Unit no. 3. "Anybody in my position that would not have taken his place in the ranks of the Communist Party at that time," Mini explained, "would have been either a coward or a hypocrite."

Over the next year or two, he worked as a labor organizer in the farm fields and was on hand in San Francisco when the city buckled under

the strain of the general strike. Mini also spent a Sunday morning in-
structing eleven young Communists how to stand up straight like soldiers and perform an acceptable left-face and right-face—a display of
martial maneuvering that the prosecution would make a big deal of at
the trial, but that came off less like the start of an armed uprising and
more like a little practice for a youth club parade.

Throughout the trial, Mini sparred with the prosecution equably and
ably, laying out for the jury the ins and outs of what America would
look like if capitalism were no more. As he expounded on Marx's
theories, it was almost as if the case being tried transcended the guilt or
innocence of the fourteen individuals in the courtroom. It became, instead, a lively debate between Mini and Neil McAllister over two
sharply conflicting visions for the nation's future.

"I believe . . . in the abolishment of this old system that is outworn,
and the replacement of it by a socialist society that would raise mankind
up to a higher level of prosperity and development," Mini said as he
took the witness stand in February 1935, "introducing a classless society
and the abolishment of poverty and crime and prostitution and war."

"In other words," McAllister asked him, "all the profit system would
be abolished entirely?"

"That is right . . . . All the people in the United States would own
the productive resources, the resources of nature in the United States,
communication, transportation and so forth. They would use it for the
development of everybody, not for the development of the small parasite class."

"What do you call the small parasite class?" McAllister asked.

"The capitalists," Mini answered, "the people that live without doing
any work, live on the labor of others."

"Don't you give them credit . . . at least for their capital having built
it up, having built up industry for the purpose of giving the people
work? . . . You don't think that after people came to this country, settled
in this country in the early days, when it was a wilderness, and went to
farming and built up manufacturing industries . . . built railroads

through the Rocky Mountains . . . that if the stockholders of the Southern Pacific Company had spent a lot of money spanning the entire continent . . . that the people who had put up the money for that
investment would not be entitled to a profit?"

Mini didn't miss a beat. "The people that built the Southern Pacific
Railroad were not the stockholders," he replied, "but exploited . . . labor
brought from China under the most miserable slave conditions. They
built the railroad over the mountain."

At a different point, McAllister tried to demolish Mini's assertion
that "the workers are inevitably forced to struggle against their bosses."
Didn't this idea completely discount people's industriousness? Wasn't
this to disregard that America was, at its core, a meritocracy?

"Did you ever hear of a man going into work as a laborer and finally
. . . owning the shop or place where he was working?" McAllister asked.

"I imagine," said Mini, "it could be done."

"Did you ever hear of a clerk going into a large corporation and in
years to come being president of the corporation, as was Charles M.
Schwab?" McAllister inquired, referring to the man who had started out
in the late nineteenth century as a dollar-a-day stake driver at Andrew
Carnegie's steelworks and rose to run Carnegie Steel Company, U.S.
Steel, and Bethlehem Steel.

"I have heard of that."

"So you mean to imply . . . that the working class of people have absolutely no chance in this world to get along?"

"In general they have no chance," Mini said. "And the chance becomes increasingly less as capitalism becomes more and more decayed."

As Mini continued to testify, he didn't deny that those who followed
Marx, Lenin, and Engels might well use force to ensure "a victorious
revolution." Violence, he went so far as to say, was practically "an inevitable thing" in the Communist blueprint. But to get to that stage, he
told the jury, lots would have to happen first: Capitalism would have to
further deteriorate and the current system of government cease to function; a "vast majority" of people in the country, after coming together to

Norman Mini, shown here in his West Point uniform, traded in his military manual for *The Communist Manifesto.* (Courtesy of Kleo Mini)

form workers' councils, would have to favor a change in government control; and a different breed of political party, representing the "oppressed classes," would have to step in and redistribute the nation's wealth. At that moment, "when the workers take over the capitalist system and use society for their own benefit," Mini said, "they are just going and taking what rightfully belongs to them—that which has been taken away from them by the capitalists."

Even then, Mini stressed, violence would not automatically occur—though McAllister pushed him on just how the workers would go about acquiring the assets of most industries.

"I assume they would pay for them in some way," the prosecutor said.

"No," Mini answered. "They wouldn't pay for them."

"Nothing at all?"

"No."

"Wouldn't even give them an IOU or a promissory note?"

"No, not the big industries. They have already been amply compensated for a long time with super-bloated profits."

And what would happen, McAllister asked, if the owner of a factory—a guy who had built a $1 million business "through hard earnings, working day and night"—resisted giving up his property to this new Socialist workers' state? "What would you do then?"

"He would be arrested."

"Supposing he resisted arrest?"

"This minority, any time like that, would be revealed in true light—they would be revealed as enemies of society and of the people, and they would be arrested."

"Supposing he actually . . . resisted arrest to the extent that he shot and killed one or two of your militia right in the office? What would you do?"

"I would arrest him with all force necessary."

"Would you kill him, shoot him back?"

"Not necessarily—not unless it was necessary."

It came down, then, to this: no, the Reds were not afraid of using violence. But if you accepted as true Mini's version of how Communism was supposed to take hold in America—and his step-by-step explication was certainly convincing—then violence wasn't the opening gambit. It was, if anything, more of a last resort.

———————

The same month that Norman Mini was pleading the Communists' case in Sacramento, Bill Camp was nearly three thousand miles away in Washington, embroiled in his own fray with those on the Far Left. The California cotton pioneer had been called in to help oversee the Agricultural Adjustment Administration (AAA), a new arm of the federal government that held two distinctions: it was the most exciting of Roosevelt's New Deal agencies, because so many crucial policy decisions were being made there, and it was also the most fractionalized.

Part of the AAA was run by a coterie of old-line farming experts who hoped to save the nation's faltering rural economy by working with large landowners and processors. This is the group with which Camp and his boss in the AAA Cotton Section, a Tennessee-born agricultural journalist named Cully Cobb, naturally allied themselves. The other principal faction was made up of lawyers wooed to the AAA from Ivy League faculties and Wall Street investment houses. They had little, if any, farming experience; most of them barely knew the difference between a cow and a sow. But they were big thinkers and big dreamers, and under the tutelage of chief counsel Jerome Frank, they viewed the AAA not only as a tool for fixing agriculture but as a vehicle for repairing society—particularly in the South, with its long track record of racism and ill treatment of sharecroppers and tenant farmers. The two blocs "were completely contrary," Cobb said. "They were at right angles." Caught somewhere in between was Agriculture Secretary Henry Wallace.

It didn't take a lot for George Peek, the crusty AAA administrator, to become repulsed by the intellectuals. "Boys with their hair ablaze!" he called them. To Peek, the AAA had one job and one job only: to increase farm prices; anything else was just "foolish stuff." Frank and his followers "blame all ills on capitalism," Peek said, "and were for abolishing it—either by degrees or at once." Left to their own devices, he added, the AAA was to become "a means of . . . breaking down the whole individualistic system of the country."

Bill Camp reached the same conclusion, telling people that he once was shown "a detailed plan" from the AAA reform crowd for "the complete collectivization of American agriculture." According to Camp, the country was to be divided into six regions, each with a "czar" who'd direct every U.S. farmer "in the Russian style." Camp said he was stunned by the plan, and he made it a point from then on to look for a way to get rid of Frank and the others behind "all of this monkey business."

Although it's hard to believe that Camp ever really saw a proposal as inordinate as the one he described, he finally got his chance to help torpedo Frank and the AAA Legal Section in early 1935. A showdown had been taking shape for months over whether the AAA's cotton program, which all but mandated a reduction in plantings in a bid to raise prices, was causing a huge hardship: the eviction of poor tenant farmers from their land, often without getting their proper share of Uncle Sam's subsidy payments.

Anticipating this problem, one of those on Frank's legal staff had suggested early on that all government checks be made out jointly to landlord and tenant. But this proposition from Alger Hiss, a twenty-nine-year-old who had clerked for one Supreme Court justice (Oliver Wendell Holmes) and was the protégé of another justice-to-be (Felix Frankfurter), didn't go over very well with Senator Ellison DuRant Smith, a tobacco-spitting South Carolinian and a staunch foe of FDR. Smith, better known as "Cotton Ed," stormed into Hiss's office one day, unannounced. "You're going to send money to my niggers instead of me?" the Democrat barked. "I'll take care of them." Hiss soon gave up on the idea.

Hiss and his colleagues did, though, manage to insert other language in the AAA's cotton contract that was meant to protect share-croppers. But these agreements were still riddled with loopholes that the big growers happily cashed in on, and the basic administration of the program was stacked in their favor: it was left to local committees, generally made up of the landlords' cronies, to settle disputes on the ground. These men "have been in the habit of exploiting the economic, social and political weakness of their tenants," an April 1934 report in the *Chicago Daily News* concluded. "They cannot be expected suddenly to mend their ways in the spirit of the New Deal. Tenants have no representation on these boards . . . . It is not surprising that the luscious fruits of the New Deal should fall largely into the hands of the powerful planters."

All along, Cobb and Camp insisted that there was no big problem with tenant farmers, black or white, being evicted without fair payment. Sure, there may have been a few unscrupulous landlords out there. "But the charge that the AAA has been responsible for any appreciable displacement of tenants . . . just isn't true," Camp said. "Certainly, trained observers who came south to investigate charges such as these have found nothing to support them." Actually, Camp's sanguine assessment notwithstanding, there was plenty to support them: numerous news articles; a thorough study from a Duke University economist; a long list of grievances from the Southern Tenant Farmers Union, which sent a delegation to Washington to complain directly to Secretary Wallace; and an internal investigation by a lawyer who, though not part of the AAA's liberal wing, had ascertained that the landlords had "openly and generally violated" their contracts. The report she ultimately submitted on the situation was so hot, it was buried by Chester Davis, who'd replaced Peek as the AAA's top official and had aligned himself squarely with Cobb's Cotton Section.

Despite Davis's posture, Frank's Legal Section continued to try to make things right. Hiss, for one, had raised additional concerns after an Arkansas planter named Hirman Norcross booted twenty-two of his sharecroppers out of their homes—all of them members of the tenant farmers' union. Hiss zeroed in on section 7 of the AAA contract for 1934–35. The accord already contained a stipulation that landlords had to keep the same number of tenants from year to year. Yet obviously, this provision had failed to offer genuine security for those who needed it most. A whole family, for instance, might be kicked off the land and replaced by a single tenant. Or paper tenants might be swapped for real people. Not to mention that benefit checks could easily go missing as new tenants replaced old ones. And then there was what Norcross had done—evicting his tenants, as Hiss noted, "simply and solely because they were members of a union."

Hiss's solution was to help draft a new legal interpretation: section 7, the thinking now went, not only required growers to retain an equal number of tenants on their plantations; they had to keep the same exact ones. Sensitive that Davis would never approve of this analysis, which emasculated the big growers and was on shaky legal ground to boot, Frank waited until the administrator went out of town. Then he had county offices throughout the Cotton Belt informed of the new policy—and he made sure it was issued under the name of Henry Wallace, no less.

Alger Hiss, pictured here, tussled with Bill Camp over the direction of federal farm policy at the Agricultural Adjustment Administration. Hiss's actions eventually helped lead to the so-called Purge of the Liberals from the AAA. (Photo by Gjon Mili, Time & Life Pictures/Getty Images)

By the time Davis returned to Washington, a tremendous fuss was underway. An irate Arkansas congressman and the head of the state's farm bureau had already descended upon Secretary Wallace to voice their displeasure. Wallace, who hadn't even realized that any section 7 directive had gone out, was able to mollify them. But he was ambivalent about what to do next. Most accounts of what transpired cast Chester Davis in the role of leading man. After preparing a hasty refutation of the lawyers' section 7 opinion, he gave Wallace an ultimatum: either Frank and his young Turks would have to go—or he'd go. Wallace, though apprehensive, acquiesced. Frank was the first to be given his walking papers. Four others were also fired, including Francis Shea, who had helped Hiss construe section 7. Interestingly, Hiss himself was spared. Apparently, Davis felt that the hardworking attorney was just being loyal to Frank, his boss. Cobb had his own take: "Hiss," he said, "was more clever at covering up" the full extent of his radical thinking "than were the other members of his group."

As time rolled on, Cobb and Camp would offer up something of an alternative version of the so-called Purge of the Liberals. Rather than

Davis engineering the dumping of Frank and the others, they said, it was Camp who was most adamant that something drastic needed to be done—or the whole cotton program might implode. As Camp remembered it, he walked into Davis's office to deliver the message in no uncertain terms.

"What's the matter, Bill?" Davis asked him.

There will be "no more cotton program," he warned, "unless action is taken."

Unsatisfied with Davis's response, Camp said, he then took it upon himself to convene a meeting of southern senators, including "Cotton Ed" Smith, Joe Robinson of Arkansas, and Pat Harrison of Mississippi. He alerted the lawmakers to the liberals' plans and suggested that what was happening with section 7 of the cotton contract was only the beginning of their dangerous schemes. By the time Camp was done, his high-ranking guests vowed to take the matter straight to President Roosevelt—and tell him that they'd bottle up all of his legislative priorities if Frank and his cohorts weren't thrown out of the AAA.

Whether Camp inflated his part in all this for posterity is hard to say. Either way, he and Cobb felt vindicated when, years later, it was disclosed that a Communist cell had in fact been operating inside the AAA—a secret alliance that at first called itself the "Cling Peaches" after a marketing agreement that the agency's lawyers had just hammered out. The cell's primary charge, it was said, wasn't to collectivize agriculture or to commit espionage, but to groom recruits who could one day penetrate the highest echelons of Washington.

Members of the cell met once a week at a Connecticut Avenue music shop belonging to the sister of Hal Ware, a longtime consultant to the U.S. government on Soviet agriculture and the son of Communist stalwart Ella Reeve "Mother" Bloor. There, the Ware Group (as it came to be called) studied Marx and Lenin and, over time, passed along reports and other documents they thought the party might find useful. Jerome Frank, who was anti-Communist in spite of his strong liberal leanings, wasn't in the group. But Alger Hiss was accused of being a member.

That allegation, by Whittaker Chambers in August 1948, would become a watershed in American history, catapulting Richard Nixon to national prominence, setting the stage for the McCarthy era, and turning Ronald Reagan on a rightward path. Hiss would always deny that he had been a Communist or a Communist sympathizer (much less a Soviet spy), and over the decades a welter of conflicting information on whether he was or wasn't would be amassed. But Cobb and Camp, who kept a file on the controversy around Hiss, never had any doubt about his guilt.

Looking back on his days at the AAA, Cobb expressed great relief that Hiss and those "Communist-front agitators" at the tenant farmers' union hadn't been able to undermine what those in the Cotton Section were trying to accomplish. "It was intuition or something that protected us," Cobb would tell Camp in 1949. "Above all, perhaps, it was an abiding faith in the eternal rightness of the fundamentals that lie at the foundation of our way of life . . . . And it was our sense of right and wrong that . . . led us to deeply distrust those who wanted to completely rework everything overnight." Best of all, said Cobb, was that Hiss seemed at long last to be getting what was coming to him. "Time has caught up with our enemies," he said, "and there isn't much that we could want done that time hasn't and isn't doing."

Camp, who had returned to California thirteen years earlier, remained less sure about that. "Most of those skunks are still living," he replied to Cobb, warily, "and they may yet have an opportunity to do some more of their dirty work."

———————

As the Sacramento Conspiracy Trial crept into March 1935, Neil McAllister continued to parry with the Communists on the stand—the interchanges filling the jurors' heads with two completely different pictures of what America looked like and where it was going. It was akin to the blind men and the elephant, only in this case it was a blind adherence to ideology—with one side describing a free-market utopia, the other a collectivist paradise—that prevented each from recognizing in the slightest what the other could see so clearly.

"Is it for you to say . . . that those people who work in this or that or the other mine or factory or oil well don't get paid enough, and for that reason you will take it away from the owner?" McAllister asked Caroline Decker, the petite, blonde labor agitator who'd joined the Young Communist League at age sixteen and then went off to organize the Kentucky coal mines at nineteen and the California cotton fields at twenty-one.

Decker promptly turned the whole thing right around: "Is it for you to say the owner has the right to keep it from the people?"

"The people haven't the right to what doesn't . . . belong to them," McAllister shot back.

"It does belong to them. That is where you and I differ."

"Under what theory do you say it belongs to the people? Under what theory?"

"Well, I don't know," said Decker. "It seems to me that under any moral, human theory you couldn't help but believe that. Why a handful of people—capitalists—should be permitted to exploit the whole human race and exploit natural resources . . . while the millions of people, the best brains, the engineers, the professionals, the workers are destitute, are insecure—don't know where their next month's rent is coming from, don't know where their next meal is coming . . . . By what moral right should any condition like that exist?"

"Our present legal system," McAllister reminded her, "provides for the ownership of private property."

"I am sure . . . the people . . . are going to find it necessary to reframe the legal provisions of this country so that they will protect the human rights and interests of the masses instead of the private property of the handful."

"Don't you know—don't you know as a matter of fact that there is a very small minority of agitators in the country today that are preaching and teaching against our government—a very small minority of Communist agitators dissatisfied with our country today?"

"Mr. McAllister," Decker replied, "Jesus Christ was called an agitator."

And so on and so forth it went, until the trial reached its eighteenth week. And then, at last, the two sides rested. Leo Gallagher's closing argument focused mainly on the many inconsistencies and obfuscations that had been uttered by the witnesses for the prosecution. He also rebutted his opposing counsel's proclivity for finding isolated sentences or paragraphs in the Communists' writings that seemed, at a glance, to endorse violence. It was just as easy, all in all, to identify pieces that were pacifistic in tone and content. And besides, to pick out a damning phrase was to ignore the broader context: any contemplation of the use of force was dependent on a whole series of events (as outlined by Norman Mini) that might or might not ever occur. Gallagher didn't rely on logic alone, however, to try to sway members of the jury; he also preyed on their fears. "I dare you to convict these defendants," he shouted before the court, and then added ominously, "There is no doubt that there will be an outbreak of violence when this case is settled."

Such theatrics, though, were nothing compared with McAllister's. He began by thanking Judge Lemmon and apologizing for any impertinence on his part. "During the course of this trial, many things have been said that shouldn't have been said." And then he started in, calling the defendants "traitors." "I'll say 'traitors' many times during the course of this argument because that is what they are—traitors!" The attorney general of California, McAllister said, "considers this the most important case ever tried in the state . . . . You are here today making history. We stand today at a crossroads. One road points to Americanism"—and with that, McAllister went up to the Stars and Stripes near the witness stand, grasped its edge, and pulled out the folds. "The other road points toward Communism." And then he gestured toward the defendants.

He condemned the notion that those on trial were being prosecuted because of their union organizing. "That's an excuse in this case . . . . They care nothing about labor. Their aim, their object, their purpose is what they call worldwide Communism . . . not to better anyone's conditions except as incidental to winning the masses, as they call it . . . so they can carry out their plots and plans.

"Now let us consider the position of the Associated Farmers," said McAllister. "What are the farmers to do in the state of California? Sit idly by while these conspirators . . . these propagandists, these agitators . . . tell them how to run their farms, or are they going to organize to maintain their own rights as property owners, as toilers and as thrifty people?"

As the noon recess neared, he started to roll through the exhibits, quoting from them (very selectively) once again: "'Only a violent defeat of the bourgeoisie, the confiscation of its property, the annihilation of the entire bourgeois governmental apparatus,' etc., etc. . . . . There you have it . . . . That's the literature of the Communist party. It isn't mine! I didn't write it, circulate it, distribute it. I didn't have it in my possession.

"Treason, ladies and gentlemen. That's what it is! . . . They call it freedom of speech. Well, the court will give you instructions that advocating criminal syndicalism is in violation of free speech. This country stands for free speech, but not for advocating the overthrow of the government.

"Out of this primitive wilderness, ladies and gentlemen, sprang up the greatest democracy in the world . . . . Think of the covered wagons, think of the Donner Party coming through the snow and getting frozen to death and lost. Think of the hardships of those days. Think of that class of pioneers. We have a new class of pioneers, but a different sort of pioneers! They don't propose to come here and by their own toil earn a living! Nooo. They propose to agitate the country and take away from you what you have and overthrow the government! From Moscow! They are paid by Moscow!

"They remind me of termites. That's what they are—termites! Undermining everything with which they come in contact.

"Now, I am just about through, but I want to say that a very serious duty evolves upon you in this case. I told you before that the eyes of the nation are on you, asking you, begging you, pleading with you to stamp out this insurrection—this advocacy of revolution and the overthrow of the government and institutions which you love, honor and revere and which you hope to pass down to your children and your children's children. And what do you want to pass down? The red flag?"

Like something out of a B movie, McAllister then walked over to the witness stand, mounted the marble steps, and faced the American flag. Placing his notes in one hand, he saluted with the other. "I now pledge allegiance to the flag of the United States of America," he said. "One nation, indivisible, with liberty and justice for all.

"Ladies and gentlemen, I ask you to think of that flag in that jury room, and I ask you to think of what it stands for. I ask you to bring in a vote for that flag, for the good old U.S.A., for 'My Country 'Tis of Thee,' for 'The Star-Spangled Banner,' for my own United States, and God will bless you."

———•———

Judge Lemmon's courtroom went silent as the jury shambled in to relay the defendants' fate. It had taken sixty-six hours—and 118 ballots—to reach a verdict. A battery of policemen stood watch, prepared for a possible riot. But no fists were to fall. Only tears.

The jury convicted eight of the fourteen—Norman Mini and Caroline Decker included—and set free the other six. McAllister praised the outcome as "a step backwards for Communism, not only in the state of California but throughout the nation" and "a step forward for Americanism and all that America stands for." It was also a giant leap forward for the Associated Farmers, which had been so involved in shaping and shepherding the case.

Gallagher had a different reading on things. "It will facilitate the introduction of Fascism in California," he said. "It is impossible to believe the long struggle for human liberty has been set back."

The verdict is read at the Sacramento Conspiracy Trial.
Eight of the fourteen defendants were convicted, effectively
wiping out the agricultural workers' union that had flexed its
muscles the year before. (Sacramento Archives and Museum
Collection Center)

Those convicted would go on to make a few more high-minded pro-
nouncements during their sentencing, but that would be the last of it.
"Our standing here is no accident," Mini told Judge Lemmon at the
hearing in April 1935, just before he was sent away. "Our conviction is
the result of the class struggle—the same class struggle that . . . will
someday generate an irresistible wave that will forever sweep away everything that this country and state represents. With this knowledge, we
can face our sentence confidently, as we know the future belongs to us."
Mini was given three years in San Quentin; the one-time West Point

cadet, second class, was now prisoner no. 57606. Caroline Decker was sentenced to five years at the women's prison right outside Tehachapi (the same spot, incidentally, from which the Joads would look down, in awe and wonder, at the vineyards and orchards of the valley).

Gallagher went to work straight away on an appeal. So did Raymond Henderson, who was brought in to represent Mini. The briefs he submitted to the court concentrated on the contingent nature of the Communists' call for violence. "The Social Revolution is not conceived of by the Communists as a Spartacist uprising of a small fraction of the underprivileged classes, nor yet as a Catalinian conspiracy of a little group plotting to take over the power of the state by assassinating the present leaders, nor yet as a Napoleonic coup d'etat," Henderson wrote. "There is not one word in this record to show that they countenance violence until it becomes absolutely necessary in the revolutionary struggle of a majority of the working class . . . . The violence contemplated by the Communists will occur only in the future and under conditions which do not now exist and which in all reasonable probability never will exist." Ever erudite, Henderson then quoted many of the greatest minds of the ages on freedom of speech: Jefferson, Lincoln, Plato, Milton, and more.

The judges would find none of that persuasive. But they were moved by one other line of reasoning that Henderson and Gallagher had raised. Originally, the defendants in the case had been hit with two separate—if very similar—indictments. The jury, in handing down its convictions, had found Mini and Decker and the others guilty of two counts from the first indictment, while exonerating them on all charges from the second indictment. Here, though, was the rub: the second indictment had accused the defendants of resorting to "written or spoken language or personal conduct" in the abetting of criminal syndicalism. If they were acquitted of all these things, then how could they have been found guilty of abetting criminal syndicalism in the first indictment? "It is impossible to reconcile these verdicts," the court declared in September 1937, adding that a not-guilty verdict on the second indictment was "conclusive proof" that there should have been an identical finding on the first. Therefore, it ordered "the appellants . . . discharged from custody" immediately while cautioning that "no good will be served by a second trial."

Being released from prison had to bring feelings of joy and relief and thankfulness. Still, there was no escaping that these men and women had lost several years of their lives. Much had changed since they were first incarcerated. The agricultural union that Decker had helped direct, the CAWIU, had been ruined because of the case, though many of those who had participated in its activities had since found their way to Donald Henderson's new labor organization, UCAPAWA. The Communist Party had also transformed itself from a detached, doctrinaire cult into a proponent of the Popular Front—the all-embracing movement that included a wide variety of liberal groups united in the fight against Fascism and for which *The Grapes of Wrath* would become such a strong rallying cry.

"By the summer of 1939," political scientist Harvey Klehr has noted, "American Communists had come a long way from those days when they talked largely to themselves. Few liberal organizations were without a significant Communist presence . . . . Hundreds of prominent intellectuals, performers and artists applauded the Soviet Union's every action."

Norman Mini, having surfaced from San Quentin full of fire, was still clamoring for "a hangman's rope for capitalism" in '39. But Caroline Decker had lost her spark. "My life had taken a different turn," she said. "Almost three years in prison really gets you out of things." She was put off, too, by reports of Josef Stalin's incredible brutality. The real breaking point for her, though, was to occur on this very day—Wednesday, August 23.

That's when the Soviet Union signed a non-aggression pact with Nazi Germany. For many Communists in America and their Popular Front partners, the news that Stalin had suddenly changed course and cut a deal with a Fascist like Adolph Hitler brought an overwhelming sense of confusion and betrayal. "My own association with the Communist Party went pow," Decker would later recall. The head of the party in the United States, Earl Browder, quickly engaged in verbal gymnastics to justify Russia's about-face. But the Communists would never regain the political strength and legitimacy that they had come to relish over the previous few years. The Popular Front was instantly shattered.

And yet for all the commotion that the Nazi-Soviet pact produced, many on the left just kept doing what they were doing—especially those, like Ray Henderson, who could never stomach the Communists anyway. There were, after all, still lots of worthy causes to pursue, many of them much closer to home. "The world was shocked and surprised" by the agreement between "the two great totalitarian states, Germany and Russia," Henderson said. But what was more shocking, he suggested, was what the Board of Supervisors in Kern County had done with *The Grapes of Wrath*. "That is the philosophy of fuehrers and dictators," Henderson said. "That is what they do over in Italy and Germany and Russia and Japan."

CHAPTER FIVE
Thursday

The Joads had been lucky. They got in early enough to have a place in the boxcars. Now the tents of the late-comers filled the little flat, and those who had the boxcars were old-timers, and in a way aristocrats.

T HE BLOCK IN Bakersfield sat mostly empty, save for the three men gathered in front of a small metal trash can and the photographer who had been summoned to snap their picture, if not necessarily for the ages then at least for the afternoon paper. The man to the left, a Kern County cotton grower, gin operator, and Associated Farmers board member named L. E. Plymale, wore a fedora and scuffed shoes and a smirk on his face. Off to the right stood Bill Camp, arms akimbo. He donned a crisp white shirt and black bow tie and his trademark broad-brimmed hat, which offered a welcome touch of relief from the searing valley sun. He stared impassively through wire-rim glasses at the man in the middle, who, bent like a reed, was dangling over the trash can a copy of what Camp called, simply, "that damnable book."

A match would soon be struck, and *The Grapes of Wrath* would go up in flames. As far as book burnings go, this was pretty small-scale stuff. But the picture of the trio, taken by a photographer who'd fade into anonymity, would find its way into the late edition of the *Californian* and, a few months hence, grace the pages of *Look* magazine. In its own way, the image says as much about 1930s California—its pervasive poverty, its people, its polarizing politics—as the most celebrated works of Horace Bristol and Dorothea Lange.

The *Kern Herald*—the liberal, pro-labor counterpoint to the *Californian*—also ran a story on this day, August 24, 1939, in which Supervisor Stanley Abel had anticipated the conflagration with a certain degree of delight, almost as if he were inviting folks to a county pie-eating contest. "Well, are you going to come see us burn those . . . books?" he asked Thelma Miller, a local writer, who then recounted the conversation in her column. Miller began by noting that Abel hadn't actually read *The Grapes of Wrath*, though he professed to having gone through some of it and to having been told about the rest.

"Did the Associated Farmers have anything to do with your action in banning the book?" Miller asked him.

"Associated Farmers?" Abel replied. "I don't even know any Associated Farmers." Then, on second thought, he allowed, "Oh, I might know one or two of 'em. But plenty of other people have complained to me about the book."

"Would you say, then, that the action of the supervisors in banning *The Grapes of Wrath* was in response to popular demand?"

"I should say so, yes."

Miller went on to report the actual number of objections to the novel received by Gretchen Knief and her staff at the library. The grand total—zero—made Abel look like a fibber or a fool. Meanwhile, she couldn't resist toying with her interview subject just a bit more. "Mr. Abel, do you think that the Board of Supervisors should act as censors of the books in the county library?"

"I certainly do think so," he said, "when the books are filthy."

"Mr. Abel, are you aware that there are a number of books in the county library written by young American authors, Steinbeck's contemporaries, that might be considered just as obscene as *The Grapes of Wrath*?"

Farm worker Clell Pruett
burns *The Grapes of Wrath*
as his boss, Bill Camp, and
L. E. Plymale watch the
novel go up in flames.
(Kern County Museum)

Abel paused, obviously thrown off stride. "I was not aware of it," he said, before recovering quickly. "I'll have to speak to Miss Knief about it. Yes sir, I'll certainly have to speak to Miss Knief."

Miller wasn't the only one to serve up such barbed commentary. The *Selma Irrigator*, in its pages this same day, described the conduct of Abel and the other supervisors as "absurd," while a writer for the *Dinuba Sentinel* had this to say about the "terrible stew . . . brewing" in Bakersfield: "Take it from me, Steinbeck hasn't a thing on Rabelais or Boccaccio; he doesn't even come close to their frank vulgarity."

Abel may have hoped that Kern County would attract some publicity out of the book ban, but with the criticism piling up as fast as fresh-picked bolls tossed into the back of a cotton wagon, the question loomed ever larger: At what price? The burning was designed to answer all this. Camp's notion wasn't merely to set the novel on fire. He was intent on conveying a message that would blunt those smart alecks in the newspaper and reduce some of the resulting pressure that now threatened to overturn the supervisors' ban at their next meeting, suddenly just four days away.

The key to it all was the man sporting denim overalls and flanked by Camp and Plymale: Clell Pruett, the worker who had never read *The Grapes of Wrath* but who'd been riled up earlier in the week by Ruth Comfort Mitchell's radio broadcast from the Palace Hotel in San Francisco. By having the clean-cut twenty-four-year-old torch the book, it was a declaration that the big growers weren't the only ones offended by it; the migrants themselves were angry—"and I didn't blame them," Camp said. Others soon ran with the same idea. *The Grapes of Wrath,* said Philip Bancroft, a swashbuckling Associated Farmers vice president and conservative political fixture in the state, "was not only a libel against the farmers and other good people of California, but a still worse libel against the fine, hard-working Americans coming from the region . . . called the Dust Bowl."

Although the book burning was a publicity stunt, Camp had managed to tap into feelings that were real enough. Steinbeck may have seen great virtues in the migrants—"I admire them intensely," he said, "because they are brave . . . kind, humorous and wise"—but many of the subjects of his work were ambivalent, at best, about the way they'd been represented. "It's a lot of exaggeration," said James Lackey, who landed in Kern County from Oklahoma in 1936. Some feared, in particular, that the novel made them look like white trash—a stigma that they were having a hard enough time shaking.

"We were all very poor, but we didn't have some of the morals that were in that book," said Lula Martin, who made the journey from eastern Oklahoma to California in 1935. "It was very harsh." Another native Oklahoman, Frank Manies, held a similar opinion. "I resented John Steinbeck using that kind of language," he said. "I didn't use it . . . and I know many of my friends and relatives did not." Vera Criswell, who relocated from Texas, was turned off by what she saw as the excessive promiscuity in Steinbeck's work. "I think he did a disservice to an awful lot of people," she said. For Clara Davis, yet another migrant who wound up in Bakersfield, the bottom line was simple: "The people from Oklahoma do not have any use for Steinbeck."

The Grapes of Wrath wasn't the only piece of art to bring out such ill will. Dorothea Lange's photograph "Migrant Mother"—a figure who, along with Tom Joad, would become one of the two preeminent icons of the 1930s—was eyed distrustfully by at least one Oklahoma transplant: Migrant Mother herself. Her real name was Florence Owens Thompson, and later in her life she'd grumble about having been exploited by Lange. "I wish she hadn't of taken my picture," she said.

Thompson didn't deny that she was dirt poor, and at times truly desperate. "When Steinbeck wrote *The Grapes of Wrath* about those people living under the bridge at Bakersfield—at one time we lived under that bridge," Thompson said. "It was the same old story. Didn't even have a tent then, just a ratty old quilt. I walked from what they'd call the Hoover camp at the bridge to way down on First Street to work in a restaurant for 50 cents a day and leftovers. They'd give me what was left over to take home, sometimes two water buckets full. I had six children to feed at the time." But evidence would emerge over the years that Lange had been loose with the facts behind the famous photo. Thompson wasn't living in the washed-out pea-pickers camp at Nipomo, as Lange claimed. Her car just happened to break down there when Lange showed up. Nor was Thompson so hard up that she sold the tires on her car to feed her kids, as Lange's field notes indicated.

Beyond that, there was something embarrassing about the picture, at least to Thompson's family. Many people saw in "Migrant Mother" a quiet dignity beneath her sad mask. "She has all the suffering of mankind in her, but all the perseverance too," said Roy Stryker, the head of the Resettlement Administration's photography project, in which Lange took part. Yet Thompson's three daughters, who are clinging to their mom in the 1936 photograph, didn't view it that way. There was, on balance, so much more to Thompson: for one thing, she was active in the union, UCAPAWA, organizing meetings and negotiating wages in Kern County. "She was a very strong woman. She was a leader," said the youngest of her girls in the

The reaction by Florence Thompson and her family to Dorothea Lange's "Migrant Mother" underscores the ambivalence felt by many migrants over how they were portrayed, even by those sympathetic to their plight. (Photo by Dorothea Lange, Library of Congress)

picture, Norma Rydlewski. "I think that's one of the reasons she resented the photo—because it didn't show her in that light."

That Bill Camp was so intent on highlighting the migrants' bitter reaction to the way Steinbeck had depicted them was ironic, to say the least. After all, many of those now in his corner (local businessmen, health officers, and Associated Farmers officials) had been the ones to stereotype the Okies in the first place—and they did so without any of the warm feelings and good intentions that Steinbeck clearly had. As one foe of the book ban put it: "Today they tell us that the migrants are nice, God-fearing, moral people. A year ago they told us in their publications that the migrants were dirty, immoral scum who lived under crowded immoral conditions and lay naked in the fields."

Tom McManus of the California Citizens' Association, who had spoken at the Palace along with Ruth Comfort Mitchell, was among the big wheels who'd spewed his share of anti-migrant invective. Mc-Manus, whose group was closely allied with the Associated Farmers, spent most of his time denouncing state and federal policy. But he could be mean and cold on a human level, at one point asking those who were trying to mend their lives in the Golden State: "Why don't you go back to Oklahoma?" Others painted the Okies as stupid and uneducable. And still others cast them as welfare cheats. Every two weeks, "these wayfarers go for relief," said an article distributed by the Associated Farmers. "The street is crowded with good-looking cars, many of them new, and the mommas and poppas laugh and joke and stand in line for their handout."

Perhaps the most malevolent assessment, though, came from Lee Alexander Stone, health director in Madera County and a friend of Bill Camp's. Stone regarded himself as an anatomist of migrant culture, and he saw in those he studied a peculiar form of paralysis. "Ethnically," he wrote in 1938, "they are as far removed from a desire to attain the privileges" of modern life as "they were in the days before the Revolutionary War. To many, this indictment may seem too severe. But to me, it is not severe enough. The poor white of the United States has lived in close proximity to an advancing civilization . . . for several hundred years and yet outwardly has made little or no advance."

That the newcomers to California were a backward people was a common refrain among business and farming leaders in the state—one often spiced up by reports on the migrants' purported bedroom habits. So lurid were these accounts, related with an almost voyeuristic sense of excitement, that Steinbeck's occasional reference to somebody's "tit" or "pecker" looked wholesome by comparison. In the summer of 1938, for instance, the state chamber of commerce published in its magazine, *California,* an article by Loring Schuler, another of the presenters at the Palace. "There is so much unmorality among them—not immorality; they just don't know any better," Schuler quoted one farming organization official as saying. "There was a father who was arrested for outraging his daughter. His whole family appeared in court to defend him, and when he was sent to jail, his wife said, 'They oughtn't to send paw to jail for that. She's his own property and he can do what he pleases with her.'"

In the same piece, Lee Stone echoed the point: "Many of these people have inbred for years," he claimed. "They insist upon sleeping all in one room—father, mother, half a dozen kids, uncles and aunts and all the rest. The result is that daughters have children by their own fathers; sisters by brothers." At the same time, Stone had little, if anything, bad to say about the big growers who caused much of the overcrowding. Whenever a prominent farmer was challenged about conditions in his labor camp, Stone would arm him with material noting that the place had been inspected and approved by the local health department. At the bottom of the page was this postscript: "To hell with *The Grapes of Wrath* and *Factories in the Field*! Dr. Lee Alexander Stone."

With the community's muck-a-mucks and the media demonizing the migrants, it's little wonder that this became the prevailing view among many residents of the valley; hate, like water, flows downhill. A survey of more than one hundred junior college students in Modesto, for example, found that nearly half were willing to openly express their disgust for those clustered in the "Little Oklahoma" neighborhood nearby. To read their remarks is to absorb a steady drumbeat of revulsion: the migrants, they said, "live indecently." "Take jobs. Are ignorant." "Are lazy." "Many think the world owes them a living. The kids are thieves." "Are drones, not workers." "Are moochers." "Are shiftless." "Are degenerate." "Have no pride or hope." "All their women are whores." "Drag down the morals of California." "Better off dead."

To be sure, not all migrants felt the sting of words like these. Some maintained that they were never looked down upon, though whether this was a coping mechanism or their personal reality is hard to say. "I will deny it to my dying breath because it didn't happen," one Bakersfield man, Al Meadors, would insist when asked whether Okies and Arkies, like him, confronted any bigotry in the '30s. His own experience, in fact, speaks to the heartfelt compassion that some migrants enjoyed, and it underscores how their countless stories can't be neatly tucked into a single box.

In 1933, Meadors's father, Shuler, watched the bank foreclose on his 140-acre cotton farm in the hill country along the Arkansas River. He managed to keep food on the table by signing up with a WPA highway project, but prospects for the family were bleak. So in the summer of 1936, they packed up and hit the road for California—Weedpatch to be precise—where a cousin, a preacher named Jess Campbell, had already earned a reputation for his fiery Pentecostal sermons, ditch-bank baptisms, and laying of hands to heal the sick.

Meadors, then thirteen, helped his parents and siblings stuff everything they had into their '35 Dodge pickup, its makeshift trailer covered by a canopy of staves from a weeping willow. They picked up a cousin and one of Meadors's older brothers in Oklahoma, and while fueling up in Texas, two hitchhikers climbed on board as well. Now twelve people were jammed in the Dodge, and the toughest part of the trip was still in front of them: the Mojave Desert.

"We were gong about 55 miles per hour down a one- or two-percent incline, heading for a little community called Amboy," Meadors remembered. "Mamma told dad at a previous stop about 13 miles east of that, 'Step it up a little bit. We need to drive a little faster if we're going to get to Bakersfield today.' He wasn't pressing it too much, but he got to about 50. Suddenly my whole world turns upside down." The right rear tire blew, and the truck flipped over—once, twice. Meadors's wiped his head; blood glistened on his fingers. He looked around. Bodies had been thrown. His mother, Melda, died that night. His two-year-old sister, Thelma, died the next day. Nor did the anguish stop there. While the family was at the hospital, somebody stole their trailer from the side of the road and made off with all of their bedding, clothes, and cooking utensils.

Shuler Meadors staggered into Weedpatch—a distinct village just beyond the Resettlement Administration camp that Tom Collins led and that John Steinbeck would visit this same summer—without his wife, without his baby girl, without much of anything really, except a crushed elbow from the accident and the responsibility of taking care of six other kids. Weedpatch welcomed him, though, and there he found the rudiments he'd need to rebuild his life: tents to rent for $3 a month; a protective figure in Brother Jess, as everyone called him; a job on one of Di Giorgio's farms making boxes to pack fruit; and a tab he could run at the country store, thanks to the generosity of its owner, Oral Parish. A bit later, Parish would open his arms wider still. He and his wife, Iva, would take Al in and help raise him. Iva became a second mother.

This was, interestingly, the same Parish who served as judge of the Weedpatch court and who would scold the cotton strikers in '38, telling them that they had been suckered by the union. When Parish made those remarks to the hundred-plus detainees that Raymond Henderson was defending, it was easy to caricature him: the judge was a tool of the big growers, it seemed, and as such an antagonist of the migrants. But human beings are rarely one-dimensional creatures, and conflicting impulses coarse through all of us.

Years later, when he was in his eighties, Meadors would pull out a well-thumbed copy of *The Grapes of Wrath* and read aloud from a scene toward the end of the novel. In it, a woman from the government camp where the Joads are staying is sent to a nearby market for some provisions. Though she hasn't any money, she's told not to worry. "You jes' waltz right over t' the Weedpatch store an' git you some groceries. The camp got twenty dollars' credit there." Meadors looked up. "This is the Parish family," he said, smiling at the memory of their bigheartedness. "They gave credit to people they didn't even know."

Nonetheless, for all of the good that some did, it was incontrovertible that many migrants felt used and abused. The big farmers, they protested, were eager to have them around when they needed the labor and swift to shove them aside when they didn't anymore. "They treated them good when they had cotton to pick," said Eual Stone, who arrived in Kern County from Sulphur Springs, Oklahoma, at the onset of the Depression. "When they didn't, they threw 'em over a row"— sometimes bodily. "I seen them kick 'em out of boxcars and tents when the cotton was over," Stone said. More often, those who'd drifted into California felt misunderstood and forsaken, like the twelve-year-old migrant girl who wrote this poem about the prejudice she endured each day:

School rooms are not so cheery
And I think they are very dreary.
The teachers nag.
And look at you
Like a dirty dish rag.

It was a lesson the Joads themselves heard right after they crossed into California, the desert still ahead of them, the mountains of Arizona just behind. As Tom and Pa swam in the Colorado River, another man and his son tramped through the willows to take a dip and cool off. They were traveling east, they explained—back home to the Panhandle, having concluded that Manifest Destiny wasn't their destiny.

PA asked, "Can you make a livin' there?"

"Nope. But at leas' we can starve to death with folks we know. Won't have a bunch of fellas that hates us to starve with."

"What makes 'em hate you?"

"Dunno," said the man. He cupped his hands full of water and rubbed his face, snorting and bubbling. Dusty water ran out of his hair and streaked his neck.

"I like to hear some more 'bout this," said Pa.

"Me too," Tom added. "Why these folks out west hate ya?"

"What the hell! You never been called 'Okie' yet."

Tom said, "Okie? What's that?"

"Well, Okie use' ta mean you was from Oklahoma. Now it means you're a dirty son-of-a-bitch. Okie means you're scum." 🔲

Xenophobia aside, there was no getting around it: the migrants were a financial burden. Even the most understanding observers—those who had not an ounce of intolerance in them—recognized that the stresses being placed on the system were of legitimate concern. "With prospects of more refugees to come, we are apprehensive and alarmed at the cost," said economist Paul Taylor, who, with Dorothea Lange, his wife, had set down the story of this displaced generation in another indispensable book of 1939: *American Exodus: A Record of Human Erosion.*

In just two years, the number of people on relief in the five southern counties of the San Joaquin Valley had soared to more than forty-five thousand from fewer than nine thousand. To pay for this and much more—additional school buildings, increased hospital care, and numerous other services—there was little choice but to pinch more established Californians in the wallet. In Kern County, for example, property taxes shot up more than 50 percent from 1934 to '39. The migrants, complained the *San Francisco Examiner,* "are slowly strangling the California taxpayer—the goose that lays the golden egg."

Just how much public assistance to give, and when to begin giving it, had been loudly debated in the state for years. According to many on the right, California's relatively generous relief policy ($43 a month versus $36 in the drought states) was the single biggest reason that the migrants had pushed westward. This, though, was a vast overstatement—as much of one, anyway, as the suggestion favored by those on the left that the single biggest lure for the migrants were those handbills distributed by the big California growers, who were conniving to bring in a surplus of labor. Was there a bit of truth in both explanations? Sure. Some migrants were undoubtedly moved by the promise of welfare (even though California's high cost of living offset the government's munificence), others by the promise of work (even if a decent job wasn't as easy to find or as steady as one might have imagined). But it wasn't as if California had to sell itself on these things alone. People were drawn west, in large part, for the same reasons they'd always been: California was the last frontier, the edge of the continent, the end of the line. It was often a person's last stop—his last hope—and the place had naturally assumed a kind of mythical status in the American psyche. It didn't hurt, of course, that railroad barons, land speculators, and assorted other boosters and charlatans had been feeding the hype since the 1800s. In the imagination of many who had never actually seen it before, California was one big packing-crate label: a sanctuary of blue sky and warm sunshine and juicy oranges hanging low off the tree. As one proud son of Okie parents, Merle Haggard, would croon: *And then one night I heard my daddy saying to my mom, that he'd finally saved enough to go. California was his dream, a paradise for he had seen pictures in magazines that told him so.*

Somewhere between paradise and reality, the government was supposed to step in and supply a little cushion. Its efforts, however, were often halfhearted at best. In 1933, President Roosevelt established the Federal Emergency Relief Administration to help deal with the nation's growing flock of transients—those "who have no legal settlement in any one state or community." Within two years, California had become the state most dependent upon FERA funds. Each month, it pulled in $250,000 or more—twice as much as any other state received—to aid some seventy thousand people in need. But FERA didn't last long. In the middle of '35, with the high point of the Okie migration still to come, the Roosevelt administration decided that handing out cash was not the best answer—at least not at the federal level—and FERA was abandoned in favor of directing the unemployed toward New Deal public works programs.

Washington wasn't completely out of the game, not by any means. For example, the Farm Security Administration offered so-called rehabilitation loans to help rural families get back on their feet, in addition to running migrant camps like the one Steinbeck had visited in Arvin. After the horrible flood of 1937—the calamity that had so shocked and angered the author—the federal government extended to fifty thousand migrants a grant-in-aid program, which soon turned into a permanent entitlement. And thousands in the Central Valley were able to get jobs

The influx of migrants put huge pressure on California's public welfare system. (Photo by Dorothea Lange, Library of Congress)

through FDR's Works Progress Administration. But by and large, FERA's demise left California scrambling, as it transferred much of the onus for caring for the unemployed onto the state—specifically, the State Relief Administration. California politicians would spend years, in vain, trying to get Washington to do more.

The SRA's first director was Harold Pomeroy, the man who during the Kern County cotton strike of 1938 would give workers the Hobson's choice of scabbing or starving and who set the hard-nosed policy that anybody who refused to work for whatever the farmers might be offering—no matter how measly this "prevailing wage"—would be dropped from relief. All of this changed once Culbert Olson became governor and Carey McWilliams held his landmark hearing in Madera to establish a "fair wage" for chopping cotton. But ultimately, even Olson and McWilliams could only do so much to make life on the dole less dolorous.

Before long, the strain that the needy were putting on the state would become more severe than ever, and some feared that those receiving benefits were set to keep them rolling through that most American of institutions: the ballot box. "Migrants Are Becoming Voters," blared a headline in the October 1938 edition of *California* magazine. "And What Will They Vote for? More Relief. . . ." This wasn't a completely fanciful assertion. More than any other segment of the population, the Okies were unflinching supporters of a pension scheme in which the state would dispense $30 every Thursday to every unemployed Californian over the age of fifty. Known as "Ham and Eggs," the plan was panned as demagoguery of the worst sort and widely opposed as fiscal insanity—not only by those on the right but also by many on the left, including Upton Sinclair, Culbert Olson, and Carey McWilliams. For whatever reason, the migrants looked past that, focusing instead on the bankers and big businessmen who were Ham and Eggs adversaries. And if those affluent interests were against the thing, they figured, there must be something to commend it.

In the end, two different versions of Ham and Eggs would be trounced by voters—first in 1938 and then again in '39—leaving one occupant of the FSA's labor camp in Shafter to mourn the outcome:

Since Ham and Eggs has been defeated
I'm feeling kinda blue
For it's hard to make a livin'
When your family is more than two
I guess I was too optimistic
For I thought it sure would pass
But there was too many voted
From the moneyed class

More than anything, though, most migrants seemed to feel a deep sense of shame at having become a public millstone. "I hate to look a man in the face with him knowing I'm on relief and feeling that I'm such a failure in life," said Don Jackson, who had moved west to California for work, only to find himself reliant on the state for survival in the late '30s. He recalled once going into the J. C. Penney in Bakersfield to do some shopping and striking up a conversation with a clerk about whether the sales tax might be lowered. "Never a chance as long as the SRA exists," the clerk told Jackson, and then he pointed to some customers who were using their relief checks to buy shoes. "Take that for example," the clerk said. Recounted Jackson: "Of course that hurt my feelings because I happened to be one of them. That's not the only time I've run into such occasions . . . . Each and every one hurt, and are things that will never be forgotten. There's not much I can do about a situation like that but just try to shield myself, for no man is proud of relief, and I happened to have my wife with me. It hurt her, too."

At the Shafter FSA camp, a migrant named Lester Hunter put similar sentiments to song:

I'd rather not be on the rolls of relief,
Or work on the WPA,
We'd rather work for the farmer
If the farmer could raise the pay;
Then the farmer could plant more cotton
And he'd get more money for spuds,
Instead of wearing patches,
We'd dress up in new duds.

In 1939, Congress slashed appropriations for the WPA, leaving even more out-of-work Californians on the doorstep of the SRA. The shift was sudden and dramatic. In August 1938, the SRA had been responsible for less than a third of the combined federal-state relief caseload in California. By the following summer, the SRA was handling more than half, and funds in the state's community chest were running dangerously low. Politics only complicated things. Former assemblyman Dewey Anderson, a friend of the governor's, had taken over at the SRA, and his hope was to introduce a "new philosophy" that was based on production-for-use: having the state oversee, among other tasks, the canning of food and the making of clothes for the unemployed. Anderson pledged to proceed slowly and carefully, but to many in Sacramento his scheme smacked of Upton Sinclair's kookiness and thereby confirmed their worst suspicions of Governor Olson and his administration.

As if that weren't enough, by March 1939, the SRA found itself tarred with another damaging label: it was said to be Red. The epicenter of the crisis was the SRA office in Kern County, where longtime employees alleged that they were being targeted because they had carried out Harold Pomeroy's anti-labor policies during the '38 cotton strike. One member of the staff said that the SRA's social services director, William Plunkert—who had been fired from the agency by Pomeroy and then rehired by Anderson—had warned those in Kern that if they "did not see eye to eye with the present administration, you had better get out." Shortly thereafter, accusations flew from a former Communist that Plunkert was a die-hard member of the party determined to set up a relief system in accordance with Marxist ideology. Legislators demanded his ouster, and in April, the governor obliged. "I am opposed to organizations of an oathbound kind, organized to acquire political power through secretive methods and with loyalty to a secret organization," Olson said, "whether it is in behalf of Nazism, Fascism or Communism," not to mention what one Sacramento lawmaker had termed "Plunkertism." Plunkert, in response, chided Olson for a "loss of nerve under fire."

The legislature, which for months would continue to probe the "Communist infiltration" at the SRA, was now more skeptical than ever of Anderson's production-for-use plans, and the Associated Farmers tried to take advantage of the situation, as it lobbied frantically to have oversight of relief programs redirected from the state to individual counties. Olson fought off these efforts, but he was hardly in a position to do much more than play a little defense. His $73 million budget request for the SRA was whittled down to a temporary grant of about $35 million, and even that came with a bunch of strings attached: Anderson was forced to affirm that it was "not the desire nor the province of the SRA to set agricultural wages," while Olson agreed to have the state controller make a thorough audit of relief funds. In another concession, the governor called a special session of the legislature for early the following year to take up the issue of welfare.

In July 1939, a frustrated Anderson—who, on top of everything else, was also accused of nepotism—quit as chief of the SRA. By February 1940, conservatives in Sacramento would make more headway in gutting the governor's programs for the unemployed, with the legislature increasing the time one had to live in California to be eligible for aid from one year to three. Carey McWilliams predicted that one hundred thousand migrant workers would be forced off relief rolls as a result and added, somewhat menacingly, that "they are not going to take it lying down." "Hell is going to start popping before long in California," McWilliams said, "unless solutions of the relief and migratory labor problems are found."

———•———

Actually, there was one strikingly straightforward "solution" that various politicians and policymakers in California turned to throughout the 1930s: keep them out.

This strategy had been implemented most notoriously in the winter of '36, when the city of Los Angeles dispatched 136 cops to the state's border crossings with Nevada, Oregon, and Arizona in what Police Chief James Davis called "a determined effort to keep our unemployment and crime conditions to a minimum." His forces were ordered to book all hitchhikers on charges of vagrancy and arrest anybody caught riding the rails. Anyone in an automobile was told that there was no work in California and advised to turn back east. Among those caught up in L.A.'s so-called Bum Blockade was Woody Guthrie, who commemorated this trampling of the Constitution with the song "Do Re Mi":

Lots of folks back East, they say, is leavin' home every day,
Beatin' the hot old dusty way to the California line.
'Cross the desert sands they roll, getting' out of that old dust bowl,
They think they're goin' to a sugar bowl, but here's what they find—
Now, the police at the port of entry say,
"You're number fourteen thousand for today."
Oh, if you ain't got the do re mi, folks, you ain't got the do re mi,
Why, you better go back to beautiful Texas, Oklahoma, Kansas,
   Georgia, Tennessee.
California is a garden of Eden, a paradise to live in or see;
But believe it or not, you won't find it so hot
If you ain't got the do re mi.

Many cried foul, and even the conservative *Los Angeles Times* had to admit that a police cordon might be over-the-top—though it was a measure of how much the migrants were despised that, in the next breath, the paper tried to justify the action. "It is the kind of an outrage that ought to have been perpetrated in California several years ago," the paper contended. "If it had, we would not now be struggling with a $70,000,000 deficit. If it had, our citizens would have been spared many of the depredations of our present army of imported criminals. If it had, California would not now be the paradise for radicals and troublemakers that it is."

The Bum Blockade lasted about two months before it was abandoned in the face of mounting disapproval and an ACLU legal challenge. L.A., though, wasn't the only jurisdiction to adopt such an approach. A number of counties, which provided assistance for poor

Woody Guthrie, who commemorated the Los Angeles Police Department's "Bum Blockade" in his song "Do Re Mi," wrote a message on his guitar that was a real sign of the times. (Photo by Lester Balog, Woody Guthrie Archives)

children, the elderly, and others out of their own budgets, were inclined to act similarly. In their case, though, the tactic tended more toward move-'em-along than turn-'em-back. In 1934, supervisors in San Luis Obispo allotted $2,500 to ensure that pea pickers had enough gasoline to make it to the next county when the harvest was over. Neighboring authorities were so upset that they vowed to meet the pickers at the county line, guns in hand. In Fresno County, officials were known to cover the cost of license plates for migrants' cars on one condition: that they continue down Highway 99 to live off the relief offered by L.A. County. At the same time, a relief administrator in L.A. was reported to have knocked six hundred families off relief and steered them toward Imperial County near the Mexican border.

Herding people like cattle was a long-standing tradition in California, dating to at least the Chinese Exclusion Act of 1882, and many others would feel the prod over time, including Mexicans and Japanese. But discrimination toward the Okies was most unusual, given what normally brought out the worst in Americans: they were under attack based on class, not race.

Nowhere was this spelled out more clearly than in the state's Indigent Act, otherwise known as the "anti-Okie law." Passed in 1933 and modified four years later, it made it a crime to bring a destitute person across state lines into California. The statute hadn't been trotted out very much until 1939, when several district attorneys in the Central Valley began to go after dozens of migrants who had helped their poor relatives move to California. Civil libertarians, including Raymond Henderson, would eventually challenge the law, and, in 1941, the case of a man named Fred Edwards would reach the U.S. Supreme Court.

Edwards had left his home in Yuba County to pick up his brother-in-law, Frank Duncan, in Spur, Texas. The two then drove back to California, where Duncan arrived with all of $20 to his name. He turned to the FSA for assistance—and Edwards was slapped with misdemeanor charges under the Indigent Act. Writing for the high court, Justice James F. Byrnes would acknowledge the huge financial drain California was grappling with. "The grave and perplexing social and economic dislocation which this statute reflects is a matter of common knowledge and concern," Byrnes would write. "We are not unmindful of it." Nevertheless, he'd go on to say, "this does not mean that there are no boundaries to the permissible area of state legislative activity. There are. And none is more certain than the prohibition against attempts on the part of any single state to isolate itself from difficulties common to all of them by restraining the transportation of persons and property across its borders."

Following this line of reasoning, the court would strike down the Indigent Act on fairly narrow grounds, finding it "an unconstitutional burden upon interstate commerce."

But others saw wider implications. In his concurring opinion, Justice William O. Douglas would argue that *Edwards v. California*—a case that would stand as an important precedent during the civil rights battles of the 1960s—was about something more fundamental than business or trade. In his mind, it went straight to what it meant to be a national citizen. "The right of persons to move freely from state to state," said Douglas, "occupies a more protected position in our constitutional system than does the movement of cattle, fruit, steel and coal."

To allow California to continue enforcing the Indigent Act, he added, would be to "introduce a caste system utterly incompatible with the spirit of our system of government. It would permit those who were stigmatized by a state as . . . paupers or vagabonds to be relegated to an inferior class of citizenship. It would prevent a citizen because he was poor from seeking new horizons in other states."

It would, that is to say, flagrantly disregard what millions upon millions of Americans have yearned to do since the East Coast was first settled hundreds of years ago: turn west in pursuit of a brighter future.

———•———

Clell Pruett didn't think a whole lot about the future as he was growing up on a little farm in southeast Missouri, outside the town of Oran. Life just kind of came at him, like a running river. No sense fussing about it too much. It seemed to go where it wanted to go, unbidden. And, anyway, his dad and mom had always done all right, even with a houseful to clothe and feed.

They were an industrious, if uneducated, couple, Oscar and Myrtle Pruett. He had grown up in a one-room cabin with a dirt floor near the foothills of the Ozarks, while her roots stretched to Tennessee's Indian country. She had an uncanny ability to grow things, and she told Oscar where to plant his crops and when.

The old man didn't ooze much warmth. He was apt to lose his temper in a flash and prone to cussedness. Once, Oscar got into a row with his brother Joe—the particulars long since lost—and decided, in effect, to disown him; he changed the spelling of his name to "Pruitt" on the spot, replacing the *e* with an *i*. He then had Clell's five youngest siblings—all those born after the argument—do the same. (The clan would relish its tri-annual Pruett-Pruitt reunions for years to come.) Yet even though he was basically humorless, Oscar earned the deference of his children and, for the most part, "he was good to us," Clell said. His boys, in return, were good to him. "We never did fight among us," Clell said. "We just done what he told us to do."

What he told them to do, above all, was work hard. Clell attended school through eighth grade, but that's as far as he got. When he was about sixteen, the family moved to Bloomfield, about thirty miles from Oran. The Depression was well under way by now. For the Pruetts, though, this proved a time of opportunity. A manager with Metropolitan Life Insurance was looking for somebody trustworthy and responsible to tend a 640-acre tract that the company owned. Oscar Pruett was their guy. It didn't hurt that he came with a built-in workforce. "The kids was all getting big enough now to plow and to work in the fields," Clell explained, and that's just what he and Herschel and Emmett did, watching over the corn and soybeans and threshing the wheat.

They lived in a big white house on a knoll. There was no electricity or indoor plumbing. But there were four rooms upstairs and four rooms down, and a big porch that wrapped all the way around the front of the place. Nobody would have described these as fat years, but they weren't terribly lean either, especially considering the adversity so many families were going through. Myrtle conjured her magic in the garden, cultivating cabbage, carrots and corn, beans and beets. "She'd have enough stuff canned to last us all winter," Clell said. Meantime, his dad would plant a hundred bushels of spuds. "He'd plow them out and then cover them up with dirt so they wouldn't freeze. Then that winter he'd go out there and get them and we'd eat potatoes." Lots and lots of potatoes. They had hogs and a few cows, too, and sold some of the cream they churned.

There wasn't much money for fun, but the boys dated some of the neighbors' girls, waiting patiently to give their dad's Model T a spin. "We had to take turns," Clell said. "We didn't get the car but about once every week or so." Still, the brothers barely got jealous or fought. "We just respected one another." When they weren't working or running around, they made music. Herschel was partial to the fiddle, Emmett the guitar and mandolin. Clell thumped on the guitar a little bit himself. Some of the families around Bloomfield—the Linkhearts, the Smiths—would empty the furniture out of their living rooms, and the boys would play and play, and their friends would dance and dance until their legs drooped like limp noodles.

In 1936, during a slow stretch on the farm, Clell took a job for $5 a week, helping care for a blind man who lived south of Bloomfield, in the town of Gideon. Clell stayed with him through the winter and into the spring of '37, planting his fields with cotton. As part of Clell's compensation, the man let him keep two acres for himself. But Clell grew homesick, and he soon returned to the family farm. Myrtle and Oscar were glad to have their son back, but it didn't take long for him to realize that things had changed.

Herschel, the oldest boy, had married and gone off to California, where his wife had kin. And there was less and less for Clell to do. A couple of younger brothers, who were now old enough and strong enough to drive the teams of horses and mules, had stepped into Clell's boots. Now twenty-one and with a steady girlfriend on his arm, Clell looked around for what he was going to do next. The alternatives were few.

The Pruetts' Missouri spread lay quite a distance from the hundred million acres that had been ravaged by the black blizzards of the Dust Bowl proper. But the economy of Bloomfield was sick nevertheless. Apart from what there was on the homestead, Clell said, "There wasn't no work around there for young guys like me." So, after lying about for a few weeks, he made up his mind. "I believe I'll go to California," he told his parents. He made $50 by selling a cow that his dad had given him a few years earlier and used the money to buy a train ticket to Los Angeles. He still had thirteen bucks left over as the locomotive chugged out of the station at Poplar Bluff.

Going to California by rail, especially having paid the proper fare, wasn't the classic mode of migrant travel, but it had one thing in common with all those flivvers on Route 66: it was sufficiently uncomfortable. "It was just an old, hard coach," Clell said. When the train pulled in to L.A., Herschel was there to greet him. Clell's big brother had done rather well for himself. He'd taken a job as the groundskeeper at the Thousand Oaks summer home of actor Henry Wilcoxon, who'd made a splash playing Marc Antony, opposite Claudette Colbert, in Cecil B. DeMille's *Cleopatra*. Clell found a job at a nursery not far from where his brother worked, and he soon sent back to Missouri for his girlfriend, Mace, who had a sweet face to match her sweet personality. They married and rented a small cottage about fifty miles northwest of Los Angeles amid a scattering of oaks along Sherwood Lake.

It all seemed to be going beautifully—but, as so often happened in the precarious economy of the 1930s, their good fortune withered as fast as it had come. Business slowed at the nursery, and Clell was laid off after only a few months. He had no idea where to turn. Just then, he ran into a neighbor and told him about his bad break.

"What are you going to do?" the man asked. "I don't know," Clell said.

"Well, did you ever pick cotton? My boy has a boss up in Bakersfield named Bill Camp, and they got a lot of cotton to pick."

That's all Clell needed to hear. He and Mace loaded a two-burner camp stove into their Chevy and made a beeline for the Central Valley. They had $25 between them, tops. "You talk about kids going out and starting from scratch," Clell said. "That was some scratch."

What Clell did possess, in unstinting amounts, was that old Pruett work ethic, the one his daddy had instilled in him back in Missouri. With it, he rose rapidly from picking cotton for Bill Camp to supervising others, making sure they snatched every last bit of fiber they could from the sea of white. "I was just a watchdog out in the field," Clell said. He also began to manage that most critical of functions in the arid West: irrigation. That first season, "I irrigated the potatoes, and they said that was one of the best crops they had in a long time," Clell recalled. "I'd done well."

For her part, Mace was no second-rate sidekick. Clell, a strapping six-footer, could pick about two hundred pounds of cotton a day. His wife, though not a big woman, sometimes outpicked him by one hundred pounds. Clell didn't seem ruffled, though. "She was just quicker, I guess."

———•———

Unlike most of Bill Camp's workers who lived in tents (and, later, in tiny cabins), the Pruetts were invited to move in to the small collection of converted railroad refrigerator cars at Camp's headquarters operation, Georgianna Farms. A handful of other families—mostly young couples like Clell and Mace—were asked to stay there too. Working in potatoes for thirty-five cents an hour wasn't exactly a bonanza, and the railcars were adequate at best, with doors that didn't close tight, allowing swarms of mosquitoes to invade and eat you up at night. But nobody complained. A job was a job, and a roof over your head was a roof over your head. "It was about as nice as it could be back in them days," Clell said.

Reminders of what could have been were ubiquitous. One day, when he was out irrigating, Clell saw a wagon rolling down the highway. From a distance, it looked a little like one of the horse-drawn plows he had guided in Missouri. But as it got closer, he saw that it wasn't a horse in the lead. It was a man hooked up to some kind of harness, lumbering along, pulling a buggy with his wife and baby on top. "It was the saddest thing I'd ever seen," Clell said.

Ira and Ortha Taylor, who also lived at Georgianna, were certainly appreciative of all they had. He was a good-looking man (a mix of Irish and Native American blood) with thick, dark hair and blue eyes, and she was a skinny little thing with a lovely smile and the most delightful dimple on her chin. They'd grown up near Cleveland, Oklahoma, in oil country, and married in 1937. She had just turned twenty; he was twenty-two. With no work in sight, the newlyweds decided to join the procession to California. They crammed their Model A full of every-

Clell and Mace Pruett, pictured here with their young daughter, Darlene, were sanguine about living in a railcar on Bill Camp's farm. "It was about as nice as it could be back in them days," he said. (Courtesy of Ortha Taylor)

thing they owned: a kerosene stove, a small feather bed, two pillows, and a double blanket cut in two, so it would fit better. They refused to strap anything to the top or the sides of the Model A, however. "We had too much pride to put stuff outside the car," Ortha said.

Slowly, they made their way west, picking cotton in New Mexico and Arizona before finally reaching Shafter, where they'd heard there was a need for farmhands. They lived in the Model A for a little while, and meals were meager: a can of kidney beans, with two spoons—his and hers—digging through the goo. Work was grueling. During cotton picking, "I thought my back would break," Ortha said. And when it was time to pick grapes, wasps buzzed among the vines, and the sticky blend of juice and dirt would make the blisters on her fingers sting. Eventually, the Taylors saved enough to rent a tent. An electric cord, which powered a single light bulb, snaked inside. They bought a card table too. It wasn't a palace, but they were grateful to be out of their car. "We hugged each other and danced all over that tent," Ortha said.

After a while, they got on steady at Georgianna Farms, and were offered an even grander abode: the railcar next to the Pruetts. "From a tent to a boxcar," Ortha said. "We were really going uptown now." The Taylors took considerable care to fix up their new dwelling. Ira removed an oil pan from the Model A, painted it white and turned it into a sink, complete with a drain running out to the cesspool in the back. Ortha made tea towels and bed sheets out of old potato sacks.

The Pruetts and Taylors became fast friends, bound together by their shared labors and common values. They were mild-mannered and honest and, while not Holy Rollers, had faith in the Lord above. Clell would sneak out for a beer from time to time, if Mace didn't catch him. But neither he nor Ira were big on drinking or brawling or shooting dice, like some of the hell-raisers in the tent cities around Shafter. "We didn't want any part of that," Ortha said. "We were raised by decent families. Moral." Equally tame were the men from the other families in the railcar encampment and their friends in "the Flats," the migratory camp north of headquarters—the Phillipses and the Monks and the Hesters. Bill Camp wouldn't have put up with much carrying on anyhow. And their days were too long and wearying for much frivolity, what with the foremen in the service yard spitting out orders before 7:00 a.m. and work often lasting past dusk.

Now and again, they'd slip into town to see a movie—cowboy pictures, mostly. And once, the Taylors and the Pruetts went to the pier in Santa Monica to try the thrill rides. Ortha was so terrified, she bawled until they let her off. The excursion was well worth it, however: she got to stick her toes into the ocean and splash around, which she'd never done before. Mostly, they all took pleasure in just being together, twenty-somethings far from their parents, trying to inch their way to a better station in life. "Us women had a great time, even when we were hoeing out in the heat," Ortha said.

When they weren't in the fields or the packing sheds, the bulk of their time was spent right around the railcars, in the shadow of a eucalyptus stand, visiting with one another. Sometimes, Clell would take out his mandolin and strum a little. Or they'd listen to the radio—Gene Autry singing "Back in the Saddle Again," maybe, or Bob Wills and His Texas Playboys plucking their way through "San Antonio Rose." Mainly, they'd talk, chattering about this and that with a perspective that Ortha would later describe as "naïve and unworldly."

One thing they didn't do much, if ever, was grouse about the boss—though Ortha noticed things about Bill Camp that sure bugged her. There was, for instance, the time that he tried to drive up the price for first-class potatoes by having a crew haul a mountain of them out to the desert, douse them with gasoline, and burn them to a crisp. Knowing how tough it was for the Taylors and the Pruetts and the others on the farm to get even a little bit ahead, Ortha said, "I wondered why he didn't let us have some first." (The episode would find an echo in *The Grapes of Wrath*, where Steinbeck wrote of guards with shotguns patrolling a citrus grove, "so a man might not pick an orange for a thin child, oranges to be dumped if the price was low.") Another thing that would always stick with her was the way that Camp would never give any of his workers a ride if he was rumbling down the road in his big Buick and one of them happened to be walking in the same direction. His wife, Georgia Anna, would always stop if she was behind the wheel. But he'd just speed on by. "He didn't want close relationships with his hands," Ortha said. "He wanted us to understand that we could be let go at anytime. This was not our permanent home."

Still, they made it home. Less than a year after she and Clell came to Georgianna Farms, Mace had a baby girl. They named her Darlene. Later on, Ortha would have a son, Darrell Leon. When Darrell was about fifteen months old, he got sick and stopped taking his bottle. Ortha took him to a doctor in the town of Wasco and then, when he didn't improve, to another in Bakersfield. Finally, the Taylors admitted

Ortha Taylor and her husband came to California to find a better life, only to lose their baby boy. (Courtesy of Ortha Taylor)

the baby to the hospital and were told to pick him up the next day. "We went home, but we were very upset," Ortha said. Later that afternoon, one of Camp's foremen came by to deliver the news: Darrell was dead. "My shoulders were shaking so hard," Ortha said. "When he was born I felt like I was walking two feet off the ground. Then your baby is gone."

The autopsy pointed to two causes of death, but Ortha would have a difficult time acknowledging either one. The first cited was bronchial pneumonia. "It was damp from September to April, damp and chilly north of Bakersfield—foggy," Ortha said. "But those boxcars were thick. We had a small oil burner. I don't think it was that." The coroner's other finding—malnutrition—was even tougher to accept, for it implied that the Taylors couldn't provide for their family, just like all those Okie haters would've had you believe. "That has bothered me all the rest of my life," Ortha would say many years later, fighting back the tears. "Believe me, it wasn't malnutrition."

The Taylors wanted to bury Darrell in the motherland, in Oklahoma, but by this time the United States was entangled in World War II and fuel was being rationed. At first, it looked like they might have to put the baby in a mausoleum in California temporarily, and then ship the body east later on. But Bill Camp called in a few chits in Washington and obtained the necessary gasoline stamps for the Taylors to return to Oklahoma and bury their boy. It was a kindness that Ortha Taylor would always remember—one that more than offset some of the less considerate acts she had seen Camp engage in. Indeed, at the end of the day, when she toted up the ledger, it contained more pluses than minuses. "We were grateful for a job, believe me," Ortha said. "And for what he did for us when our son died."

Clell Pruett, likewise, thought well of the boss—well enough that he didn't dither for an instant when Camp swung by the fields and asked if he'd burn a copy of *The Grapes of Wrath*. In part, it was a matter of fidelity, of doing right by the guy who had given him the most precious thing of all in 1930s America: a job. "I burned the book because Camp come by and wanted to know if I'd burn it," Pruett said. "It was that simple."

Besides, if all those things that the woman at the Palace Hotel had said about Steinbeck were true—and Camp thought they were—then why not?

How dare Steinbeck characterize the big growers as a gang of bandits—men who treated their workers, said Pruett, "like dogs and hogs and put them on the farms to pick this stuff and then cut their wages." This didn't jibe with the world he knew. Camp "wasn't one of these bosses who just pushed their labor around," Pruett said. "He was a good guy to work for." Pruett also didn't like the way the book was said to have demeaned the migrants, how it made them seem dirty and bawdy and uncouth. "It degraded us," Pruett said. "We weren't drunkards or outcasts or beggars." He saw in himself something different, something finer. "I had the ambition of making money if I could find a place to do it," Pruett said. "Saving money and making my own way and making a good living. I wanted to grade myself up.

Every one of them that lived there at the camp felt the same way. They just wanted to get higher up."

Nor was he the only one tempted to set *The Grapes of Wrath* ablaze, as the Okie poet Dorothy Rose would lay out in verse:

> *I hate him   I hate him   Charlcia said*
> *His book is a bunch of lies*
> *Dirty filthy nasty lies   Mary Elizabeth said*
> *Steinbeck sells our hearts*
> *Our guts   Our pride   Royce said*
> *He makes things worse*
> *For all the Okies in California   Louise said*
> *Better to leave it alone*
> *Unwritten   untold   Grandma said*
> *It should be banned   Gerald Ray said*
> *Daddy everyone is reading the book*
> *How can we go to school tomorrow   I said*
> *With your heads held high   Mamma said*

CHAPTER SIX
Friday, Saturday, Sunday

Tom stepped clear of the ditch and wiped the sweat out of his eyes. "You hear what the paper said 'bout agitators up north a Bakersfiel'?"

BESIDES STANLEY ABEL, no other member of the Kern County Board of Supervisors cut as commanding a figure as did Charles Wimmer. He was a solid six-footer, a horseman, and a hunter. As a businessman, he had been a resounding success. And his family's history was stitched tightly into the tapestry of California.

Peter Wimmer, his grandfather, helped oversee construction of a sawmill for John Sutter on the American River. Peter's wife, Elizabeth, was the camp cook. It was late January 1848, when Peter and James Marshall, Sutter's general foreman, chanced upon something glittering in the water. Though many of the workmen dismissed the find as fool's gold, Elizabeth had panned for the real thing as a teenager back in Georgia—and she believed that this nugget was genuine. As a test, she submerged it in a kettle of lye soap that she had prepared for washing clothes. And when she pulled out the quarter ounce of ore the next morning, it was still sparkling—a sign that it was in fact gold. Marshall gathered up some other pieces and took them for further chemical testing. Two months later, the first news account of the discovery hit— "GOLD MINE FOUND"—and the California Gold Rush was on. Marshall gave Elizabeth that original lye-soaked chunk as a memento, and she carried it in a leather bag, worn around her neck, for the next forty years. It would become known as "the Wimmer nugget."

For his part, Charles made a mint as a contractor, entering the transportation business in San Francisco around the turn of the century, before moving on to build roads near Santa Barbara, and later clearing heavy timber in the oil country around Taft. He lost much of his multi-million-dollar fortune during the Crash of '29, but he was still quite well-off when he entered politics and won his supervisor's seat in 1932. Perhaps it was because of his standing that Wimmer was willing to do something anathema to many politicians: concede error. Or perhaps there was a touch of guilt involved. According to a story passed down through his family, he had once helped lead a vigilante attack on a group of migrants squatting along the Kern River at a spot called Gordon's Ferry. "After it was over with, he was pretty remorseful," Wimmer's grandson would later say. "He regretted his participation." Or perhaps he was simply more independent than some of his colleagues on the Board of Supervisors; certainly, Wimmer was no toady for Stanley Abel, whom he was never afraid to oppose on a big issue.

Whatever the reason, Wimmer picked up the phone on this Friday, August 25, 1939, called Gretchen Knief at the library, and told her that he'd be reversing his vote at Monday's meeting. He was now opposed to banning *The Grapes of Wrath*. "It's not the board's business," Wimmer said, "to censor Kern citizens' reading matter." Nor was he the only one believed to be moving in this direction. Also on this day, the *Californian* ran a front-page article headlined "Migrant Book Ban May Be Rescinded by Board." The report noted Wimmer's switch and predicted that Supervisor C. W. Harty would do the same. That would mean a majority—Ralph Lavin, Wimmer, and Harty—was coalescing against the ban—with only Abel and Roy Woollomes, the board's chairman, now in favor of continuing the restriction.

For anybody paying attention to the political dynamic in Kern County, Wimmer's turnaround on *The Grapes of Wrath* was, depending on your point of view, heroic or horrifying; but either way, it wasn't a total shock. Though not as liberal as Lavin, Wimmer often found himself on the same side of things. Back in the spring, for instance, the two had tried in vain to preserve Ralph Abel's job as secretary of the Kern County Water Association. They'd band together, as well, on key votes regarding health care and welfare policy. But an about-face by Harty, the newest member of the board, would be truly stunning. Since joining the Board of Supervisors earlier in the year, the longtime grocer had formed a solid bloc with Abel and Woollomes. The three marched in lockstep and, as a result, were rarely forced to compromise on anything.

That Harty would gravitate to Abel and Woollomes was only natural. Abel's raw power was evident. And Woollomes was likewise no slouch as a political pugilist (or, for that matter, when it came to the sweet science itself; indeed, he loved nothing better after a long day at the office than to come home and work up a good sweat by pounding away at the punching bag he'd hung near the chicken pens in the backyard). Elected to the board in 1928, Woollomes had been, most recently, a bank cashier and an insurance man. But he was no office stiff. Born in 1889 in the Arizona mining town of Pinal, Woollomes's dad had operated a stagecoach and, as the son would tell it, once met up with Billy the Kid along the trail. Woollomes had earlier in his career laid pipe for the Santa Monica Edison Company, unloaded cargo ships at the Los Angeles harbor, and muddied his hands in the oil fields of Coalinga. All told, there was a peculiarly western brand of toughness about him—a trait that must have been especially appealing to a down-to-his-core conservative such as Harty.

Even Gretchen Knief didn't think Harty insincere regarding his discomfort with *The Grapes of Wrath*. "The question of censorship and all that

it implies was something new to him," she said, "and since he is undoubtedly not familiar with modern literature, it was easily understandable how
Steinbeck's book would have affected him at the thought that any adolescent boy or girl might read it." Still, if this latest news account was to be
believed, Harty suddenly and unexpectedly seemed to be breaking out on
his own. The paper didn't quote him, so nobody could be sure exactly what
he was thinking. But maybe the constant pressure from all the civil libertarians and commentators had given him pause and made him reevaluate
his position. Maybe he had somehow decided that for a man who preferred keeping the government out of people's lives, it was intellectually in-
consistent for the Board of Supervisors to tell folks what books they were
forbidden to read. Regardless of Harty's motivation, "rescinding of the ban
by a 3 to 2 vote . . . appears probable," the *Californian* asserted.

Not that Steinbeck's opponents were ready to pack it in. Another area
paper, *North of the River News,* ran its own review of the situation, and it
was as sharp-tongued as anything the Associated Farmers had ever
served up. The article—whose headline, "Kern Kounty Komment," was
clearly designed to antagonize with its hateful acronym—praised local
officials for providing the migrants with medical care, housing, and other
necessities. And it commended Emory Gay Hoffman for highlighting
this humanitarianism in his film, *Plums of Plenty.* "How anyone could say
what Steinbeck did about Kern County is most sickening," the piece
added, concluding that the author "has been misinformed or is a plain
liar." It ended with a rousing call to keep the ban on the novel in place:
"Kansas City libraries took *The Grapes of Wrath* off their shelves, terming
it obscene and unfit for public reading. Yet the book was published about
conditions in California. Mostly about Kern County. It's Kern County
that should take action. Will we? If the book tells the truth, more power
to it; if it tells the untruth and is tainted with Communism, as accused,
let's take it out of our public libraries and out of our homes."

The last word on this Friday, however, would belong to those anxious
to revoke the ban—in particular to Raymond Henderson. As evening descended, the blind attorney leaned into the microphone at radio station

KERN in Bakersfield and began: "Ladies and Gentleman . . . . It has been many years since any book has captured the public's attention" like *The Grapes of Wrath*. "Critics have hailed it as the great American novel," he said, "and it tops the lists of bestsellers." Echoing some of the remarks he'd made in his labor journal article, Henderson went on: "It is not a sweet book. It is modern realism in its most realistic form. It is coarse, plain, brutal—as nature is coarse, plain, brutal. The author attempts to portray a phase of American life as he sees it." Because of this, Henderson said, "it was natural that many readers" would be offended by the book. But banning *The Grapes of Wrath* in reaction, he continued, was "positively revolutionary"—a phrase that must have rung in a few of the supervisors' ears, given that it was Steinbeck who was supposed to be the subversive. "The Board said: 'This book shall not be in our libraries.' If it can say what shall not be in our libraries, of course it can say what shall be in our libraries. If it can do this thing about one book, it can do the same thing about other books." With his customary scholarly flair, Henderson then summoned a half-dozen sources to stress how dangerous it was to substitute "the will and opinions of the rulers for the will and opinions of the people": the U.S. Constitution, the California Constitution, Voltaire, Milton, Saint Paul, and William James. He closed his protest this way:

> If you want to make Kern County a hiss and a byword wherever free people live, let it be known that our public officials have set themselves up as arbitrators of public taste, as dictators as to what people shall read. These would-be dictators must be given to understand that this is a free country and that we will have none of their censorship.

By the time Saturday's paper hit people's doorsteps in Bakersfield, the prospect of having the book ban canceled seemed more certain than ever. A story in the *Californian* this day, August 26, 1939, reported that C. W. Harty was now in the middle of reading *The Grapes of Wrath* and, for the first time, it quoted him directly about where he stood. The supervisor explained that his final position was "still undetermined" but he was "inclined to believe" that he'd vote to rescind the board's order. Once again, the newspaper proclaimed the weeklong battle all but over: "Harty's Vote Expected to Lift County Ban on Migrant Novel."

The backlash to the publication of *The Grapes of Wrath* was strong. But as a frantic week drew to a close, the backlash to the backlash was starting to look like it might be even stronger.

———

Over the big hill in Los Angeles, the debate about the novel had taken on a different flavor. Nobody in L.A. was pushing to censor *The Grapes of Wrath*. There were, though, Angelinos keen on countering it—not only by attacking Steinbeck but, in at least one case, by doing something far more interesting: offering up an alternative version of the story.

To that end, careful readers of the *Los Angeles Times* on this Saturday may have spotted on page 2, right next to an ad for the Italian Village restaurant on Eighth Street—"Cocktails 25 cents. NO COVER CHARGE!"—the following item: "'GRAPES OF GLADNESS' Answers Steinbeck. All bookstores. $1.25." The tiny, two-line announcement had been running all month, placed there by the author of the tract.

Marshall Valentine Hartranft, better known (depending on the audience) as M.V. or Uncle Marsh, was a classic California operator—equal parts dreamer and dreammonger. Born in Pennsylvania in 1871, Hartranft (pronounced hart-raft) learned at an early age that making your own way often required getting a little dirt under your fingernails. Hartranft's father died when he was five years old, and his mother supported him and his siblings by having them till the family garden and sell the crops. He later worked in a nursery and, after almost becoming a clergyman in New Jersey, started his own produce market. The enterprise collapsed in 1893, and two years later he moved west. Hartranft launched an agricultural newspaper called *Los Angeles Daily Fruit World,* and it became an essential periodical for growers and brokers tracking prices, transportation routes, crop forecasts, and futures trading. But

Marshall Hartranft, author of *Grapes of Gladness*, was a classic California operator—equal parts dreamer and dreammonger. (Bolton Hall Museum)

while Hartranft built a booming business supplying all this information, he remained wary of farming on a commercial scale—still feeling burned, perhaps, by the failure of his produce market back east. "To grow crops to sell is to speculate like hell," he liked to say. "But to grow crops to eat keeps you standing on both feet."

Equipped with this jingle and steeped in the teachings of Bolton Hall—the author of *Three Acres and Liberty* and *A Little Land and a Living*—Hartranft began to establish colonies of gardeners and small growers fifteen to twenty miles from bigger cities. He'd acquire options on virgin parcels, which were at least one thousand acres in size, and then sell bonds, mainly to subscribers of his new publication, the *Western Empire*. If he raised a sufficient sum to buy the land in the clear, he'd go through with the purchase. If not, the bondholders would get their money back. Once the land was paid for, Hartranft would subdivide it into small farms and erect a town site. He'd then put in roads and other infrastructure. Once the bonds matured, holders could either cash them in at a profit or exchange them for land—one acre for $300 worth of securities. Hartranft used this formula to establish several communities in the early 1900s, including the Kern County town of Wasco, about twenty-five miles from Bakersfield.

His most ambitious venture, though, was the subdivision he started on the northern outskirts of Los Angeles in 1913 called Los Terrenitos (Spanish for "Little Lands"). Hartranft's partner on this particular deal was a man every bit as starry-eyed as he was, if not more so. William Smythe had, at an earlier stage of his career, been a zealot for another cause: bringing water to the West so that the region would thrive and, he hoped, spawn the Progressive Era's answer to agrarian democracy. Through his journal, *Irrigation Age,* and, later, his book, *The Conquest of Arid America,* Smythe had helped galvanize a national movement that resulted in the landmark Reclamation Act of 1902, under which the federal government built massive dams and canals and delivered water to farms beyond the hundredth meridian. "I had taken the cross of a new crusade," Smythe later wrote. "To my mind, irrigation seemed the biggest thing in the world. It was not merely a matter of ditches and acres, but a philosophy, a religion, and a programme of practical statesmanship rolled into one." From this first ideal flowed a second: the development of Little Landers colonies, organized around one-acre subsistence lots, up and down California. These communities were intended to be close enough to the city to take advantage of its cultural offerings but far enough away for residents to carve out their own cooperative, communal utopia—a vision extremely close to Hartranft's own.

The two made quite a pair—Smythe, a sober-looking character with a dark beard and sad eyes, and Hartranft, who drove around in a Studebaker sedan with balloon tires, wore leather spats, and peered through pince-nez balanced atop his nose. They set aside 240 acres in Los Terrenitos, nestled in a rift between the San Gabriel and Verdugo Mountains. Six lots were sold the very first day the land went on the market. Within two years, more than five hundred people called the place home. The colony boasted a community center that hosted dances, musical performances, literary programs, and town meetings. There was a coopera-tive store, a post office, and efficient coach lines to and from L.A. Thou-sands of fruit trees were planted. "The water is the sweetest I ever tasted," one newcomer said, "and as for the scenery, well, I want to live there the rest of my days." But paradise didn't last long. By 1917, Los Terrenitos started to crumble, a victim of rocky soil, marauding gophers, and concerns by a state commission (later proven unfounded) that set-tlers were being exploited. Many residents soon gave up on farming, sliced up their one-acre lots, and sold out. In 1925, the area was incor-porated as Tujunga, and seven years later it was annexed by Los Angeles. It would remain a lovely spot with a proud history—but it would never again embrace Hartranft's notion of "a little land and a living."

Nonetheless, Hartranft never stopped believing in the power of fam-ilies acquiring a small piece of ground on which they could grow their own food, and as the Depression hit and hundreds of thousands of out-of-work migrants swarmed into California, it only deepened his convic-tion. *Grapes of Gladness*, then, wasn't just a rebuttal to *The Grapes of Wrath* in the same way that Ruth Comfort Mitchell's *Of Human Kind-ness* was. Hartranft's book was, more than anything, a monumental sales job by a tireless salesman.

Over 113 poorly written pages, it tells the story of Ma and Pa Hoag, who leave drought-ravaged Beaver, Oklahoma, for a fresh start in the Golden State. As their car trundles over the Cajon Pass, they begin to see giant billboards along the highway: "We are authorized by one of the largest banks in Los Angeles to loan an acre garden . . . to 500 fam-ilies of enterprising and worthy people. You need make no purchase payment down, for five years, except the interest of 6% . . . . We have built many communities on this plan for the past third of a century." Pa is skeptical, worried that he's being "suckered into a somethin' for nothin' game," but Ma urges him to drive on and find out more. So he does, absorbing one road sign after another: "Welcome to the Land of Sunshine, Fruit, Flowers, and Marvelous Industrial Development . . . . Now that you are here in California . . . the leaders of this state greet you and want to help you make yourself into useful home-owning citizens, instead of becoming landless migrants to be incited into revolution by sensational writers." The billboard went on: "If you can put a pig in a barrel and collect the answer to daily prayer for bread from your own garden—then you are an acre-culturist—a little lander of California—and we . . . welcome you even in this storm of economic upheavals that we are going through."

Hartranft's tale continues with all the subtlety of a backhoe leveling the land to make way for one of his residential projects. Ma and Pa and another family they meet on the road, the Simpsons, reach the colony of Shore Acres (part of present-day Manhattan Beach), where they're told that they are about to become a part of a broad movement tracing itself to Moses, William Penn, and Brigham Young. Eventually, they meet Uncle Marsh, who adds another name to the pantheon: "You know we try to live, think and operate on Thoreau's philosophy out here. You'll find the book *Walden Pond* in most all the homes." Just ten miles away, they're informed, are the bustling factories of Ford and Firestone—perfect for people who want "one foot on a garden and one foot under the desk or workbench."

With such a splendid setup, the Hoags come to understand, all it takes to prosper is a little gumption. "But if you are what some fictional writers describe as Oakies: profanity-belching, sex-mongering or property stealing," *Grapes of Gladness* warns, "don't try to enter" Shore Acres or any other such development. In case anybody missed the reference, a footnote goes on: "Californians have too much respect for their sister state to designate as Oakies such low characters as Mr. Steinbeck has invented. Having absorbed so much unnecessary profanity and morals of the barnyard from his book, we instinctively think of his 'loved associates' as steinbitches—without social or community value."

Hartranft didn't confine the peddling of his ideas to the pages of *Grapes of Gladness*. By 1940, he'd form an organization with the backing of the Salvation Army called Social Adjustments Inc., which likewise saw endless opportunity in one-acre homesteads. "The disease of unemployment has cursed all the civilizations of recorded history," Hartranft would write in a proposal to "save California," which he shared with, among others, Carey McWilliams. "God made one job for man big enough to go around. That is feeding yourself from your own garden."

It sure worked out, anyway, for Ma and Pa and their friends. There's no stillborn baby in their story, no flood, no starving stranger. Instead, by their third year at Shore Acres, the Hoags and the Simpsons each own a sow and are blithely producing raisins, olives, and honey. They've even started bottling and selling pomegranate juice. And Ma has become a Thoreau aficionado.

If Marshall Hartranft had his own peculiar set of goals—focused as much on hawking real estate as on hammering *The Grapes of Wrath*—George Thomas Miron was burdened by no such divided agenda. His little counter-book, *The Truth about John Steinbeck and the Migrants*, had but one aim: to tear apart the most popular novel in America. His twenty-six-page treatise began, as Miron explained it, as a letter to a friend, who suggested "the material might be of interest to other readers in view of the fact that very little has been written on the growers' side of the controversy." The friend, Miron couldn't help but add, "was quite surprised that the question actually had two sides."

What Miron's answer may have lacked in gracefulness was more than made up for by his vehemence. He opened by condemning "all revolutionary-proletarian fiction" for its "over-simplification" of the issues—and then proceeded to go after Steinbeck in a manner that can only be described as oversimplified. Miron called *The Grapes of Wrath* "a novel wherein naturalism has gone berserk, where untruth has run amuck drunken upon prejudice and exaggeration, where matters economic have been hurled beyond the pale of all rational and realistic thinking."

Those were bold words from a guy who'd be remembered years later by his nephew as "a lifelong struggling writer." Born in 1906, Miron was raised in a Los Angeles that had yet to be transformed from a big town into a real city; still to arrive were the hundreds of thousands of calloused hands and hunched shoulders—mainly from the Midwest—that would assemble autos and airplanes, forge steel and tires, dig for oil, and make fantasies flicker across the big screen. No child of privilege, Miron grew up with a father who worked in the delivery department at the Broadway department store downtown and, later, operated a bulldozer for the Los Angeles Shipbuilding Company, bending steel beams to the contour of cargo vessels. Ultimately, he became a contractor. Miron himself took a job at General Petroleum Corporation and then wore the hardhat of a telephone lineman, repairing wires from L.A. to Kern County and beyond. He could have, that is, been any one of the working stiffs Tom Joad encountered on the road—men who, according to Steinbeck, were angry and anxious and ready to challenge a system that was rigged against them. As a writer, Miron claimed to have found inspiration from H. L. Mencken—Carey McWilliams's mentor. Miron read Mencken voraciously and corresponded with him. Mencken's mordant columns and essays, Miron said, "symbolized our generation of protest."

But for all that, Miron seemed to flinch from protest. In 1937, he set out to make "a first-hand study of the agriculture-work problem," and this months-long survey carried him through the San Joaquin Valley, over to the coast, and all the way north to the Oregon line. What he discovered, he said, was 180 degrees different from what Steinbeck and McWilliams later depicted. Most of the migrants Miron met "were receiving more money per day than they ever had before in their entire lives," he wrote. He conceded that migrant children often got sick. But he chalked this up to tender tummies "gorging fresh fruits." In the end, *The Truth about John Steinbeck and the Migrants* was a tenacious defense of the status quo. Miron knocked McWilliams for his "prejudice" against large landowners in *Factories in the Field*. And he bristled at the "revolutionary borscht" that Steinbeck had cooked up. "I can think of no other novel," said Miron, "which advances the idea of class war and promotes hatred of class against class, in the most classless society in the world, more than does *The Grapes of Wrath*."

Such fierce reaction to a work of literature was not without precedent. Harriett Beecher Stowe's *Uncle Tom's Cabin* (itself an enormous best seller) had resulted in a counteroffensive that was every bit as potent as what Steinbeck would face. By one count, twenty-seven books were written by Southerners in response to the antislavery novel between its appearance in 1852 and the Civil War. Among the most famous was Mary Henderson Eastman's *Aunt Phillis's Cabin*—a title that, just like *Grapes of Gladness* or *Plums of Plenty*, left no doubt as to what work it was trying to skewer. Yet as cheeky as some of these "anti-Tom" books were, it's important to recognize that, just as with their 1930s counterparts, they were driven primarily by one thing: fear. Fear that a wildly popular novel had shined a light on an inherently iniquitous system. Fear that society might rise up as a result. Fear by a fortunate few that the world they sat atop might soon come unglued. The abolition movement, Eastman wrote, was "nurtured in violence and disorder . . . accomplishing nothing good, forever creating disturbance." Another anti-Tom tome, *Ellen; or, The Fanatic's Daughter,* put the abolitionists' aspirations into terms that would have seemed right at home in the '30s: they "had resolved upon a total revolution in Southern affairs."

This is not to imply that the treatment of slaves in the antebellum South and the treatment of farm workers in Depression-era California—the new Cotton Kingdom—were equivalent; the former was obviously far, far worse. But it's notable that Stowe's opponents employed some of the very same techniques in their counter-works that Steinbeck's would—arguing that the plantation was a perfectly fine place to live and that blacks were content in their bondage. Consider, for example, this exchange from another book meant to take a swipe at Stowe, *Antifanaticism: A Tale of the South:*

"Would you not like to be free, Rufus?"

"Well, I think not massa; 'caze den nobody would care for Rufus den . . . ."

"You are very happy, then?"

"Oh, yes! Mighty happy . . . ."

Some seventy years later, remarkably similar sentiments could be found in the work of Frank J. Taylor, a reporter who'd write a piece in the November 1939 issue of the *Forum* called "California's 'Grapes of Wrath.'" In it, he'd tell about a group of migrants in Madera who were mighty happy themselves—so much so, that when the county health director, Lee Stone, proferred train tickets so they could get back to Oklahoma, Arkansas, and Texas, he was met with silence. Wrote Taylor:

> Finally, one of the men spoke up. "Thanks, Doc," he drawled. "Here we be and here we stay and we ain't a gonna leave the promised land."
>
> "No sirree, we ain't a gonna leave California," chorused the rest. And they didn't.
>
> Almost all the counties in the San Joaquin and Sacramento Valleys have standing offers of free transportation back home for any migrant family. Not one family in a hundred has accepted.

Taylor was, undeniably, highly selective with his facts. But so, arguably, was Steinbeck. One simply homed in on all the things that the other chose to completely ignore. Where Steinbeck saw a system of large-scale farming that was in desperate need of being shaken up, if not altogether torn down, Taylor saw a modern miracle that only needed protection from "the strike menace" the Communist-backed unions had unleashed. California, he said, was blessed with "the greatest agricultural empire the world has ever known," and the only thing that anybody needed to worry about, in his estimation, were the "terrorists" bringing "labor trouble."

For both men, their perceptions fueled their predictions. "There is little question in my mind," Steinbeck said, "that the principle of private ownership as a means of production is not long with us. This is not in terms of what I think is right or wrong or good or bad, but in terms of what is inevitable." Taylor, by contrast, was convinced that the migrants were not so interested in being organized collectively, be it on government-sponsored cooperative farms (or, it might be inferred, into labor unions, either). "And so, in spite of the good intentions of the Farm Security Administration, the Governor's Committee on Unemployment, the Simon J. Lubin Society, the John Steinbeck Committee and other organizations," Taylor wrote, "the highly individualistic newcomers probably will work out their own destiny in their own way."

If Taylor was chary of those who hoped, as Steinbeck put it, that the country was about to adopt "a new system and a new life, which will be better than anything we have had before," he came by his feelings honestly—as honestly, one might reason, as Steinbeck came by his. Taylor had, after all, gotten an up-close and personal look at the society that many held out to be the model for what was supposed to materialize in America: Communist Russia.

It was 1918, and Taylor thought that he'd enter World War I as an ambulance driver, having organized an American Field Service unit when he was still at Stanford University. Instead, he made his way to Europe as a young United Press correspondent. "I filled my notebook with human interest items gleaned from doughboys, officers, nurses, chaplains," Taylor later wrote. "Everybody had a story to tell." After the armistice was signed in November, Taylor traveled from France to Germany (where he excelled as a reporter, in part because he spoke the language) and then, reluctantly, to Russia—with the promise from his editor that if he'd "take a fast look" around, he'd be able to finally get home to California to marry his sweetheart. His introduction to the Red regime was paved with a letter from Lincoln Steffens, the left-wing journalist (and later friend and admirer of Steinbeck) who happened to be visiting Berlin at the time and agreed to do Taylor a favor. With the note tucked away in his knapsack—along with some cheese, a hunk of bread, extra socks, a shirt, underwear, and $800 in U.S., British, French, and German currency—Taylor boarded the night train for Lithuania and, outside Kovno, entered the no-man's-land separating once-warring German and Russian troops.

"With two German officers, I climbed a huge haystack used as an observation post and gazed through the twilight at Bolshevik Land," Taylor later recounted. "They regaled me with tales of tortures the supposedly barbaric Bolsheviki inflicted on their captives. I thought of calling off my foolish junket. There was still time to turn back and report to the Boss that I couldn't get through the lines."

Instead, Taylor pushed on. After a sleepless night, he boarded a *droshky,* a Russian carriage, and "set out across the quiet meadow separating the two armies." Three German officers on horseback accompanied him. All of a sudden, three Russian officers, also on horses, trotted out of the woods to meet Taylor and his party. Out of earshot from Taylor, the six military men conferred. When their powwow ended, the Russians signaled back toward the woods. "A long line of bedraggled German soldiers, who had been prisoners of the Bolsheviks, filed past us," Taylor recalled. "When the last soldier stumbled by, the Russian and German officers saluted. My *droshky* driver cracked his whip. We followed the Russian horsemen. I didn't know yet what the deal was, but it looked as though the Germans had swapped one American for about eighty prisoners."

Sure enough, as the caravan made its way deeper into Russian territory, Taylor's driver leaned over and began speaking to him in German.

"You're an agent of President Wilson, no?" he asked.

"Who told you that?" Taylor answered.

"I heard the Germans tell the Bolsheviks you were."

The next thing he knew, Taylor was on his way to a Russian army installation. From there, he was put on a train, under guard, to Moscow. "Most of the time," said Taylor, "we rode in a boxcar equipped with shelves for those passengers who did not stretch out crowded like sardines on the floor. The train puffed ahead and backed onto sidings for four days. At every station, women in bright peasant shawls presided over samovars from which they drew hot tea, which they sold along with boiled eggs and black bread. To my delight, I discovered that I

Like Steinbeck, Frank Taylor's worldview was shaped by his experiences—one of which, in his case, was being detained in Communist Russia shortly after the revolution. (Courtesy of Pat Taylor)

could communicate with some of them, not only by gestures and smiles, but in German—words which were akin to their Yiddish." It was "like a chicken conversing with ducks," but it worked.

After the train pulled into Moscow, Taylor's guard escorted him to police headquarters. Unsure of what to do with "the first enemy correspondent to invade the city," as Taylor called himself, the officials there quickly turned him over to Maxim Litvinov, a senior Soviet diplomat. He found Taylor a sparsely furnished room in the old Hotel Metropole.

"Don't try to go outside without a guard we'll assign you," Litvinov told him in perfect English, "or you may wind up in Lubyanka Prison."

What followed was a most bizarre bout of captivity. That first night, Litvinov invited Taylor to join him at a restaurant reserved for high Bolshevik commissars and, later, took him to the ballet. Taylor was, it had been made clear, in no way free to come and go on his own. But "every evening for the ensuing week, Litvinov or one of his English-speaking colleagues sprang me from what amounted to house arrest." They'd go out for a nice dinner and then "usually strolled and talked in the long Moscow twilight. They fed me propaganda but . . . during the day I was allowed to sightsee, followed always by a shadow, often a husky woman in soldier's uniform with a carbine slung over her shoulder. My guard faithfully followed me into the men's room, which I would never have been able to distinguish from the powder room, the markings on the door being in Cyrillic script."

Despite his "curtailed liberty," Taylor observed quite a bit of Russian life: "food, clothing, prices, working conditions." He even scored an interview with Georges Tchicherin, the foreign minister. At one point, Taylor said, Litvinov explained to him that without the letter from Steffens, "giving me good character," he likely would have been treated much more harshly.

After two weeks, Taylor was summoned to Litvinov's office and told he was being deported to Finland, along with five American infantrymen who'd been taken prisoner on the Archangel front. At the border, the Russian general in command took all of Taylor's dollars, pounds, francs, and marks. After Taylor complained, the general handed him two freshly printed sheets, which contained a million rubles. "It was the first and only time I have been a millionaire," Taylor said. It was barely enough to buy a simple meal for the six of them. "For dessert," Taylor added, one of the soldiers "kissed the soil of Finland."

Before he left Moscow, Taylor was permitted to write a number of stories, which the Russians promised to send along to the United Press bureau in Paris. By the time these dispatches reached France two weeks later, Taylor was already there. "The stories had been rewritten with a decidedly Bolshevik slant," Taylor said. "I rewrote them with my own slant, which was probably as biased as theirs."

After visiting Russia the same year that Taylor had, Lincoln Steffens famously declared, "I have seen the future; and it works." Taylor, though, came away with precisely the opposite impression, confident that Russia would collapse within a decade. That didn't happen—not nearly so fast anyway. But as Taylor went on to write about California agriculture for magazines such as *Country Gentleman* and eventually author hagiographies on United Airlines, Union Oil, and the Southern Pacific, he painted big business as a force to be venerated and any threat to capitalism as something to be resisted.

Steinbeck hated Taylor's take on things, dismissing him as "the propaganda front of the Associated Farmers." (The growers' group did gladly reprint and distribute his *Forum* article, which was also picked up in *Reader's Digest*.) What's funny, though, is that on the surface, the two men had much in common. One can even picture them striking up a friendly conversation over a couple of beers—as long as they stayed far away from discussing politics. They'd both attended Stanford. They both had wry senses of humor. And they both loved to garden. "Just born to the hoe, that's me," said Taylor, who raised fruit, vegetables, and flowers on his ten-acre ranch in Los Altos. As for Steinbeck, "He was always starting something from seeds," Steinbeck's third wife, Elaine, would later recall. "Salad greens, lettuces, tomatoes, squash, onions, everything." His tendency was to push his methods of cultivation as far as he could. "He always tried a revolutionary way," she said.

Elaine was speaking, innocently enough, of plantings in the backyard. Her comment, however, could well have applied to so much more.

———•———

Sunday, August 27, 1939. With the supervisors' vote just a day away, another newspaper story on censorship and *The Grapes of Wrath* plunked down on the front porches of the people of Bakersfield. Like the others, it suggested that those hoping to suffocate Steinbeck's work were losing their grip. On Friday, Wimmer's flip had been reported. On Saturday came Harty's pledge to reconsider his stance on the book ban. And now this from the *Kern Herald*: "Kern Plea Is Ignored By

Fox." The article below quoted Harry Brand, publicity director for Twentieth-Century Fox, as saying that despite the county's resolution requesting that the film version of *The Grapes of Wrath* not be completed, the studio was pressing ahead as planned. "Our intentions are not partisan," Brand told the paper. "But there is a great dramatic story in John Steinbeck's book . . . . And that is precisely what makes it great motion picture material."

It may have sounded from the breeziness of Brand's remark that those behind the movie were wholly unaffected by the dispute over the novel. That, though, was far from the case. "Lord knows there was an awful lot of talk around about whether it should be done or not," recalled Nunnally Johnson, who'd completed the screenplay in July, just a few months after the book had been published. The movie wouldn't hit theaters until early 1940, but the project was deemed so sensitive that when a camera crew was sent out to shoot footage along the highway in Oklahoma, Fox ginned up a fake name for the film; the studio claimed they were working on a silly comedy called "Highway 66." Producer Darryl Zanuck took other precautions as well. He told Johnson that instead of having the first script mimeographed and widely distributed, "as is our usual custom," he should make only three copies: one for the screenwriter and two for Zanuck himself. The cast and crew would receive only partial scripts each night during production. Otherwise, Zanuck believed, the press might be leaked a copy of the full thing and prematurely pick it apart. "A number of more or less unfriendly newspapermen are waiting . . . to actually find out what we have done with this great book," he said.

Zanuck thought he might have to tiptoe around his financiers as well. Shortly after purchasing the film rights to *The Grapes of Wrath*, he ran into Winthrop Aldrich, the chairman of Chase National Bank, Twentieth-Century Fox's biggest shareholder, in New York. Steinbeck's book didn't have too much nice to say about men in Aldrich's position. As it framed things, bankers were often the ones who coldly and anonymously kicked tenant farmers off their property in the dust-choked

Southwest. It was as if the bank "were a monster," insatiable in its greed, Steinbeck wrote. "The bank—the monster has to have profits all the time. It can't wait. It'll die . . . . When the monster stops growing, it dies. It can't stay one size." Zanuck, who was known for indulging popular tastes with gangster flicks, magnificent musicals, and Shirley Temple films, had been told that Aldrich "would probably raise hell with me" once he heard about the Steinbeck acquisition. Before Zanuck even had a chance to raise the subject, though, Aldrich startled him. "I hear you have purchased a book titled *The Grapes of Wrath*," the banker said. Zanuck braced himself for the blowback—but it never came. "My wife, Winnie, is crazy about it," Aldrich continued, "and I started reading it last night, and it was so fascinating I couldn't put it down. It should make a wonderful movie."

Not everyone concurred. The California Chamber of Commerce joined the supervisors in Kern County in their opposition to the making of the picture, and the Associated Farmers and Agricultural Council of California went so far as to call for a boycott of all Fox films. But it wasn't just big business that was dismayed over what Zanuck might do with *The Grapes of Wrath*. On the left, rumors flew that he had bought the film just so he could bury it. And despite a special clause in Steinbeck's $70,000 studio agreement that the movie must "retain the main action and social intent" of the novel, the author expressed concern that Zanuck was going to bleed it of its core principles and pathos. "When Steinbeck came out here for the first story conference," Zanuck remembered, "he was highly suspicious and told me that he had been . . . warned that the whole scheme was for the purpose of taking the social significance out of the novel." The author, Zanuck added, relayed that "he would never have sold the book to me if he had realized this company was actually controlled by big banking interests."

Zanuck assured Steinbeck that he was committed to telling the story right. This was no snow job, either. The producer had hired a firm of private eyes to verify that the migrants' suffering was as bad as Steinbeck had made it. If anything, they reported back, the novel had understated the

situation. *The Grapes of Wrath*, Zanuck concluded, is "a stirring indictment of conditions which I think are a disgrace and ought to be reme-
died." Still, the public was distrustful of Zanuck too. He said he received
some fifteen thousand letters during the making of *The Grapes of Wrath*,
99 percent of which predicted that he'd never finish the film because he'd
ultimately succumb to the desires of the business community.

By November, with Zanuck getting squeezed from both the right
and the left, *Look* magazine would take it upon itself to ask: "Is *The
Grapes of Wrath* Too Hot for Hollywood?" A range of personalities,
from Governor Culbert Olson to Agriculture Secretary Henry Wallace,
from radio host Walter Winchell to writer Ruth Comfort Mitchell,
were invited to offer an opinion on whether the novel should still be
turned into a film in light of the ongoing uproar. (Somewhat surpris-
ingly, they all said yes—even Mitchell, who contended that if the movie
were true to the book, it could play a valuable role by helping "make us
aware of the rapidly spreading menace of Communism.")

Really, though, there was only one opinion that mattered, and Darryl Zanuck wasn't wavering on the project in the least. "Some agricultural groups have threatened to boycott us if we make the picture," he
said. "Liberal organizations insist that we make it, but threaten to boycott it if we do not do it to suit them. I am paying no attention to either
side." Nunnally Johnson noted that nothing tended to spur on Zanuck
as much as speculation that he wasn't going to complete a film. "His
spirits rise, soft drinks flow like water in his office, and it is a first-rate
time to hit him for a raise or a vacation," Johnson said, adding that the
incessant nay-saying had led Zanuck to exclaim: "Show me a man that
can prove that I spent $70,000 in order to shelve it, and I'll make a pic-
ture about him!"

The movie they'd turn out, under the direction of John Ford, was not
a carbon copy of Steinbeck's book, and critics have cited numerous
places where the film all but silenced the author's willingness to name
those he thought responsible for the migrants' woes, including heartless
banks, shady used-car salesmen, power-hungry big farmers, masochistic

Darryl Zanuck was under fire from both the right and the left while making *The Grapes of Wrath*. (Academy of Motion Picture Arts and Sciences)

sheriff's deputies, and fruit ranch foremen disposed to cheat pickers at the scales. On screen, one student of cinema would find, *The Grapes of Wrath* imparts no better than "a cop-out analysis, which avoids blaming any individual or institution for the plight of the Okies." Muted, above all, was Steinbeck's most radical language, his most incendiary ideas:

ONE man, one family driven from the land; this rust car creaking along the highway to the west. I lost my land, a single tractor took my land. I am alone and I am bewildered. And in the night one family camps in a ditch and another family pulls in and the tents come out. The two men squat on their hams and the women and children listen. Here is the node, you who hate change and fear revolution. Keep these two squatting men apart; make them hate, fear, suspect each other. Here is the anlage of the thing you fear. This is the zygote. For here "I lost my land" is changed; a cell is split and from its splitting grows the thing you hate—"We lost our land." . . . This is the beginning from "I" to "we."

You won't find any passages like this in the film. That's not surprising. Ford, who had just directed *Stagecoach* and *Young Mr. Lincoln*, said that what attracted him to *The Grapes of Wrath* were the "simple people," not the sectarian politics. In Steinbeck's yarn, the filmmaker was able to tease out a thread of universality. "The story was similar to the famine in Ireland, when they threw the people off the land and left them wandering on the roads to starve," he said. "That may have had something to do with it—part of my Irish tradition—but I liked the idea of this family going out and trying to find their way in the world." Ford added: "I was only interested in the Joad family as characters .... Before all else, it is the story of a family, the way it reacts, how it is shaken by a serious problem, which overwhelms it. It is not a social film on this problem; it's a study on a family." Pushed further on the social import of *The Grapes of Wrath*, Ford announced: "I love America ... I am apolitical."

Zanuck's own politics were more complex. He was known to be a Republican. "Always had been," Johnson said. But Steinbeck's story revealed in him a deep desire to help those whom the unseen hand of the marketplace had let slip through its fingers. "Many things in Socialism appeal to me," Zanuck confessed years later to the director Elia Kazan, "probably the same instincts that made me want to produce *The Grapes of Wrath*." There were limits, though, to how far Zanuck was willing to go. In particular, he was concerned that Socialism invariably seemed to yield to something pernicious. "I have repeatedly seen Socialists ensnared and used by Communists and then swallowed whole," Zanuck said. "Both Communists and Fascists have used Socialists as stepping-stones. Hitler did and so did Mussolini .... I guess what I detest more than anything is any form of regimentation or any type of suppression of the individual. So far as I can see, or as far as history will let me see, the Democratic system is the only chance for survival, and the free enterprise system (call it Capitalistic if you like) is the only form of commerce that results in general prosperity."

The biggest differences between the novel and the film were in the sequencing of the narrative and in their respective endings. Johnson moved around various events so that instead of the Joads first coming to the government labor camp, where life was relatively happy and good, and then going on to work for miserable wages on a peach ranch, the order was reversed. Coupled with the final scene, in which Ma Joad delivers her celebrated stemwinder to the family ("We're the people that live. They can't wipe us out. They can't lick us. We'll go on forever, Pa, 'cause we're the people"), the effect was to go out on a classic Hollywood high note. Steinbeck had placed Ma's speech, by contrast, about two-thirds of the way into the novel. "The only real change I made—and I had to make it—was in the ending," Johnson said. "There had to be some ray of hope—something that would keep people who saw it from going out and getting so drunk in utter despondency that they couldn't tell other people that it was a good picture to see." Steinbeck, Johnson maintained, had himself "agreed on the necessity for a more hopeful ending."

Still, for all the changes, those both behind and in front of the camera went out of their way to ensure that the movie didn't stray too far from the essence of Steinbeck's novel, or from real life. "Nine-tenths of the dramatic action of the book is in the screenplay," Johnson said, "and, to the best of my purpose and ability, the same sociological emphasis." To that end, Goodwill supplied the costumes. Ford banned his actresses from spritzing any perfume on the set; "expensive odors," according to a Fox press release touting the edict, "weren't in keeping with the spirit of the production." Makeup was prohibited too. And Ford demanded that Jane Darwell, the actress who played Ma Joad, really weep in all her tragic scenes. He wanted no fake tears. To add another dash of authenticity, migrant families were given $5 if they'd drive alongside the Joads' jalopy and be filmed for a few minutes, but finding willing participants on the road wasn't easy. They thought it was "some hoax," recalled cameraman Charles Clarke. "Most of them wouldn't do it, though they surely needed the money. A few others seized on this as a blessing." Ford and cinematographer Gregg Toland studied the documentary films of Pare Lorentz and the photography of Dorothea Lange, Walker Evans, Margaret Bourke-White, and Ben Shahn to get a better feel for the imagery that had so stirred Steinbeck. And Fox hired Tom Collins as a technical advisor—a move that delighted the author. "He'll howl his head off if they get out of hand," Steinbeck told Elizabeth Otis.

But they never did. Somehow, Zanuck, Johnson, and Ford managed to walk a perfect line, keeping the basic integrity of the novel intact without running afoul of the Hays Office. This was the arm of the motion-picture industry that regulated itself—"self-censored" is actually a more accurate way to say it—so that every film would adhere to certain moral standards. In the 1920s, rocked by a series of sex scandals and afraid that hundreds of regional film boards across the United States would begin to impose their own notions of decency, Hollywood published a list of "do's and don'ts" to guide moviemakers. Hired to keep the studios in line was Will Hays, onetime chairman of the Republican National Committee and former postmaster general in the Harding administration. By 1930, the "do's and don'ts" had been supplanted by a formal production code, written by a priest from St. Louis. It wasn't until 1934, however, that the so-called Hays Code got some teeth. Under steady assault from the Catholic Church's National Legion of Decency, the industry agreed to hit anyone who produced, distributed, or exhibited a film that hadn't received Hays Office approval with a $25,000 fine. Scholars have long debated whether the Hays Office undermined artistic expression or whether it was, as one study terms it, primarily "window dressing." There is absolutely no doubt, however, that of particular concern to the office's chief censor, Joseph Breen, were films that fell into the "social category." Citing "industry policy," he had been actively discouraging the making of such movies for years. By 1939, Breen was pleased to inform Hays that fewer than 10 percent of all Hollywood productions featured any serious social or political connotations.

Moralistic and anti-Semitic—he'd blame the Jews for degeneracy in Hollywood—Breen had started his career as a newsman in Philadelphia before going on to serve two causes he believed in passionately: Catholicism and capitalism. He worked for a couple of church organizations and also as a flack for Peabody Coal, using both as perches to preach against the perils of Communism. One can only imagine, then, what someone as conservative and pious as Breen would have made of *The Grapes of Wrath*—a story that, as Joseph Di Giorgio was eager to remind the Hays Office, "promotes class hatred and incites to revolution." Amazingly, though, Breen had little bad to say about the film. His minions called on Fox to make some tweaks to the movie, including removing any explicit mention of Tulare County so as not to upset the local congressman. Breen also suggested that the studio agree to another dozen or so changes to the script, most of them dealing with language and taste. In one scene, for example, he advised that "the toilet gag about Granma should be entirely eliminated." In another, he asked to "please eliminate the word 'hell' from Pa's speech."

A couple of Breen's petitions were more overtly political. For instance, he pushed to erase a reference in one of Tom's speeches to "the association" (aka the Associated Farmers). Another line, which described a Red as someone unwilling to work for starvation wages—and that had been flagged by Breen—was also altered so as to become innocuous. What's more, the studio apparently fiddled with the script even before it got to Breen, in anticipation of what he might object to. Specifically, Jason Joy, a former Hays Office official who'd joined Fox in 1932, thought it would be wise to cloud the issue of just who lured the migrants to California. Joy "feels we must express . . . doubt where the handbills came from—so we don't give the definite impression that the big growers did it," Zanuck told Johnson in July.

But that was about it. All in all, Breen was satisfied that whatever Marxist propaganda was coursing through Steinbeck's book had been satisfactorily drained from the film. "Frankly," he'd tell Hays, "we here do not worry very much about the question of policy, which may have been suggested by the original novel." He thought the film was adequately balanced, for while it depicted "certain employers who do enforce bad working conditions . . . there are other farmers in the fruit belt who are decent about it all, and honest and honorable." The main thing, Breen said, was that *The Grapes of Wrath* "can well be defended as legitimate drama."

Henry Fonda as Tom Joad in the big-screen version of *The Grapes of Wrath.* The filmmakers walked a tightrope, trying to be faithful to the spirit of the novel while not running afoul of Hollywood's censors. (Academy of Motion Picture Arts and Sciences)

Still, Breen wasn't naïve. He knew that some measure of controversy was "inescapable." Everyone did. "The Fascists will say it is purely Communistic because it shows nothing but greed, villainy and cruelty in the minds of all those who are not paupers," Nunnally Johnson predicted before the movie was released. "The Communists will say it tends to Fascism, because it subtly shows that the country ought to be regimented, regulated and controlled from the top, so that such utter and crushing poverty in the midst of surplus and plenty could not take place."

And yet the film was much more than a flash point for those at the far ends of the political spectrum. Like the novel, it would have its biggest impact on the masses in the middle, who made it Fox's highest-grossing film of the year (with more than $1 million in box office sales). For despite all the compromises it made, despite quashing Steinbeck's most rebellious pronouncements, despite turning a clarion call for collective action into what Breen described as "really a story of mother-love," *The Grapes of Wrath* was still an astonishing film for its day. It would, as George Bluestone wrote in his seminal study, *Novels into Film*, come as close as any movie "in Hollywood's prolific turnout to exposing the contradictions and inequities at the heart of American life."

The Grapes of Wrath would open to mostly glowing reviews and go on to be nominated for seven Academy Awards, including best picture. Henry Fonda would receive a nomination for best actor for his portrayal of Tom Joad, and Nunnally Johnson for his screenplay. Two would win Oscars: John Ford for best director and Jane Darwell for best supporting actress. Perhaps most impressive, the man who was probably the toughest critic of all—and surely the most dubious initially—would also express great pleasure over what the film had achieved. "Zanuck has more than kept his word," Steinbeck told Elizabeth Otis. "He has a hard, straight picture in which the actors are submerged so completely that it looks and feels like a documentary film and certainly no punches were pulled—in fact with descriptive material removed, it is a harsher thing than the book, by far. It seems unbelievable but it is true."

Besides its coverage of Zanuck's movie in the making, the *Kern Herald* carried two more articles on *The Grapes of Wrath* in its Sunday edition. One of them centered on Ralph Lavin, who'd had a busy weekend. On Saturday, he'd sat down to write a letter to John Steinbeck, telling the author about the furor in Kern County and asking for his take on the situation. Steinbeck would write Lavin back a short while later—the author's only known comments on the censorship struggle:

I have your letter of August 26 for which I am grateful. Quite apart from the fact that it was my book you defended, I am glad for your defense. It required courage of course but the kind of courage that is necessary if we are to maintain our democracy. It is good to know that such men as you function in our local government . . . .

I have not felt it necessary to defend myself against the Associated Farmers or the Pro America group. Their stupidity in applying the vigilante methods of their labor relations to literary criticism was immediately obvious to the people of California for whom they presume to speak . . . .

Thank you again for your defense. I am sure it will be available when any attempt is made against the civil liberties of Americans.

Meanwhile, the *Herald* reported, a *Time* magazine correspondent had paid Lavin a visit. The writer from *Time* "told him he was national news. That the action of his fellow supervisors in banning Steinbeck's book . . . was receiving wide comment." Lavin, whom the left-leaning *Herald* dubbed Kern County's "Patrick Henry," explained that his own views had been shaped from "rubbing shoulders with the common man." He also talked about how he had been caught off-guard by the resolution to censor the novel. "Like other things," he said, "why should the majority tell the minority about what is going to happen?"

But what was going to happen now, with the supervisors' meeting just hours away?

The other article in the *Herald* noted that C. W. Harty, who'd been thrust into the role of swing vote, was still trying to figure out what to do. Just a day before, it appeared that he was ready to throw his lot in with Lavin and Wimmer and become a hero to the open-minded. But now, according to the paper, he "said that opinions of citizens as they reached him were so nearly 50–50 for and against the ban that he was having a hard time deciding which was right." The only thing Harty was sure about was that, no matter which way he wound up voting, one side of the fight was going to be hopping mad. "It looks like I'll be the fall guy again," he said.

CHAPTER SEVEN
Some Day

"Don't you fret none, Tom. A different time's comin.'"

To the folks jammed inside room 213 of the Bakersfield court-house, it must have seemed like forever before the Kern County Board of Supervisors got around to the issue they had come to see set-tled. A run of news had swept through town in recent days. On Satur-day, the '39 cotton harvest had formally begun, and it was predicted to be a biggie. On Sunday, *The Wizard of Oz* had opened at the Fox Theater—in Technicolor, no less. The Bakersfield police, meanwhile, had announced a possible break in the unsolved murder of Methias Warren, the father of Earl Warren, now the state attorney general (and, later, California's governor and chief justice of the U.S. Supreme Court). All along, war clouds continued to gather over Europe. But on this Monday morning, August 28, 1939, there was little that anybody was focused on, except for one thing: whether the banning of *The Grapes of Wrath* would be lifted or the censorship would stand.

On the sidewalk outside the courthouse, members of the Workers' Alliance—a group that presented itself as the "union of the unemployed" and sought to organize the migrant community with the backing of both the Communist and Socialist parties—marched and clutched hand-scrawled signs: "Put the Grapes of Wrath Back on Library Shelves." "Preserve American Democracy." "Supervisors Action is a Facist Trick!" "We Want a Ban on Some Supervisors." Inside, more than a hundred local residents packed the chamber. A man peddled copies of *People's World*, the Communist newspaper.

Many in the crowd had arrived early, anxious for the meeting to get underway. But when the proceedings were called to order at 10:25 a.m., the board began by taking up the banal: the filing of three applications by local utilities for pipeline crossings; the issuing of directions to the auditor's office in connection with Kern's welfare program; the acceptance of payments owed for a new dishwasher at the county hospital, new cabinets in the sheriff's office, and fourteen other equally quotidian purchases. This exercise didn't last very long. Still, it's easy to envision those in attendance, crammed elbow to elbow, fidgeting in their seats, as the supervisors OK'd this motion and that, all unanimously, all devoid of expression, all without any hint of the raw emotion that everyone knew lay just beneath the surface.

Then at last, it broke through: the agenda turned to *The Grapes of Wrath*, with Raymond Henderson invited to speak on behalf of the ACLU. The blind lawyer dove right in, protesting the banning of the novel on the grounds that a library should be an open institution, not a partisan repository. "We are not concerned with whether *The Grapes of Wrath* is a good or a bad book," he said. "But we are concerned with whether a public board can set itself up as a board of censors to decide what the people shall or shall not read. If this sort of thing should be allowed to continue, the Republicans could ban a book written by a Democrat, and Democrats could bar a book by a Republican."

Henderson then called upon a series of others to help make his case. The first was Edgar J. "Ted" Evans, the chairman of the local branch of the ACLU and the pastor of Methodist Trinity Church. The reverend was a small man with a big heart—"a hellfire and damnation kind of preacher," as one of his congregants would remember him, who had real compassion for the migrants and organized "Sunday sings" at the labor camps.

"I do not approve of everything" in *The Grapes of Wrath*, Evans declared. "But I do believe the people should be given an opportunity to read it"—especially considering the importance of the book and the great demand for it. He noted that it was a best seller in fifty-seven cities. Stanley Abel, who'd been sitting back, fiddling with some papers, seemingly paying little attention, bore in. He had assumed the role of chairman for the day's meeting, with Roy Woollomes away on vacation.

"Are you aware," Abel asked, "that hundreds of other books and magazines are banned from the library?"

"But not by this board," Evans replied, evidently nonplussed.

"By this board!" Abel said, though there was absolutely no truth to the claim.

"Then the situation," Henderson interjected quietly, "is worse than we realized."

Abel was now on a roll. "Ninety-eight percent of people from Oklahoma don't use the kind of language used by characters in the book," he said, his tone rising. "If there are other books as filthy in the library, I'm in favor of throwing them all out into the streets."

Next up were two union men—representatives of Kern County's oil and brick workers, with a woman named Bertha Rankin sandwiched in between. A crusader for the interests of small farmers and an ACLU member, Rankin lived on a ranch in Arvin, right near the federal labor camp there. Trained as a nurse, she had married into one of the county's pioneering families in 1916 and worked on their cattle ranch in the mountains outside Bakersfield for several years. But somewhere along the way, Rankin got involved with "the very beginnings of Communism and all that stirring around," as her niece Alice Beard would remember it. "Some people are just born contrary," Beard added. "Bertha was always the topic of conversation because she was always doing something that we thought was wrong."

Protestors march before the August 28, 1939, Kern County Board
of Supervisors meeting, trying to force the ban against *The Grapes
of Wrath* to be lifted. (Kern County Museum)

On this day, what she was doing was standing in the county courthouse, defending people's right to read what they wanted to read. Ralph
Lavin asked Rankin whether she thought that Steinbeck's portrayal of
the migrants was accurate. "I do," she replied, citing the cotton strike of
1933, where workers were shot and killed. "The book is true," Rankin
went on. "Mr. Abel objects to the language of Steinbeck's migrants. It is
their regular language. When a bunch of you menfolk get together, you
use the same kind of language."

Lavin then looked toward Abel. "As a doctor of philosophy," he said, referring to the honorary degree that Abel had just picked up from Pacific Coast University, "if you were going to write a book, Stanley, would you give these Okies an Oxford accent?"

Henderson stepped forward to chip away at the same point. "You mentioned obscenity and vulgarity, Mr. Abel," he said. "Have you read *Gone with the Wind?* I can quote one passage in that book that is a great deal more intimate than anything Steinbeck wrote."

Henderson proceeded to read aloud a selection about incest between a man and his daughters. That, he said, "is from another book. It is in our library. Would you like to ban it?" Abel, usually not one at a loss for words, remained quiet. "That passage I just quoted," Henderson said, "is from the Old Testament, Mr. Abel"—the story of Lot in the Book of Genesis.

If Stanley Abel felt harassed by all this, he didn't show it. Mostly he grinned and munched on an apple, "like he was thoroughly enjoying the chaos of the whole thing," said Ralph Lavin's daughter, Hallie Killebrew.

Only now, the onslaught came courtesy of two other Abels—his brothers Ralph and L.L., who were speaking in their capacity as ACLU activists. Ralph was particularly obstreperous, blasting the Associated Farmers for being "a distinct threat to democracy" and "posing as a farm group." He accused his brother of doing the organization's dirty work by writing the resolution banning *The Grapes of Wrath.* Stanley, suddenly growing agitated, denied the accusation. The two siblings shouted each other down, with Stanley challenging Ralph to name the actual author of the resolution.

With the tension becoming ever thicker, Henderson tried to inject a little levity. "We have heard much of Plums of Plenty, Grapes of Wrath and Prunes of Poverty," he said. "Let us do away with the Apples of Discord in this fruitful land."

Discord, though, was clearly the order of the day. "These supervisors are not shocked by the language in Steinbeck's book," said Weltha

Smithson, a fifty-four-year-old grandmother and member of the Workers' Alliance, addressing Abel and his colleagues. "They've heard it all their lives. They just don't want the true conditions exposed. Sure, we have had to crowd whole families into one small tent. We didn't want to live that way. We had to.

"The migrants are proud of John Steinbeck's book. And if the migrants want to cuss, I think they've got a right to cuss. How well we know those words—'starvation wages.'"

And with that mention of starvation, the Board of Supervisors soon broke for lunch.

Around 2:30 p.m., the Board of Supervisors reconvened. What had begun as an argument over censorship and the appropriate use of language had evolved into something else: a broad—and angry—discussion about politics, penury, and pain.

A man who'd worked in the county health department told of migrant children frolicking in garbage. "The book is not strong enough," he said. A redheaded woman followed him, contending that the amount allotted to relief clients—$9 a month—wasn't sufficient to live on.

That got a rise of Stanley Abel. "Produce me somebody who is starving," he said to her.

"I'll take you and show you," she answered.

"You can't take me anywhere," Abel said, his smile wide again.

"All right, then, meet me in Hooverville, and I'll show you old men who are starving."

"I'll meet you," Abel said.

"I'll take you by the hand—"

"No you won't," Abel said. "I'll go peaceably." A few people snickered.

A bedraggled man went next, telling those assembled how tough it was to survive on odd jobs that paid twenty-five cents an hour. "When my young ones get hungry they look to daddy to do something," he said. "But I just get pushed around from one place to another. I don't want those young ones to go hungry. That's why I'm fighting for something better."

At that, a voice in the crowd pointed out that the state had recently "equalized" the amount of relief that whites and blacks were eligible to receive.

"Yeah," someone else said, "equalized so they can both starve on the same level."

Stanley Abel had had enough. "I defy anyone to show any community in the United States that is doing more for these people than Kern County," he said. "Right now we are fighting to keep the forces of reaction from stopping hospitalization for newcomers in the county." Abel maintained that the federal labor camp at Arvin—the one that Steinbeck had held up as an oasis of decency and democracy—couldn't have been established without the cooperation of the supervisors. Yet, Abel added, "the county which is doing the most for the migrants is libeled the most." For good measure, he denounced Culbert Olson, "your great liberal governor," and President Roosevelt, saying that his administration had accomplished nothing "in eight long years."

Ralph Abel jumped to his feet again, objecting to his brother's depiction of the New Deal and rekindling the clash he'd had earlier in the year over Stanley's decision to dissolve the local water association. "The Board of Supervisors went into a conspiracy with the utilities and certain big landowners to sabotage the water and power program," Ralph said. "Conditions would be improved if small farmers could get cheap water and power. It's a plot!"

"Tell the truth!" roared Stanley.

"You tell the truth!" shouted Ralph.

As the day stretched long, it occurred to at least one woman in the audience that Gretchen Knief hadn't been invited to make a comment, and she suggested that the librarian might have something to say. Abel quickly brushed her off, noting, only half-jokingly, that Knief worked for the supervisors.

Finally, Charles Wimmer stood up. "I made a mistake, and I admit it," he said of his earlier vote to censor *The Grapes of Wrath*. "I move that the ban on Steinbeck's book be rescinded." Lavin seconded the motion. Applause filled the room—that is, until C. W. Harty grabbed center stage. He'd seemed nervous all afternoon, and now he stared down at a set of prepared remarks and began to read. Harty said Lavin had been using the disagreement over *The Grapes of Wrath* for his own glory, and he accused him of conspiring with his political opponents to have him recalled from office. Lavin then lost his temper, saying that he was "too damned busy" looking after his own district to have time for such games.

Harty didn't back down, though. He taunted Lavin by daring him to read portions of *The Grapes of Wrath*. Nick Podovinnikoff, secretary of the Workers' Alliance, rushed to Lavin's rescue, saying it was unfair to take anything out of context like that. Still, Abel couldn't resist. "It's too filthy to read, isn't it, Mr. Lavin?"

Abel also offered up his reason for supporting the book ban. Before, he'd said that his vote to censor the novel had nothing to do with its so-cial implications; it was strictly because of its crudeness. Now, in a fit of pure doublespeak, he proclaimed: "When I proposed the book be banned from the library, I had just this sort of thing in mind. I wanted to get people stirred up. I wanted everybody to read the book. I want them to known the damnable conditions that exist in this state."

The crowd exploded. Some booed. Others burst out laughing. Abel smirked. The whole affair, said Gretchen Knief, had "worked itself into a Roman holiday."

When the noise died down, an elderly woman asked Abel, "Ever hear about the cuttlefish?"

"Well, I don't know," he replied.

"The cuttlefish is something with a lot of tentacles. When anything comes too close to it, it squirts black ink to becloud the issue."

When all was said and done, however, there was nothing murky about the result. A poll was taken. Lavin and Wimmer voted to lift the censorship. Abel voted to keep it in place. So did Harty, who'd failed to break ranks with his political sidekicks after all. With the board deadlocked two to two, the ban would remain in effect.

The next day, Harty issued a statement:

It should be unnecessary for me to assure you that I fully realize the gravity of my position in this matter. I am aware that the eyes of the nation are in some small way focused on this board . . . .

I have patiently listened to every word spoken. I have tried to weigh every value fairly and truly and in its proper place.

I have not been unduly influenced either by the Associated Farmers or the Workers' Alliance. I propose to be fearlessly independent of coercion from any source, not only today but every day.

This is in no sense a proposal to place a ban on the circulation of the book in Kern County along regular channels, but a well-considered decision to refuse free distribution of obscene material to children and young people at the expense of the taxpayers.

While I deplore the misinformation and deliberate falsehoods upon which the obvious propaganda of the book is based, I have no desire to limit the right of the people to read what they like.

If the obscenity were stricken from its pages, I would be the first to insist on its free circulation . . . .

My contention that the book is unfit for general circulation seemed well borne out by the loud protest of the audience, at yesterday's session, against reading selected passages . . . in public even though no children were present.

It would seem that these people would like to demand that the taxpayers circulate the book among the youth of Kern County but would prefer themselves to hide its loathsome features from public discussion while they are present.

This is exactly the attitude of the bad boy who chalks up rhymes in secret places. It is not my way.

The following week, Bertha Rankin showed up at the Board of Supervisors to request that they vote again on the book ban. Both Ralph Lavin and Stanley Abel happened to be absent from the meeting that day, and Chairman Woollomes asked for the matter to be held over to a later time. During the following year, a few more letters of protest drifted in, but otherwise the issue lay dormant.

In the summer of 1940—after *The Grapes of Wrath* had won the Pulitzer Prize—Stanley Abel learned that Gretchen Knief had given out four dozen copies of the novel to other libraries around the state for their use. He scolded her for "loaning county property" and demanded that she recall the books. That way, they could sit on Kern County's shelves, unopened and unread.

———

On a blue-sky October afternoon, sixty-five years after *The Grapes of Wrath* was published, an elderly group of Okies and their sons and daughters gathered at the old federal labor camp in Arvin for an annual celebration called Dust Bowl Days. It seemed like a good time to drive over the mountain from Los Angeles, eat a little tri-tip, and, most of all, consider all that had happened since the banning of the novel—what had changed and what hadn't.

A knot of festival-goers loitered in front of a large display of Dorothea Lange's "Migrant Mother." Others ate biscuits drowned in gravy and did their best to ignore the flies. A couple of old guys and gals two-stepped to the sound of Tommy Hays and the Western Swingsters. Then the band slowed things down a beat and launched into the Merle Haggard classic "Hungry Eyes."

> *A canvas covered cabin in a crowded labor camp*
> *Stand out in this memory I revived;*
> *Cause my daddy raised a family there, with two hardworking hands*
> *And tried to feed my mama's hungry eyes.*

Country music star Merle Haggard helped turn the term "Okie" from a pejorative into a badge of honor. (Kern County Museum)

He dreamed of something better, and my mama's faith was strong
And us kids were just too young to realize
That another class of people put us somewhere just below;
One more reason for my mama's hungry eyes.

By the time Haggard had recorded that elegy in 1968, the migrants (as well as the state and the nation) were in a whole new space—economically as well as culturally. The term "Okie" was long on its way to going from a pejorative to a badge of honor, emblazoned on belt buckles, bumper stickers, and trucker's caps. Haggard, whose family was living in a converted railcar just outside Bakersfield when he was born in 1937, had a lot to do with swelling people's chests, with songs such as "Okie from Muskogee" and "I Take a Lot of Pride in What I Am." That these tunes were Billboard chart mega-hits highlighted the degree to which those outside the migrant community had also come to romanticize the Okie experience.

The transformation in how the migrants were looked upon—and in how they looked upon themselves—was swift, but it didn't occur overnight. In late 1939, a few months after the supervisors voted for the second time to ban *The Grapes of Wrath,* a groundbreaking Senate investigation showed up in California and confirmed the "shocking degree of human misery" among the state's farm workers. The inquiry, led by reformist Republican Robert M. La Follette Jr., was centered primarily on violations of free speech and the rights of labor, and it already had examined the circumstances behind violent clashes at textile plants, auto factories, and steel mills in the East and Midwest. But Steinbeck's novel, along with *Factories in the Field,* convinced the senator that he needed to set up shop on the West Coast too.

Operating out of Los Angeles and San Francisco through early 1940, the La Follette Committee issued 500-plus subpoenas, held 28 days of hearings, heard from nearly 400 witnesses, compiled some 2,500 pages of testimony, and collected more than 7,500 exhibits, much of which centered on one villain: the Associated Farmers. Indeed, the panel would conclude that where the big growers' organization had been able to see its aims realized, "local fascism was the result." Steinbeck anticipated La Follette's probe with great eagerness, while Bill Camp bridled at it. Camp, in fact, would long preserve in his own files an Associated Farmers newsletter, which argued that "the La Follette Committee was infiltrated by Communists and practically was managed by them." Camp was so impressed by that particular passage, he underlined it, circled it, and marked it "Important."

The Grapes of Wrath remained a top ten best seller through 1940, and reaction to the book continued to generate news. In March, Philip Bancroft debated Carey McWilliams in a nationally broadcast Town Meeting of the Air titled "What Should America Do for the 'Joads'?" That same month, Woody Guthrie played at a "Grapes of Wrath Evening" at the Forrest Theater in New York to benefit agricultural laborers. Guthrie scratched his head with his guitar pick, mumbled something about the "Rapes of Graft," and began to sing. Some credit his performance that night with starting the modern folk-music movement. Also in March, McWilliams and Donald Henderson, president of the agricultural workers' union, were joined by members of *The Grapes of Wrath* movie cast at a mass meeting in Los Angeles. "So You've Seen 'The Grapes of Wrath,'" the flier for the event read. "Now . . . What is America going to do for the Joads and California's 490,000 other migrants?" As the months rolled on, however, the public seemed to lose interest in the Okies and their problems. "People sort of forgot them," the journalist Ernie Pyle noted. By late the following year, the country had more pressing things to worry about anyway: it was off to war.

The conflict proved not only a distraction; it was a powerful corrective. California's aircraft factories and shipyards sopped up the surplus labor that had long plagued the Central Valley. By the end of the 1940s, the bulk of those who'd moved to the Golden State from the Southwest had exited the fields for good and were working in solid blue-collar jobs—in construction, oil and gas, automotive services, and more. By and large, their incomes soared, and their children would make further occupational and financial gains. If this wasn't a story of rags to riches, it was certainly one of rags to respectability.

Clell Pruett didn't hang around to see the community's ascent. Once the Japanese bombed Pearl Harbor, he feared California was next, and so he and Mace abruptly left Bill Camp's employ and headed back to Missouri. For the next thirty-seven years, he worked in the Lead Belt, handling dynamite and loading shuttles going in and out of the mines.

A few months before the Dust Bowl Days celebration, Clell could be found at his small home an hour outside St. Louis. He was eighty-eight now. In front of the white clapboard house, where he'd lived since 1947, a wooden Uncle Sam was holding the Stars and Stripes. Clell still had never read *The Grapes of Wrath*, the book he'd burned, but he promised to do so now. A few weeks later, he rendered his verdict. "It was just about like I thought it was," he said. The migrants were "pretty much degraded all the way through." He said that he had no second thoughts, no regrets, about what he'd done.

Gretchen Knief left California too—though she stuck around long enough to see *The Grapes of Wrath* returned to circulation. The key was Stanley Abel's defeat in the 1940 election, after three decades as a county supervisor. In January 1941, his replacement, A. W. Noon, seconded a motion by Ralph Lavin to remove the ban on the novel and have "supervision of reading material in our library be returned to its properly qualified and trained personnel." No objections were made. "It's a sight for sore eyes to see all those *Grapes of Wrath* gone from the shelves in my office," Knief told Noon that day. "Fifteen minutes after the news was broadcast . . . a patron telephoned his request for the book. Apparently you have pleased countless residents of Kern County by your action."

In 1942, Knief departed Bakersfield for a much bigger job: she had been appointed state librarian of Washington. That same year she married. And, ultimately, she settled on a dairy farm in Alabama, where she pushed to desegregate the state library association. In 1954, she wrote a county library manual. It included one brief section on censorship: "Mature adults should not need to be shielded against so-called 'objectionable' books. Yet, since many county library stations are located in small, conservative communities, it is sometimes advisable to insert notes to the field staff regarding the nature of certain books included in the shipment. Properly indoctrinated personnel will understand that all writing is merely a reflection of the times and that there is a vast difference between sincere artistry and cheap vulgarity." Gretchen Knief Schenk died in 1989.

Meantime, the others who had been caught up in the battle over *The Grapes of Wrath* and the turbulence of the 1930s also moved along, tossed this way and that by the vicissitudes of life. Stanley Abel quit Kern County and became a public housing and redevelopment official near the Mexican border. His brother Ralph served as a union leader in Boron, California. Charles Wimmer was defeated in his re-election bid for supervisor in 1944, while C. W. Harty lasted in office until 1952 and Roy Woollomes until his death in 1964. Ralph Lavin was campaigning for his third term on the board when the fifty-three-year-old died of a heart attack in 1946. "Ralph built little monuments to the things in which he believed," a friend eulogized at his funeral.

> Many times he let his official vote stand alone on one side of an issue—not to mark a victory but to commemorate a sincere belief. In an old-fashioned way he waxed sentimental over his country and his flag. His sweep of emotion made him quaintly dramatic in his defense of what he considered the Democratic way of life . . . .
> In this groove he found his affection for his fellow Americans, especially those most humble. Like Whitman, he could have said,
>> O you whom I often and silently come where you are that
>> I may be with you,
>> As I walk by your side or sit near, or remain in the same
>> room with you,
>> Little you know the subtle electric fire that for your sake
>> is playing within me.

Raymond Henderson also never stopped advocating for those in need, becoming the first executive director of the National Federation of the Blind. His cadet-turned-Communist client, Norman Mini, quit the party in 1941, frustrated that "it had lost all it originally set out to do." He later testified against other suspected Communists, naming names. In the late '40s, Mini began to mentor a young science-fiction writer named Philip K. Dick. Mini also wrote books himself, including a work that his friend Henry Miller called "the best first novel I have ever read." He never published anything, however.

Emory Gay Hoffman, creator of *Plums of Plenty* and the actual author of the resolution banning *The Grapes of Wrath*, led the Kern County Chamber of Commerce until the mid-1950s and then ran the local parks and recreation department. Ruth Comfort Mitchell continued to write through the 1940s, while staying active in the Daughters of the America Revolution and the Christian Science Church of Los Gatos. She died in her bathtub of heart failure in 1954. *Grapes of*

Gladness author Marshall Hartranft suffered a heart attack, as well, and died at his desk—"hard at work," said one tribute, "and that is how he would have desired it to be." As for Steinbeck's other detractors, Thomas Miron wrote some satire for Red Skelton before he passed away in 1995, while Frank Taylor fell ill and decided to take his own life in 1972. He was seventy-eight.

As the years wore on, no two people remained truer to their convictions than did Bill Camp and Carey McWilliams.

Through the 1950s, '60s, and '70s, Camp was a player in conservative political circles, backing a succession of Republican candidates. He was named treasurer of the U.S. Chamber of Commerce. And as he got older, the honors and awards poured in. In 1975, the group Religious Heritage of America, which had been instrumental in getting the phrase "under God" added to the Pledge of Allegiance, feted him at a Washington banquet. In 1980, six years before he died at age ninety-two, the National Right to Work Committee, an anti-union group, named its headquarters building for Camp.

As Camp held firm to his beliefs, the migrants tacked more and more in his direction. The community that had started out voting heavily for Democrat Culbert Olson when they first arrived in California turned out to be stubbornly traditional in their mores, extremely difficult to unionize, and, by the late '60s, had realigned themselves to become dependable GOP supporters. As America shifted rightward, so did the Okies, only more so.

Carey McWilliams kept watch over all this, but as an outsider, not as a government insider anymore. On January 5, 1943, just a day after delivering his inaugural address, Governor Earl Warren undertook his first official act as Culbert Olson's successor: he fired McWilliams as chief of the state's Division of Immigration and Housing. Given that the new administration was sure to bring in its own loyalists anyway, Warren's dismissal of the *Factories in the Field* author was mainly a symbol—as potent as the freeing of Tom Mooney had been four years before. In 1945, McWilliams took a job as West Coast correspondent for the *Nation,* and in 1955 he became the magazine's editor, a post he held until the mid-1970s. He wrote about the dramas that had grown out of the ferment of the '30s: the Red Scare in the '40s, the McCarthy witch hunt in the '50s, the Sturm und Drang of the New Left in the '60s. McWilliams died in 1980, the year that America finally had its revolution—only not the one so many had foreseen. It was, of course, Ronald Reagan's.

John Steinbeck's first inclination after finishing *The Grapes of Wrath* was to forget about politics. As he set out to write his next book, the taxonomic travelogue *Sea of Cortez,* he seemed wistful about escaping the tumult that had characterized the preceding period. "The world is sick now," he wrote to his friend Carlton Sheffield in November 1939. "There are things in the tide pools easier to understand than Stalinist, Hitlerite, Democrat, capitalist confusion, and voodoo."

Over the years, however, Steinbeck moved ever more to the right, or at least that's how his critics perceived it. By the late 1960s, with a Nobel Prize in Literature now to his name, Steinbeck was seen by many on the left as a traitor. They criticized him for being manifestly "middle class." (He did rent a fancy sports car during a trip to Europe, dubbing himself and his wife "the Joads in the Jag.") Some were dismayed by his anti-Marxist comments, others by his hawkish stance on Vietnam. In truth, what Steinbeck had contested—and would always contest—was any repression of a person's spirit, be it at the hands of the Associated Farmers or Stalin's secret police. "I believe in and will fight for the right of the individual to function as an individual without pressure from any direction," he wrote in 1954.

Still, there was no question that the rage that had fueled Steinbeck's greatest novel cooled over time. "When I wrote *The Grapes of Wrath,*" he told the Voice of America, "I was filled naturally with certain anger . . . at people who were doing injustices to other people, or so I thought. I realize now that everyone was caught in the same trap. If you remember, we had a Depression at that time. The Depression caught us without the ability to take care of it."

A sign at a gas station in Kern County in the late 1930s. By the time Steinbeck
had finished *The Grapes of Wrath*, he was sick of the era's polarizing politics,
which he characterized as "Stalinist, Hitlerite, Democrat, capitalist confusion,
and voodoo." (Photo by Dorothea Lange, Library of Congress)

Stricken by clogged arteries, John Steinbeck died in New York in
December 1968. His ashes were scattered over the California coast.

As the sun lowered over the Dust Bowl Days festival, the Western
Swingsters played a few last songs before packing up their instruments.
It was time to go home. The slow road toward Highway 99 wound past
some rundown farm-worker settlements occupied by men and women
who'd journeyed from deep inside Mexico to pick clean the same fields
the Okies once had. Just to the north lay Bakersfield, where the Kern
County Board of Supervisors in 2002 had issued a proclamation declaring October "Reading *The Grapes of Wrath* Month." Some greeted their
action as if it were an apology for their predecessors' ill-conceived book

ban. Others would invoke Kern County's history of censorship a year later when a group of local parents tried to keep Toni Morrison's *The Bluest Eye* from being taught in their children's high school—one of the two thousand or so books challenged every year around the country.

In his letter to Carlton Sheffield, Steinbeck had said that, with *The Grapes of Wrath* behind him, he was ready to write about things "which are relatively more lasting." But on the four-thousand-foot climb back toward L.A., it was hard not to marvel at how enduring *The Grapes of Wrath* has been. It isn't just the hundred thousand copies of the book that are still sold each year, or the way the Joads have continued to penetrate popular culture, thanks to Bruce Springsteen and Rage Against the Machine. For many, *The Grapes of Wrath* remains the quintessential story of dignity in the face of adversity.

Then again, maybe it's something else that has made the book so ageless. In a country where nearly 40 million people don't always have enough food, where about a third of the population doesn't earn an adequate amount to cover basic necessities, and where income inequality is wider now than at any time since before the Great Depression, the central conundrum of capitalism is not much different than it was in 1939: how can there be so much want amid so much plenty? "Our people," wrote Steinbeck, "are good people; our people are kind people. Pray God some day kind people won't all be poor. Pray God some day a kid can eat."

Pray God some day we won't have such a need to remember the Joads.

Acknowledgments

Like a lot of good ideas, the one to write this book was sparked by a conversation. I was chatting with a friend of mine, a poet named Lee McCarthy, outside a bookstore in Bakersfield, when she asked if I had ever seen a photograph of *The Grapes of Wrath* being burned.

Actually, I told her, I had. I'd stumbled across it while researching my last book, *The King of California*. The image had stuck with me too. I remembered the way it showed cotton titan Bill Camp standing there, looking smug, while one of his farm workers pitched Steinbeck's novel into the fire.

"Well," Lee said, "have you heard about the librarian who fought the censorship?" That, I said, I didn't know anything about—but it intrigued me. "She was brave," Lee added. I promised to check it out.

Thus began a four-year journey that turned into *Obscene in the Extreme*—a journey on which I piled up no shortage of debts to friends, who never seemed to tire of asking me, with genuine affection, how the book was going, and to colleagues at work, who were always there to pick up the slack when my mind would wander back to the summer of 1939.

A few special acknowledgments are in order. The first is to Lee, a superb writer and a courageous fighter for social justice in her own right, for planting the seed.

My agent, Kris Dahl of ICM, and my editor, Robert Kimzey, have been enthusiastic about this project from the beginning. It is rare for a writer to have a one-two punch like them: literary champions who are extremely skilled at what they do, and awfully nice people on top of that.

Nothing is more welcome to a tired and hungry writer on the road than a welcoming place to stay. My friends Allyson and Brent Kauffman, Vera and Marc Lifsher, and John and Shirley Kirkpatrick opened their homes to me during long research trips to central and Northern California. They couldn't have been more gracious.

In L.A., I am blessed to have the love of so many others, including David Levinson, Ellie Herman, Anne Reifenberg, and Barry Greenberg. My parents and in-laws are constant sources of support as well. Whether they realize it or not, all of these folks are important catalysts for the creative process. Forget the tragic artist. I can't write well if I don't feel good. Fortunately, my rich circle of friends and family makes me smile every day.

At work, whether in the newspaper world or on campus, I've been lucky to have bosses who understand that writing books doesn't detract from my other obligations; rather, it broadens my horizons and thus strengthens everything else I do. Thanks to John Carroll, Dean Baquet, Robert Klitgaard, and Ira Jackson for their wisdom.

The gifted historian Bill Deverell has been invested in this book from the moment I told him about it. He has been extraordinarily generous in every way—with his financial backing (via the Huntington-USC Institute on California and the West, which he runs), his knowledge, and his friendship.

And then there is Mark Arax. People have asked me if it's been funny not having Mark as my coauthor this time around. The truth is, he is still always there. Hardly a week goes by when we don't have long talks about writing and about life. His voice will forever be stuck in my head, whenever I take a turn at the keyboard: "Be ruthless on yourself. Remember—include just the cream."

Then there is my most important partner of all: my wife, Randye. She edited every chapter of this book with a sharp eye and a sharp mind. A wonderfully talented writer herself, her insights grace every page.

Along with our children, Emma and Nathaniel, she has also borne the brunt of what it takes to put together a book like this: countless weekends in which I was away from home or holed up in the office upstairs, growling at anybody who dared come near; vacations that were cut short or never got off the ground; household chores endlessly put off because, well, I hadn't quite finished chapter 3.

To Randye and Emma and Nathaniel, I can only say thank you for your patience. Thank you for your indulgence. And thank you for loving me in spite of this craziness. I couldn't love you more.

Rick Wartzman
Los Angeles, February 2008

Notes

ABBREVIATIONS

AF Associated Farmers

BC *Bakersfield Californian*

BML Files of the Beale Memorial Library, Local History Room, Bakersfield, CA

BPL Records of the Buffalo and Erie County Public Library, Buffalo, NY

CCOH Cully Cobb oral history, Regional Oral History Office, Bancroft Library, University of California at Berkeley

CDOH Caroline Decker oral history, Bentley Historical Library, University of Michigan

CMcW Carey McWilliams

CMcWP Papers of Carey McWilliams, Department of Special Collections, UCLA Research Library

COP California Odyssey Project Oral History Program, Walter W. Stiern Library, California State University at Bakersfield

DBMA Dust Bowl Migration Archives, Walter W. Stiern Library, California State University at Bakersfield

DW Archives of Doris Weddell, organizer of the Dust Bowl Days Festival, Bakersfield, CA

EO Elizabeth Otis

FB *Fresno Bee*

FOX Files from Twentieth Century-Fox Film Corp., Arts Library Special Collections, UCLA

FTP Papers of Frank J. Taylor, Department of Special Collections, Stanford University

FWP Files from the Federal Writers' Project on Migratory Labor, Bancroft Library, University of California at Berkeley

GK Gretchen Knief

HHOH Helen Hosmer oral history, McHenry Library, University of California at Santa Cruz

JB Research materials for Jackson Benson's *The True Adventures of John Stein-beck, Writer,* Department of Special Collections, Stanford University

JHJP Papers of Joseph Henry Jackson, Bancroft Library, University of California at Berkeley

JS John Steinbeck

JSP Papers of John Steinbeck, Department of Special Collections, Stanford University

KCBS Correspondence, records, and meeting minutes of the Kern County Board of Supervisors, Bakersfield, CA

KCM Kern County Museum, Bakersfield, CA

KH *Kern Herald*

LAT *Los Angeles Times*

LF La Follette Committee, U.S. Senate, *Hearings Pursuant to S. Res. 266, Violations of Free Speech and Rights of Labor*

LT Lee Tulin

NJOH Nunnally Johnson oral history, Department of Special Collections, UCLA Research Library

NM Norman Mini

OP *Oildale Press*

PB Papers of Philip Bancroft, Bancroft Library, University of California at Berkeley

PST Papers of Paul Schuster Taylor, Bancroft Library, University of California at Berkeley

RCM Ruth Comfort Mitchell

RCMP Papers of Ruth Comfort Mitchell, Department of Special Collections, Davidson Library, University of California at Santa Barbara

RH Raymond Henderson

RHP Papers of Raymond Henderson, archives of the National Federation of the Blind, Baltimore

RO *The Rural Observer*

SB *Sacramento Bee*

SCT Court transcript and records from the "Sacramento Conspiracy Trial" (*The People of the State of California v. Pat Chambers et al., Criminal No. 1533*), California State Archives, Sacramento

SCTM Miscellaneous documents from the "Sacramento Conspiracy Trial" (*The People of the State of California v. Pat Chambers et al., Criminal No. 1533*), Sacramento Archives and Museum Collection Center

SFC *San Francisco Chronicle*

SFN *San Francisco News*

TC Thomas Collins's Kern migratory labor camp reports, DW

TGOW *The Grapes of Wrath*

TGOW-F Files related to the film version of *TGOW,* Academy of Motion Picture Arts and Sciences, Margaret Herrick Library, Los Angeles

UCAPAWA　Papers of the United Cannery, Agricultural, Packing and Allied Workers of America, Labor Archives and Research Center, San Francisco State University

　　WBC　Wofford B. "Bill" Camp

　WBCP　Papers of Wofford B. Camp, Special Collections, Robert Muldrow Cooper Library, Clemson University

　WCOH　Wofford B. Camp oral history, Regional Oral History Office, Bancroft Library, University of California at Berkeley

EPIGRAPH

vi　**"Somehow sacred"**: Steinbeck, "Some Random and Randy Thoughts on Books" in *The Author Looks at Format,* the American Institute of Graphic Arts, 1951. Reprinted in Steinbeck, *America and Americans and Selected Nonfiction,* 167–171.

CHAPTER ONE: DARK DAYS

1　**"I'm bolshevisky"**: Steinbeck, *TGOW,* 248.

1　**The Big Room**: Details on the Big Room and the Rock of Ages at Carlsbad Caverns are from Ford Sibley, "My Trip through Carlsbad Caverns," Southern Pacific Railroad, 1946; several documents from the Carlsbad Caverns National Park Library, including "Rock of Ages Talk as Given by Thomas Boles," 1942; Bennett T. Gale, "Rock of Ages Ceremony: Favorable and Unfavorable Aspects," 1946; and Hal K. Rothman, "A Historic Resource Study of Carlsbad Caverns and Guadalupe Mountains National Parks and the Surrounding Areas," 1998; as well as author interviews and correspondence from 2005 with Rothman and park rangers Bridget Litten, Bob Hoff, and Dave Hutson.

2　**The Roosevelt Recession**: Economic data are from Steven Mintz, "The Depression of 1937," *Digital History* (2003), http://www.digitalhistory.uh.edu/database/article_display.cfm?HHID=480; Robert VanGiezen and Albert E. Schwenk, "Compensation from before World War I through the Great Depression," Bureau of Labor Statistics, U.S. Department of Labor (2003), http://www.bls.gov/opub/cwc/cm20030124ar03p1.htm; and "About the Great Depression," *Modern American Poetry,* compiled and prepared by Cary Nelson, http://www.english.uiuc.edu/maps/depression/about.htm.

2　**"Luckiest man"**: Gehrig's farewell speech is widely cited. The full text can be found at http://www.lougehrig.com/about/speech.htm.

2　**Must have been Gretchen Knief's**: Details of her vacation were recounted in "California Libraries Are Ahead, Vacation Reveals," *BC,* August 21, 1939. Information on GK herself was gleaned from articles written by and about her; "Gretchen Knief Schenk: A Bibliography," compiled by Vi Harper, Mobile Bay Area Library Association, 1972; *Who's Who in Library Service: A Biographical Directory of Professional Librarians of the United States and Canada, 1955*; and author interviews conducted in 2004 with those who knew her, including Arnold Schenk, Carma Russell Zimmerman Leigh, Mila de Laveaga, Jean Schlottmann, Kathleen Parker, Charles Ebert, Larry Black, Francis Black, and New York State librarian emeritus Joseph F. Schubert.

3   **seventy-one branches:** See "Need for Space at Library Told as Branches Expand," *BC,* May 4, 1939.

3   **So cramped:** See photograph in *BC,* November 6, 1939.

3   **$300,000 bond issue:** Discussed in numerous articles in *BC,* including "Citizens Demand Rapid Action on New Library," May 9, 1939; "Voters Will Decide $300,000 Bond Proposal," November 6, 1939; and "Civil Service, Library Lose," November 8, 1939.

3   **four hundred thousand folks:** Gregory, *American Exodus,* 9–10. The peak years for migration were 1936 and '37, as noted in Schamberger, "Steinbeck and the Migrants," 76, citing a report of the Select Committee to Investigate the Interstate Migration of Destitute Citizens.

3   **Human tumbleweeds:** Gregory, *American Exodus,* 30.

3   **"Misery, Squalor, Disease":** *The Providence Sunday Journal,* May 21, 1939, DBMA. California newspapers, of course, also covered the migrant crisis closely. Among the most notable efforts were a twelve-part series in the *SFC* by Robert E. Girvin, which ran in March 1937; a five-part series in the *LAT* by Ray Zeman, published in July 1937; and a six-part series in the *SFN* by Theodore Smith, printed in February 1938. (These articles are among those cited in Schamberger, "Steinbeck and the Migrants," 91–94.)

3   **"Pitched their voices":** Walter Davenport, "California, Here We Come," *Collier's,* August 10, 1935, 10, DBMA.

4   **Population swell:** Stein, *California and the Dust Bowl Migration,* 46–47.

4   **Still living in slums:** Survey of Kern County Migratory Labor Problem, Supplementary Report As of July 1, 1939, Kern County Health Department, copies found in CMcWP and DBMA.

4   **"Drunks, chiselers":** Cited in the Kern County Health Department survey, copies found in CMcWP and DBMA.

4   **"Negroes and Okies":** From 2006 author interview with Okie poet Dorothy Rose, who cites the sign in her poem "Bakersfield" in *Dustbowl Okie Exodus,* 46–47. Also cited by CMcW in "California Pastoral," *Antioch Review,* March 1942, which is reprinted in Donohue, *A Casebook on The Grapes of Wrath,* 46. Recalled, as well, by CMcW in Terkel, *Hard Times,* 243. Haslam, *The Other California,* 105, says the theater sign used even harsher words: "Niggers and Okies Upstairs." But Haslam, one of the great chroniclers of the valley, didn't come of age in Kern County until the 1950s, and so I went with Rose's and CMcW's more contemporaneous accounts. Humes, *Mean Justice,* 26, says, "Signs sprang up in Bakersfield restaurants and other public places, proclaiming, 'No Niggers or Okies,' but I couldn't find anybody who remembered that firsthand. Haslam told me, "I heard that there were 'No Niggers or Okies' signs in a few businesses, but only a few. There was, however, inarguably that attitude even when I was grow-

ing up in the 1940s and '50s. Being categorized with blacks really angered Okies (who were often more southern than western in their attitudes)."

5 **Made a travesty:** See, among others, Arax and Wartzman, *The King of California;* Daniel, *Bitter Harvest;* McWilliams, *Factories in the Field.*

5 **"Manufacture it":** Quoted in Watkins, *The Hungry Years,* 341.

5 **Caste system:** Daniel, *Bitter Harvest,* 17.

5 **Ethnic parade:** McWilliams, *Factories in the Field,* 103–133; Arax and Wartzman, *King of California,* 92–93; Johnson, Haslam, and Dawson, *The Great Central Valley,* 47.

5 **"Beasts of the field":** Street, *Beasts of the Field,* xviii.

5 **Best-seller list:** *TGOW* showed up on the *LAT* best-seller list as early as April 23, 1939, just after its April 14 publication. Also on the list: *All This, and Heaven Too* by Rachel Field, *Tree of Liberty* by Elizabeth Page, *Disputed Passage* by Lloyd C. Douglas, and *Seasoned Timber* by Dorothy Canfield. Several sources, including the California Legacy Project at Santa Clara University, say *TGOW* was the best-selling book of 1939. It was also one of the top 10 for 1940, according to W. J. Weatherby, "Mighty Words of Wrath," *Guardian,* April 17, 1989. French, *A Companion to The Grapes of Wrath,* 106, also says the book was the top best seller of 1939 and one of the 10 best of 1940 (though the publication date is listed incorrectly as March 14).

5 **Already busy with the film version:** The contract between JS and Twentieth Century-Fox for the film version of *TGOW* is dated April 24, 1939, FOX.

5 **Soon record his ode:** Guthrie would record the bulk of his "Dust Bowl Ballads," including "Tom Joad Part 1" and "Tom Joad Part 2," in April 1940 in New York City.

5 **"Unforgettable experience":** See Roosevelt, *My Day,* 39. Her June 28, 1939, newspaper column on *TGOW* is reprinted in French, 131, and is cited, as well, in Donohue, 73. Also see "Mrs. Roosevelt Tours Mecca of Migrants: Inspects California Camps and Says Steinbeck Told Truth," *New York Times,* April 3, 1940.

6 **"Them big farmers":** Steinbeck, *TGOW,* 381.

6 **"500,000 Americans":** Radio address at the White House Conference on Children in a Democracy, January 19, 1940.

6 **"Grapes of Wrath" parties:** As noted in a Committee to Aid Agricultural Workers bulletin, April 1, 1940, CMcWP.

6 **Broadway actors:** As noted in Agricultural Bulletin, National Council to Aid Agricultural Workers, August 1940, CMcWP.

6 **"Meet the Joad Family":** *North of the River News,* September 22, 1939.

6 **"Joad Family in Kern":** An article by Virgil E. Combs, January 2, 1940, DW.

6 **"What's Being Done":** Article by CMcW, *New Republic,* September 20, 1939.

6 **"Joads on Strike":** Article by CMcW, *Nation,* November 4, 1939.

6 **"Joad Cap":** Noted in Bryant Simon and William Deverell, "Come Back, Tom Joad: Thoughts on a California Dreamer," *California History* 4, (Winter 2000–2001): 182.

6 **"Rock of Ages":** Words by Augustus M. Toplady; music by Thomas Hastings.

6 **"Troubled and confused"**: Gretchen Knief, *BC,* April 13, 1939.

6 **Route 66:** This would have been Knief's most likely route back to California from New Mexico.

6 **"Like bugs":** Steinbeck, *TGOW,* 249.

6 **Mother Road:** Steinbeck, *TGOW,* 151. It was JS who gave the road this name, according to the National Historic Route 66 Federation.

7 **Having briefly met:** 2004 author interview with Mila de Laveaga, who was on GK's staff at the time. She recalled that GK was busy the day JS came into the library, so she had one of her colleagues escort him to Arvin, where he was planning to do research.

7 **"Major creative writers":** Gretchen Knief, *BC,* April 13, 1939.

7 **Classical revival:** Details on the architecture and history of the building are from McDevitt, *Courthouses of California,* 204; *BC,* November 28, 1953; KCBS.

7 **Bellies pressed:** Photos of the supervisors at work can be found at KCM.

7 **Meeting of Monday:** All details of the proceedings are from KCBS.

8 **Blindsiding:** Supervisor C. W. Harty described it this way to GK, according to GK's September 2, 1939, letter to California State librarian Mabel Gillis, BML.

8 **Whereas:** The resolution can be found in KCBS; BML; Lingo, "Forbidden Fruit," 352; and Dunn and Durham, "The Grapes of Wrath in Kern County," 27.

9 **These five men:** The former building contractor was C. W. Wimmer, according to the author's 2004 interview with his grandson Charles Wimmer and his obituary in the November 15, 1948, *BC.* The bank teller was Roy Woollomes, according to his obituary in the May 12, 1964, *BC* and a 2005 author interview with his son, James. The grocer was C. W. Harty, according to the February 5, 1938, *BC.* The newspaper publisher was Abel, and the pharmacist was Lavin.

10 **"Bestial way":** United Press dispatch from Kansas City, August 18, 1939, *BC.*

10 **"Once in a while":** July 10, 1939, letter from Alexander Galt of the Buffalo Public Library to Ralph Munn, director of the Carnegie Library of Pittsburgh, BPL. The situation in Buffalo is noted in, among other places, French, *Companion to The Grapes of Wrath,* 130.

10 **Trenton:** As noted in correspondence found in BPL, which also pointed out what was happening in Detroit. The situation in San Francisco was noted by Samuel Sillen in his essay "Censoring The Grapes of Wrath," *New Masses,* September 12, 1939, reprinted in Donohue, *Casebook on The Grapes of Wrath,* 3–7.

10 **East St. Louis:** *St. Louis Star-Times,* November 14, 1939; *Publisher's Weekly,* November 25, 1939.

10 **U.S.S. *Tennessee*:** Donohue, *Casebook on The Grapes of Wrath,* 7.

10 **Postal Service:** According to Rep. Lyle Boren, *Appendix to the Congressional Record,* January 10, 1940.

10 **"The forerunner":** *BC,* August 21, 1939.

10 **Taken aback:** August 29, 1939, letter from GK to California State librarian Mabel Gillis, BML. GK's interaction with Abel when she went upstairs is laid out in the same letter.

11 **Washington had been cutting:** In *American Exodus*, 80, Gregory notes that the federal government revamped its relief programs in 1935, closing down the Federal Transient Service and moving some responsibilities to the states; and in *Olson's New Deal*, 80–81, Burke points out that the California State Relief Administration caseload during 1939 swelled, "chiefly because SRA had to take over more and more persons dropped from federal relief as WPA appropriations were reduced by Congress."

11 **"Stressed the immorality":** See Tim Kappel, "Trampling Out the Vineyards," *California History* (Fall 1982). Also cited in Rick Heredia, "What 'Wrath' Had Wrought," *BC*, April 23, 1989.

11 **"Successful struggle":** "The Joads Organize," Agricultural Bulletin, National Committee to Aid Agricultural Workers, November 15, 1939, CMcWP.

11 **Tourist travel:** *KH*, August 20, 1939.

11 **"Stands to reason":** *BC*, August 21, 1939.

11 **"One of the best":** August 20, 1934, dispatch from Lorena Hickok to Aubrey W. Williams, as reprinted in Lowitt and Beasley, *One Third of a Nation*, 313–314. Also see "Kern Growers Provide Housing for Workers," *BC*, August 24, 1939.

12 **Had made sure:** *BC*, July 25, 1939; author interview with former Kern County librarian Mila de Laveaga.

12 **Free medical care:** Stein, *California and the Dust Bowl Migration*, 54; also discussed by Lingo, "Forbidden Fruit," 354–355; Dunn and Durham, "The Grapes of Wrath in Kern County," 37; and *Role of the Kern General Hospital in Kern County: July 1, 1938–June 30, 1939*, Kern County Department of Public Health, CMcWP. The term "most enlightened" is Stein's and is also cited by Lingo as well as Dunn and Durham.

12 **"Squalor, starvation":** *KH*, August 20, 1939.

12 **"Extremely sorry":** Correspondence found in BML.

12 **"A good fight":** August 29, 1939, letter from GK to California State librarian Mabel Gillis, BML.

12 **"Idealist and a realist":** Author interview with Mila de Laveaga.

14 **"Tedious plain":** Brewer, *Up and Down California in 1860–1864*, 202.

14 **Llano:** Johnson, Haslam, and Dawson, *Great Central Valley*, 125.

14 **"So empty":** Johnson, Haslam, and Dawson, *Great Central Valley*, 133. The writer of the book, Gerald Haslam, is a Kern County native. (Stephen Johnson was the editor and designer of the book; Robert Dawson handled the photography.)

15 **Four thousand feet:** The Tejon Pass is just above this mark.

15 **"Supports no man":** Austin, *The Land of Little Rain*, 3.

15 **"The morning glow":** Steinbeck, *TGOW*, 292–293.

16 **Forbidding swampland:** See Johnson, Haslam, and Dawson, *Great Central Valley*, 125–148; Arax and Wartzman, *King of California*, 46–49.

16 **"More forlorn":** Robinson, *The Story of Kern County*, 12.

16 **Baker settled:** Ibid, 25.

16 **Thirty Indians:** Ibid, 26.

16 **By 1878:** "Homes in California, Prospectus of the Kern Valley Colony," KCM.

16 "Grand Khan": For details on Haggin and his empire, see Igler, *Industrial Cowboys*, 101–102, 215; Worster, *Rivers of Empire*, 103–104; and Arax and Wartzman, *King of California*, 80.

17 "Greatest farm": Worster, *Rivers of Empire*, 104.

17 Shamelessly manipulated: Ibid., 103–104; Igler, *Industrial Cowboys*, 102; Berg, *A History of Kern County Land Company*, 8–9.

17 Four hundred thousand acres: Worster, *Rivers of Empire*, 103.

17 Carleton E. Watkins: Street, *A Kern County Diary*, 1–24.

17 "Wild and woolly": Ibid.,13. Regarding the selling off of land, also see Berg, *History of Kern County Land Company*, 19–21.

18 Began snapping up: The pace of Miller's land acquisition in Kern is reported in Igler, *Industrial Cowboys*, 97.

18 1.25 million: Ibid., 4.

18 122,000 head: Ibid., 145.

18 Double-H brand: Ibid., 83.

18 1,200 laborers: Ibid., 123. For more on what it was like for Miller's workers, also see Street, *Beasts of the Field*, 551–552.

18 "The Cattle King": Edward F. Treadwell's 1931 hagiography of Miller is titled *The Cattle King*.

18 Picture of Miller: Igler, *Industrial Cowboys*, 163.

18 Lux hobnobbed: Ibid., 17.

18 Smoking and swearing: Arax and Wartzman, *King of California*, 74–76.

18 "Burned up": Igler, *Industrial Cowboys*, 99.

19 *Lux v. Haggin*: Regarding the case and its aftermath, including all the direct quotations used, see Igler, *Industrial Cowboys*, 103–112; and Worster, *Rivers of Empire*, 104–108. Also see Berg, *History of Kern County Land Company*, 8–15.

19 Miller died: Igler, *Industrial Cowboys*, 180.

19 Haggin had passed: See "Great Tract In Kern Will Be Thrown Open," *LAT*, October 21, 1914.

19 Since the 1860s: Latta, *Black Gold in the Joaquin*, 25.

19 "Loud as a cannon": Ibid., 248–249.

19 Began in earnest: Ibid., 26–27; "The Kern County Oil Industry," San Joaquin Geological Society (2002).

19 A bona fide gusher: Berg, *History of Kern County Land Company*, 36–38. The Ten Section Field was discovered in 1936.

19 Eighty million barrels: Data from the San Joaquin Geological Society.

19 Nine thousand wells: "Kern County, California: The Land of Diversified Opportunity," Kern County Chamber of Commerce (1937), KCM.

20 Furnishing the federal government: Turner, *White Gold Comes to California*, 42.

20 Nile Delta: Arax and Wartzman, *King of California*, 119.

20 Japanese spinning mills: In *White Gold Comes to California*, Turner, 80, notes that by the late 1930s, it was estimated that 89 percent of San Joaquin Valley cotton was being sold to Japanese mills.

20   "**Industrial cavalcade**": "Kern County, California: The Land of Diversified Opportunity," Kern County Chamber of Commerce (1937), KCM.

20   **Strung up and hanged**: Boyd, Ludeke, and Rump, *Inside Historic Kern*, 194.

20   **Poem penned in 1925**: "Salutation" from Blodget, *Little Dramas of Old Bakersfield*, 9.

21   **Steinbeck had set out**: Benson, *True Adventures of John Steinbeck*, 411.

21   "**Always wondered**: As quoted in John C. Rice, "John Steinbeck Turns His Wrath on *The Grapes of Wrath* Publicity," included in Fensch, *Conversations with John Steinbeck*, 15. Also quoted in St. Pierre, *John Steinbeck: The California Years*, 100.

21   "**Nuts about fairs**": Benson, *True Adventures of John Steinbeck*, 411.

21   **You could eyeball**: Details gleaned from the *Official Guide Book, Golden Gate International Exposition on San Francisco Bay* (1939).

21   "**One big toy**": Fensch, *Conversations with John Steinbeck*, 16.

22   **Which occupied a building**: *Official Guide Book, Golden Gate International Exposition on San Francisco Bay* (1939), 67.

22   **Had paid $25,000**: Records of the Kern County Chamber of Commerce.

22   "**Bakersfiel'**": Steinbeck, *TGOW*, 382.

22   **Radio station KFI**: Transcript located in WBCP.

22   "**Employed by Di Giorgio**": TC report for week ending March 21, 1936.

23   **Fresh fruit grower**: See LF, Part 48.

23   **A major fund-raiser**: As reflected in various AF financial documents, WBCP; LF, Part 48; *RO*, January 5, 1940. Among other things, Di Giorgio raised money for a special AF public-relations fund.

23   **Its state treasurer**: A year-by-year listing of all AF officers can be found in Chambers, *California Farm Organizations*, 212–215.

23   "**The Farmers' Association**": Steinbeck, *TGOW*, 378.

23   **Had emerged**: Chambers, *California Farm Organizations*, 39–45; Orlando J. Wiebe, "Report on Associated Farmers of California Inc.: Its Structure, Aims and Activities," University of California at Berkeley political science paper (1938), CMcW; "Development of Associated Farmers of California Inc.," PST; "The Associated Farmers," *Propaganda Analysis*, August 1, 1939, CMcWP; "Who Are the Associated Farmers," *Survey Graphic*, September 1939, CMcWP.

23   **One crop after another**: Jamieson, *Labor Unionism in American Agriculture*, 427.

23   **Fifteen thousand pickers**: Ibid. The 1933 cotton strike has been widely covered. See, for instance: Arax and Wartzman, *King of California*, 137–157; Daniel, *Bitter Harvest*, 167–221; Weber, *Dark Sweat, White Gold;* Taylor, *On the Ground in the Thirties;* LF, Part 54; SCT.

24   "**Right to grow**": "From Apathy to Action," Annual Report of President Garrison, AF bulletin, December 14, 1937, CMcWP.

24   "**Known radicals**": Annual Report of President Garrison. Specifically, he said, "Our records show that 90 percent of these C.I.O. organizers are known radicals."

24   "**Led by racketeers**": Chambers, *California Farm Organizations*, 62, quoting Holmes Bishop. Stein, *California and the Dust Bowl Migration*, 234, makes the

point that "claiming at first that they opposed only 'communist unions,' the Associated Farmers, when confronted with noncommunist AFL unions, opposed them too." In a February 21, 1940, address to the League of Women Voters in San Diego (found in PB), AF official Philip Bancroft declared that any unionization—even by the AFL—would be "absolutely ruinous to us, as well as to the laborers themselves." He went on to explain: "If the American Federation of Labor, as at present constituted, could control farm unions the matter would be debatable; but even if that organization should form such unions, the chances are that the foreign or native-born radicals would sooner or later get control of them, just as they did with the longshoremen's union." Also see Loftis, *Witnesses to the Struggle,* 94.

24 **Committee for Industrial Organization:** It would become the Congress of Industrial Organizations in 1938.

24 **"Anti-God":** Noted in Orlando J. Wiebe, "Report on Associated Farmers of California Inc.: Its Structure, Aims and Activities," University of California at Berkeley political science paper (1938), CMcW.

24 **Associated Farmers backed:** The group's agenda is captured in Arax and Wartzman, *King of California,* 168. Also see LF, Parts 46, 48, 53, 62; Johns, "Field Workers in California Cotton," 73–98.

24 **Incited a mob:** Mooney and Majka, *Farmers' and Farm Workers' Movements,* 133–134.

24 **Nightriders attacked:** Jamieson, *Labor Unionism,* 125–127.

24 **Stockton canneries:** Ibid., 149–152; Chambers, *California Farm Organizations,* 70–72.

24 **Fifty people:** *LAT,* April 26, 1937.

24 **"Bad boys":** Chambers, *California Farm Organizations,* 222, cites the *SFC* of December 8, 1938, quoting an unnamed AF official.

25 **"A silk glove":** Quoted in Chambers, *California Farm Organizations,* 49–50.

25 **Well regarded:** WBC's life story is recounted in Briggs and Cauthen, *The Cotton Man,* albeit in the most obsequious terms.

25 **Fifty thousand miles:** Briggs and Cauthen, *Cotton Man,* 62.

25 **Admonish his daughter-in-law:** 2004 author interview with Bill Camp Jr.

25 **"Stand up close":** 2004 author interview with Don Camp.

26 **He was hardened:** Author interview with Bill Camp Jr.

26 **"I have faith":** WBC, undated interview by Pat Killoran, transcript in CMcWP.

26 **Bagged 353 pounds:** Ibid.

26 **"I understand":** Ibid.

26 **Railroad car:** Details from author interviews with Bill Camp Jr. and Don Camp; WCOH.

26 **"No discomfort":** WCOH.

26 **"Very happy":** WBC, interview by Pat Killoran.

26 **"I don't think Dad":** Author interview with Bill Camp Jr.

27 **"Mammy" and "Pickaninny":** Author interview with Don Camp.

27 **"Battle Hymn":** See Benson, *True Adventures of John Steinbeck,* 387. Also see Schamberger, "Steinbeck and the Migrants," 11.

27   **Ribier and Thompson:** *BC*, August 18, 1939.

27   **He directed:** Noted in an April 22, 1959, letter from Emory Gay Hoffman to John Edward Schamberger, BML.

27   **Just how generous:** As described in the *Arvin Tiller*, August 25, 1939. The August 20, 1939, *KH* notes that the film "shows familiar scenes of Kern County agriculture, commerce and wealth and is designed to eradicate a possible mental image of Kern County as a land of squalor, starvation and despair."

27   **Six-thousand-word testimonial:** April 22, 1959, letter from Hoffman to John Edward Schamberger, BML. Also cited in Schamberger, "Steinbeck and the Migrants," 64–65. Hoffman explained that the six-thousand-word draft of the story was removed from his office and lost, but "from the notes we published a short movie."

27   **Included shots:** As noted and depicted in *Look* magazine, October 24, 1939.

28   **Spent $6.72:** Ibid.

28   **Prairie schooner:** Ibid.

28   **A fast talker:** Details on Hoffman are from author interviews conducted in 2004 with Robert Bovee and Jimmy Radoumis, who worked with Hoffman at the Kern County Chamber of Commerce.

28   **Hoffman posed:** *SFC*, August 13, 1939.

28   **"A nickel raise":** Meister and Loftis, *A Long Time Coming*, 35. This echoes dialogue straight from Steinbeck, *TGOW*, 382–383: "A red is any son-of-a-bitch that wants 30 cents an hour when we're payin' twenty-five!"

29   **"Exceptionalism":** Lipset and Marks, *It Didn't Happen Here*, 22–24. Also see Denning, *The Cultural Front*, 432; Peeler, *Hope Among Us Yet*, 40, 107.

29   **FDR's skillful hijacking:** Lipset and Marks, *It Didn't Happen Here*, 74–76, 208–210, 219, 232. Also see Dyson, *Red Harvest*, 116–119, 202; and Pells, *Radical Visions and American Dreams*, 80.

30   **"All generalizations":** Chase, *A New Deal*, 251–252.

30   **"Karl Marx" stogies:** Lipset and Marks, *It Didn't Happen Here*, 120.

30   **Milwaukee in 1939:** Ibid., 119.

30   **Between 1918 and 1940:** Ibid., 56.

30   **"Grand American cranks":** Mitchell, *The Campaign of the Century*, xvi.

30   **In a pamphlet:** A copy of the cover is reprinted in Mitchell, *Campaign of the Century*; Coodley, *The Land of Orange Groves and Jails*, 201; and Arthur, *Radical Innocent*.

30   **Bellamy's utopian novel:** Coodley, *Land of Orange Groves*, 201. See also Mattson, *Upton Sinclair and the Other American Century*, 173.

30   **Putting private factories:** The specifics of Sinclair's EPIC plan are laid out in Mitchell, *Campaign of the Century*, 22–23; Arthur, *Radical Innocent*, 254–259; Watkins, *Hungry Years*, 248–251; Mattson, *Upton Sinclair*, 173–174; and Newton, *Justice for All*, 78.

31   **Won more votes:** Mitchell, *Campaign of the Century*, 7.

31   **"Nearest thing":** Lipset and Marks, *It Didn't Happen Here*, 209–210. Despite that, the Communist Party lashed out at Sinclair, characterizing him as a "Social-Fascist." (See Klehr, *The Heyday of American Communism*, 173–181.)

31 "Strange twist": Newton, *Justice for All*, 83–84.

31 The White House: After a one-on-one meeting with FDR, Sinclair came away with the impression that the president would back EPIC, but the president abandoned him in the end. See Schlesinger, *The Politics of Upheaval*, 120; Mitchell, *Campaign of the Century*, 471; Arthur, *Radical Innocent*, 277; Watkins, *Hungry Years*, 250; and Kennedy, *Freedom from Fear*, 226.

31 "Won't stop shiverin'": Mitchell, *Campaign of the Century*, 513–514.

31 Sinclair lost: The final tally is noted in Burke, *Olson's New Deal for California*, 4; and Arthur, *Radical Innocent*, 277.

32 "Rouse a flicker": Burke, *Olson's New Deal*, 23.

32 Assumed leadership: Olson's background and policies are detailed in Burke, *Olson's New Deal*, 4–13.

32 "Privileged interests": Burke, *Olson's New Deal*, 11.

32 "Watch Your Step!": Ibid., 29.

32 Harper Knowles: The *LAT* of October 30, 1938, said Knowles was on leave from his AF position.

32 Wearing pinstripes: Photo from Capitol Hill in *LAT*, October 25, 1938.

32 Denouncing all sorts: "Educators Deny Red Charges," *LAT*, October 26, 1938.

32 "Easy to smear": Bentley, *Thirty Years of Treason*, xvii.

33 Shirley Temple: The childhood actress was one of six movie stars listed as having "loaned their names to Communism" by sending greetings to the French newspaper *Ce Soir*, which was said to be Communist-owned, *LAT*, August 22, 1938. Also see JS's essay "A Primer on the '30s," *Esquire*, June 1960, reprinted in Steinbeck, *America and Americans*, 17–31.

33 "I am sorry": Burke, *Olson's New Deal*, 30.

33 Nearly 59 percent: Ibid., 33.

33 "Human needs": As quoted by various newspapers throughout the state. See, for instance, "Olson Pledges Self Help Plan," *FB*, November 9, 1938. Also quoted in Burke, *Olson's New Deal*, 36.

33 Tom Mooney: This episode is recounted in Burke, *Olson's New Deal*, 48–58.

33 Liberal martyrs: Denning, *Cultural Front*, 66.

33 In manacles: Newton, *Justice for All*, 101.

33 "Not unmindful": Gentry, *Frame-Up*, 422–423.

34 "California finally elected": Burke, *Olson's New Deal*, 56.

35 Was hospitalized: Ibid., 60.

35 Tried to appoint: Ibid., 63.

35 Suspected Communist: Bridges underwent two failed deportation attempts to his native Australia between 1938 and 1945 for his alleged affiliation with the Communist Party. Transcripts of the proceedings are found at the Harvard Law School Library.

35 Lost a number: Olson's troubles are covered in detail in Burke, *Olson's New Deal*, 61–77.

35 "Dickie": His shenanigans are covered in Burke, *Olson's New Deal*, 60–61.

35 **"Tom, Dick and Harry":** Gentry, *Frame-Up,* 429; Burke, *Olson's New Deal,* 149.

35 **Carey McWilliams:** His background was gleaned from Richardson, *American Prophet;* McWilliams, *The Education of Carey McWilliams;* and Loftis, *Witnesses to the Struggle.*

36 **Began writing:** Richardson, *American Prophet,* 73–78.

36 **The *American Citizen:*** Copies of the paper can be found in CMcWP. Also cited in Starr, *Endangered Dreams,* 183.

36 **"I have worked":** December 26, 1937, letter from CMcW to Adamic, CMcWP.

36 **Internecine conflicts:** See, for instance, Lipset and Marks, *It Didn't Happen Here,* 208.

37 **"Cause more trouble":** AF, February 3, 1936, organization memorandum, LF, Part 62.

37 **"A small c":** Denning, *Cultural Front,* xviii. Also see Diggins, *The Rise and Fall of the American Left,* 174.

37 **"Farmer fascism":** Loftis, *Witnesses to the Struggle,* 142.

37 **He toured:** Richardson, *American Prophet,* 78–79; McWilliams, *Education of Carey McWilliams,* 75; Loftis, *Witnesses to the Struggle,* 141–143.

37 **"Little imagination":** McWilliams, *Education of Carey McWilliams,* 75.

37 **Spirited magazine:** Denning, *Cultural Front,* 18.

37 **"Methods of Marx and Lenin":** This and the other quotations are cited in Richardson, *American Prophet,* 79.

38 **Pike claimed:** Roy M. Pike, "Facts From the Fields," El Solyo Ranch, Vernalis, California, November 1939, CMcWP.

38 **"Collective agriculture":** McWilliams, *Factories in the Field,* 324–325.

38 **"Life-or-death threat":** December 3, 1939, telegram to WBC from Harold Angier, president of AF regional district no. 3, WBCP.

38 **George Soule:** See Soule, *The Coming American Revolution.*

39 **In January:** Richardson, *American Prophet,* 93.

39 **Been moribund:** See "Migratory Labor in California," State Relief Administration of California (1936).

39 **Inserting himself:** Richardson, *American Prophet,* 93–98; also reflected in numerous documents in CMcWP.

39 **"Cover to cover":** August 2, 1939, letter from J. W. Hawkins to Culbert Olson, CMcWP.

39 **Barely knew each other:** McWilliams, *Education of Carey McWilliams,* 78. Also see CMcW, "A Man, a Place and a Time," *American West* 7, no. 3 (1970).

39 **"Here is the data":** Starr, *Endangered Dreams,* 263–64.

40 **"Termites Steinbeck":** *Pacific Rural Press,* July 29, 1939. Also cited in Loftis, *Witnesses to the Struggle,* 163.

40 **Not unheard of:** See, for example, Terkel, *Hard Times,* 35, 123, 423.

40 **Not by toppling:** See, for instance, Ybarra, *Washington Gone Crazy,* 168.

40 **Climbed to six hundred:** The *FB* of August 22, 1939, put the number at five hundred. GK used six hundred, though, in her letter sent to members of the Board of Supervisors dated August 21, 1939, BML.

40 "A rough book": July 28, 1938, letter from JS to EO, his friend and literary agent, as quoted in DeMott, *Working Days*, 154. The full quotation is: "This is a rough book, as rough as the people it deals with. It deals with them in their own terms. So in choosing a publisher (if you must) be sure there are neither moral traits nor reactionary ones, because a revolution is going on and this book is revolutionary. And I wouldn't want it changed to fit the policy of an old house."

CHAPTER TWO: MONDAY

41 "Pa'll be glad": Steinbeck, *TGOW*, 34–35.

41 Six hundred guests: Details on the luncheon and the speakers are from *Pro America*, September 1939, RCMP; *LAT*, August 22, 1939; *SFC*, August 22, 1939; and *BC*, August 22, 1939.

41 Rose Room: Description from a 1922 booklet on the facilities of the hotel, made available by the Central Pacific Railroad Photographic History Museum, http://cprr.org/Museum/Palace_Hotel_SF/.

42 Oil tycoon: A. C. Mattei was head of the Honolulu Oil Corp.

42 Merritt saluted: The speakers' remarks are carried in *Pro America*, September 1939, RCMP.

42 "Ranchers' side": *LAT*, June 29, 1939.

42 Green clothes: Noted in Susan Shillinglaw, "California Answers *The Grapes of Wrath*," an essay found in Hayashi, *John Steinbeck: The Years of Greatness, 1936–1939*, 145-164.

42 "Stimulating lash": Shillinglaw essay in Hayashi, *John Steinbeck: The Years of Greatness*, 148.

42 Born in 1882: Biographical details and other information on RCM's writing career are drawn from RCMP.

43 "Stream of lizards": As described in Bierce, *The Devil's Dictionary*, 121.

43 "The bright view": From the *New York Times* obituary for Ruth Comfort Mitchell, as cited in Shillinglaw essay in Hayashi, *John Steinbeck: The Years of Greatness*, 148.

43 "Superior abilities": September 18, 1900, letter to RCM from W. C. Morrow, RCMP.

43 "Your own plans": September 28, 1900, letter to RCM from W. C. Morrow, RCMP.

44 "Needs no introduction": *The Argonaut*, September 6, 1935, RCMP.

44 "Similarities in perspective": Shillinglaw essay in Hayashi, *John Steinbeck: The Years of Greatness*, 147.

44 Yung See San Fong: Information on the house and on Senator Young is from RCMP, as well as from the National Register of Historic Places, http://www.cr.nps.gov/nr/travel/santaclara/yun.htm. Also see Conaway, *Los Gatos*, 99. For additional information on Proposition 1, see LF, Part 61.

44 Assumed the helm: *LAT*, May 7, 1939.

44 Mitchell announced: *LAT*, June 29, 1939.

44 **"More accurate one"**: "Valley Authoress Prepares Rancher's Reply; Other Side to 'Wrath' Migratory Problem," *San Jose Mercury Herald,* October 1, 1939.

44 **Handbills**: See Steinbeck, *TGOW,* 118, 154, 188–189, 243, 315–316, 364, 377, 520.

45 **No such circulars**: *San Jose Mercury Herald,* October 1, 1939.

45 **"I'm still waiting"**: Noted by CMcW in the "Correspondence" column of the *New Republic,* September 2, 1940, as reprinted in French, *Companion to The Grapes of Wrath,* 140–142.

45 **Mitchell was right**: Starr, *Endangered Dreams,* 259–260. Also see Schamberger, "Steinbeck and the Migrants," 19–21, 51–52, 57.

45 **"Only bring hardship"**: Transcript of radio talk, apparently from 1939, on Oklahoma City's WKY, WBCP.

45 **For inspection**: See French, *Companion to The Grapes of Wrath,* 142.

46 **Official acknowledged**: See the testimony of Henry Strobel, LF, Part 53. Also see Part 52, in which a migrant recounts being part of a group of cotton pickers in Texas who had "some handbills threw at them demanding them to come to California, guaranteeing them they could make more money. . . ." In Dunn and Durham, "The Grapes of Wrath in Kern County," 9, a migrant named Eual Murmduke Stone says of the handbills: "You better believe they exist. They exist cause I seen 'em."

46 **That Steinbeck exaggerated**: See Stein, *California and the Dust Bowl Migration,* 18–22.

46 **Sentence by sentence**: Schuler's analysis is found in RCMP. Notably, Steinbeck's work would continue to be parsed for accuracy decades later. See, for example, Keith Windschuttle, "Steinbeck's myth of the Okies," *New Criterion,* June 2002.

46 **Partisan document**: This was CMcW's exact phrase in "Glory, Glory, California," his July 22, 1940, essay in the *New Republic,* reprinted in French, *Companion to The Grapes of Wrath,* 140–142.

46 **"Energy and thrift"**: Mitchell, *Of Human Kindness,* 5.

46 **"Happy-go-lucky"**: Ibid.

46 **"Been ground down"**: Ibid., 81.

46 **"Willow slim"**: Ibid., 205.

47 **"Not to be confused"**: Review found in RCM's scrapbook, RCMP.

47 **"Compulsory reading"**: Letter to RCM from Grace Stone Woodbridge, RCMP.

47 **"Honey-tongued"**: Confidential News Service, Simon J. Lubin Society Inc., August 1939, CMcWP.

47 **"In limousines"**: "Befurred 'Farmers' Settle Migrant Problem Their Way," *People's World,* August 25, 1939. The *People's World* story is also cited by Samuel Sillen in his essay "Censoring *The Grapes of Wrath,*" *New Masses,* September 12, 1939, which is reprinted in Donohue, *Casebook on The Grapes of Wrath,* 3–7.

47 **"California neighbors"**: Mitchell's speech is reprinted in *Pro America,* September 1939, RCMP.

48 **Mutual Broadcasting**: Noted in *Pro America,* September 1939, RCMP.

48 **Didn't much like**: 2004 author interview with Clell Pruett.

248

48 **"The riot act"**: As quoted in a letter to RCM from Robert Franklin, a publicity man for the AF, August 25, 1939, WBCP.

49 **One bookseller:** *Polk's Bakersfield City Directory,* 1939.

49 **130 copies:** The *KH* of August 24, 1939, noted that Davy's store, The Bookshop, had received a shipment of 125 copies of the book on Monday, August 21, and also had five copies in its "circulating library" and thirty requests on file.

49 **$2.75:** As widely advertised.

49 **Loaf of bread:** It fetched about eight cents, according to Bureau of Labor Statistics data.

49 **"Want to read":** August 26, 1939, letter to GK from Mrs. O. S. Hughes, BML.

49 **Inventory of forty-eight:** A listing of how many books were sent where can be found in BML. Other reports, including the *FB* of August 22, 1939, put the Kern County Library's total number of copies of *TGOW* at sixty.

49 **"Thrilled to receive":** November 22, 1939, letter to GK from Minerva Waterman.

49 **League of American Writers:** August 23, 1939, letter to the Board of Supervisors, KCBS.

49 **Vice president:** Folsom, *Days of Anger, Days of Hope,* 67. As discussed in the book, the FBI considered the league a major "Communist front organization," and there were certainly strong ties between the league and the Communist Party. Also see Keith Windschuttle, "Steinbeck's myth of the Okies," *New Criterion,* June 2002.

49 **National Council:** August 25, 1939, letter to the Board of Supervisors, KCBS.

49 **"Obscene in the extreme":** *BC,* August 22, 1939.

50 **"Debauches the imagination":** Boyer, *Purity in Print,* 21.

50 **Only one book:** Sova, *Banned Books: Literature Suppressed on Social Grounds,* 275. The local prosecutor in Detroit banned the Hemingway book.

50 **"Abused far more":** Boyer, *Purity in Print,* 250.

50 **Ultimately be seen:** See Boyer, *Purity in Print,* 249–274. There were exceptions, of course. Among them: Sinclair Lewis's *Elmer Gantry* was banned from the U.S. mails in 1931. In 1934, the New York Society for the Suppression of Vice brought a complaint of obscenity against Viking for publishing Erskine Caldwell's *God's Little Acre.* And Jim Tully's *Ladies in the Parlor,* published in 1935, also became the subject of an obscenity case. (For details, see Sova, *Banned Books: Literature Suppressed on Social Grounds;* Sova, *Banned Books: Literature Suppressed on Sexual Grounds.*)

50 **Aesop was hurled:** "Banned Books: 585 BC to 2003 AD," a list compiled by the Seattle Public Library.

51 **Pope Paul IV:** Bald, *Banned Books: Literature Suppressed on Religious Grounds,* xiv. The index would remain in effect until 1966.

51 **Comstock Law:** "Fact Sheet on Sex and Censorship," Free Expression Policy Project, NYU School of Law, http://www.fepproject.org/factsheets/sexandcensorship.html.

51 **Around the country:** Boyer, *Purity in Print,* 5.

51 "Pestiferous evil": Ibid., 13.

51 90 percent of the time: Ibid., 10.

51 "Immoral tendency": Ibid., 31.

51 "Lustful" Huns: Ibid., 53–57.

51 "Borderland" literature: Ibid., 52.

52 New generation: Ibid., 70–71.

52 "Into opposing camps": Ibid., 101–102.

52 Imbroglio unfolded: Details on this episode are from Jules Tygiel's foreword to Sinclair, *Oil!;* Boyer, *Purity in Print,* 186–187; Karolides, *Banned Books: Literature Suppressed on Political Grounds,* 372–377; Arthur, *Radical Innocent,* 211–212; and Mattson, *Upton Sinclair,* 142.

52 "Seashore this summer": From a piece that Sinclair wrote for the *New Yorker,* which is reprinted in Karolides, Burress, and Kean, *Censored Books,* xxiii–xxvi.

53 The Germans: Boyer, *Purity in Print,* 268.

53 Top-hatted gent: Ibid., 250.

54 Old Saxon words: Ibid., 258.

54 "No longer taboo": Ernst and Lindey, *The Censor Marches On,* 21.

55 Diego Rivera's mural: Green and Karolides, *Encyclopedia of Censorship,* 469–470.

55 David Alfaro Siqueiros: Information from the Santa Barbara Museum of Art, http://www.olvera-street.com/html/siqueiros_mural.html.

55 *Cradle Will Rock*: Denning, *Cultural Front,* 287. "Dangerous" was the word used by Hallie Flanagan, director of the Federal Theatre. Also see Terkel, *Hard Times,* 365.

55 *Pins and Needles*: Denning, *Cultural Front,* 302–303.

55 Trotsky's works: Karolides, *Banned Books: Literature Suppressed on Political Grounds,* 427.

55 Harold Rugg: Karolides, Burress, and Kean, *Censored Books,* xiii.

55 "In vogue now": Moore, *The Novels of John Steinbeck,* 96.

55 Paine and Marx: Steinbeck, *TGOW,* 194.

56 "And the great owners": Ibid., 306.

56 "Using bad words": Ibid., 30.

56 Three whores: Ibid., 124.

56 One-legged gal: Ibid., 231.

56 A little "screwin'": Ibid., 28–29.

56 "The dirtiest language": Quoted in Marsh L. Weisiger, "The Reception of The Grapes of Wrath in Oklahoma: A Reappraisal," *The Chronicles of Oklahoma* 70 (Winter 1991–1992): 394–415.

57 Steinbeck's litmus test: The quotations by JS are noted in "Steinbeck and the Wrath of the Censors," an outline of a speech given by Cindy Mediavilla of UCLA's Department of Information Studies, as part of the Steinbeck centennial. Also quoted in Benson, *True Adventures of John Steinbeck,* 389–390.

57 Otis coaxed: Parini, *John Steinbeck: A Biography,* 217; Benson, *True Adventures of John Steinbeck,* 389; St. Pierre, *John Steinbeck: The California Years,* 96.

57 Was the end: The ending of *TGOW* has been much discussed by scholars as it relates to the Bible and religion, the role of women, and the meaning of community.

For a taste of this, see Ditsky, *Critical Essays on Steinbeck's The Grapes of Wrath*, 116–124; and Theodore Pollock, "On the Ending of *The Grapes of Wrath*," and Jules Chametzky, "The Ambivalent Endings of *The Grapes of Wrath*," both reprinted in Donohue, *Casebook on The Grapes of Wrath*, 182–184 and 232–244, respectively.

57   **Related years earlier:** Benson, *True Adventures of John Steinbeck*, 47–48; Benson, *Looking for Steinbeck's Ghost*, 71–72.

57   **"A punch point":** From Benson's interview with Frank Kilkenny, tape recording in JB.

57   **"Survival symbol":** January 16, 1939, letter from JS to his editor, Pascal Covici, as quoted in Benson, *True Adventures of John Steinbeck*, 390. Also quoted in St. Pierre, *John Steinbeck: The California Years*, 96–97.

57   **Francis Spellman:** Starr, *Endangered Dreams*, 258.

58   **"Black, infernal creation":** *Appendix to the Congressional Record*, January 10, 1940. Also cited in, among others, Starr, *Endangered Dreams*, 257; Benson, *True Adventures of John Steinbeck*, 418–419; Martin Staples Shockley, "The Reception of *The Grapes of Wrath* in Oklahoma," reprinted in French, *Companion to The Grapes of Wrath*, 125–126, and in Donohue, *Casebook on The Grapes of Wrath*, 58–59.

58   **"Make a cuss word":** 2004 author interview with Mara Daniel.

58   **"A prude":** Author interview with Bill Camp Jr.

58   **"Bring the blushes":** Donohue, *Casebook on The Grapes of Wrath*, 73.

58   **"Half-way apologetic":** Quoted in "Steinbeck and the Wrath of the Censors," an outline of a speech given by Cindy Mediavilla of UCLA's Department of Information Studies, as part of the Steinbeck centennial.

58   **"Fornication is the keynote":** August 22, 1939, letter from Alexander Galt of the Buffalo Public Library to *Dallas Morning News* president G. B. Dealey, BPL.

58   **"Fact of the matter":** From Joseph Henry Jackson, "Why Steinbeck Wrote *The Grapes of Wrath*," *Booklets For Bookmen*, Limited Editions Club, DW; JSP.

59   **Relatively tame fare:** For a revealing portrait of America in 1939, see Peters, *Five Days in Philadelphia*, 3–15.

59   **Nude Ranch:** Information from the Virtual Museum of the City of San Francisco, http://www.sfmuseum.net/bio/rand.html.

59   **"Coarse in spots":** See Roosevelt, *My Day*, 39–40.

59   **Cries against censorship:** Correspondence in KCBS. Also see "Oil Workers in Move to Rap Book Action," *BC*, August 24, 1939.

60   **Sons of a California rancher:** Family history and details on the brothers are gleaned from author interviews conducted in 2005 with Barbara Brown, Stanley Abel's niece; Brown's brother-in-law, Harry Perry; Pattie Zeigler, stepdaughter of Ralph Abel; and Linda Franson, daughter of Lindley Abel. There was also a fifth brother, Bob, who lived in Texas, as well as two sisters.

60   **"Steinbeck was right":** Author interview with Linda Franson.

60   **Foment "civil war":** Quotes are from Edson Abel's article "The Communist Menace to Agriculture," *Pacific Rural Press*, February 3, 1934.

60   **"Aiding and abetting"**: "California's Present Farm Labor Problems," 1934 radio talk by Edson Abel, PST.

60   **"Paid propagandists"**: *Pacific Rural Press*, February 3, 1934.

61   **Laying the groundwork**: Edson Abel's role is detailed in "Development of Associated Farmers of California, Inc." and other documents found in PST.

61   **Boxed competitively**: Mentions of Ralph Abel's exploits in the ring can be found in issues of the *LAT* from May and June 1936.

61   **"Wonderful Communism was"**: Author interview with Barbara Brown.

61   **"Abels Clash"**: *BC*, March 14, 1939.

61   **"Corporate interests"**: *BC*, May 9, 1939. Also see *RO*, June 1939.

61   **"Corporate stooges"**: *OP*, August 31, 1939. Also cited in Lingo, "Forbidden Fruit," 359.

62   **Had a hand**: At the time, Stanley Abel denied that the AF had a direct hand in the resolution. But WBC's comments to the *BC*, published the morning of August 21, leaves little doubt that the AF knew a ban was about to be implemented in Kern County: "We hope [Kansas City's] action will be the forerunner of a widespread denouncement against the book before schools open and our boys and girls find such filthy material on the shelves of our public libraries." What's more, in WCOH, WBC uses the phrase "*we* tried" (emphasis by author) when talking about aspects of the ban. In "Forbidden Fruit," 359, Lingo also concludes that Abel had an "alliance with the Associated Farmers."

62   **Born in 1891**: Basic biographical details from *Who's Who in Kern County, 1941*. Also see Rick Heredia, "What 'Wrath' Had Wrought," April 23, 1989, *BC*.

63   **"Beer was cheaper"**: Humes, *Mean Justice*, 24.

63   **Blacks weren't welcome**: Ibid. Also see Haslam, *The Other California*, 124–134, which contains the essay "Oil Town Rumble: The Young Men of Taft."

63   **Honorary doctorate**: *BC*, June 26, 1939.

63   **Family lore**: Author interview with Barbara Brown.

63   **Ku Klux Klan**: The story of the Klan in Kern and Abel's involvement with it is drawn from various sources, including "The Ku Klux Klan in Kern County in 1922," a 1992 Cal State Northridge master's thesis by Kent Miller, BML; "The Invisible Empire in Kern County, 1922," a Cal Poly San Luis Obispo history paper by Kenneth E. Farmer, BML; local newspaper clippings from the period; J. W. Hicks, "Intolerance Unmasked: A Story of the Late Ku Klux Klan," BML; and Rintoul, *Oildorado*, 165–185.

65   **He was in charge**: 2004 author interview with Hallie Killebrew, daughter of Supervisor Ralph Lavin.

65   **"Progressive"**: Author interview with Killebrew.

65   **Had served**: Biographical details on Ralph Lavin are from author interviews with Killebrew; Lavin's obituary in the May 10, 1946, *BC*; and *Who's Who in Kern County, 1941*.

65   **"Salute our flag"**: According to KCBS, Lavin's motion was introduced on July 8, 1940, apparently in response to charges that Communists had taken over the welfare office in the county.

65 **"Business administration"**: *BC*, May 6, 1938.

66 **Two drugstores**: The story of Lavin's troubles during the Depression and his confrontation with Abel and the other supervisors is from the author's interview with Hallie Killebrew.

67 **"One finger"**: Author interview with Killebrew.

67 **Far more agreement**: As reflected in KCBS.

67 **"No love lost"**: Author interview with Killebrew.

67 **"Lie and a libel"**: *BC*, August 28, 1939.

67 **"Grace of God"**: Inscription seen by author.

CHAPTER THREE: TUESDAY

69 **And the rain fell**: Steinbeck, *TGOW*, 555.

69 **"Suffering arthritis"**: INS news dispatch, *FB*, August 23, 1939.

69 **"Almost dead"**: DeMott, *Working Days*, 91–92. Also quoted, in part, by Parini, *John Steinbeck: A Biography*, 208.

70 **Tonsils out**: See Benson, *True Adventures of John Steinbeck*, 91–92, regarding JS's health troubles. Also reflected in January 23, 1939, letter from JS to Pare Lorentz, included in Lorentz, *FDR's Moviemaker*, 121–122.

70 **"Can't smoke"**: Undated letter, clearly from this period, from JS to Joseph Henry Jackson, JHJP.

70 **Fifty to seventy-five letters**: Benson, *True Adventures of John Steinbeck*, 405; June 22, 1939, letter from JS to EO, reprinted in Steinbeck and Wallsten, *Steinbeck: A Life in Letters*, 185.

70 **Unlist his number**: Same letter, cited above, from JS to Joseph Henry Jackson, JHJP. Also noted in Benson, *True Adventures of John Steinbeck*, 414.

70 **"Why do they think"**: "'Grapes of Wrath' Author Guards Self From Threats at Moody Gulch," *LAT*, July 9, 1939. The article is included in Fensch, *Conversations with John Steinbeck*, 18–20. It's also quoted, in part, in DeMott, *Working Days*, 98.

71 **"Carol doesn't like me"**: August 20, 1939, letter from JS to EO, JSP. Also noted in Benson, *True Adventures of John Steinbeck*, 412.

71 **"Lovely and clever"**: Benson, *True Adventures of John Steinbeck*, 148.

71 **Depended on Carol**: Ibid., 181, 257.

71 **Thought up the title**: Parini, *John Steinbeck: A Biography*, 207; Benson, *True Adventures of John Steinbeck*, 385. Also see DeMott, *Working Days*, 161.

71 **"Pulled him up"**: Benson, *True Adventures of John Steinbeck*, 181.

71 **Boozing it up**: See Parini, *John Steinbeck: A Biography*, 187; Benson, *True Adventures of John Steinbeck*, 416, 355; and Benson's recorded interviews with Francis Whitaker and Horace Jones, JB.

71 **Joseph Campbell**: Parini, *John Steinbeck: A Biography*, 121–123.

71 **Band singer**: Benson, *True Adventures of John Steinbeck*, 403–404; Parini, *John Steinbeck: A Biography*, 229; DeMott, *Working Days*, 99–100.

71 **The fighting**: See Parini, *John Steinbeck: A Biography*, 232–233.

71   **Gotten pregnant:** Ibid., 227. Harmon, *John Steinbeck: An Annotated Guide to Biographical Sources,* 241, notes that Susan Shillinglaw, "the authorized biographer of Carol Henning Steinbeck Brown, has told this author that there is a possibility that Carol Steinbeck had several abortions, dating back to 1932, one of which may have been in Mexico or while she was in Hawaii . . . . Parini apparently got his information from Alison Harley, a friend of Carol's."

71   **Stealing fruit:** Benson, *True Adventures of John Steinbeck,* 179; Parini, *John Steinbeck: A Biography,* 95.

71   **"Good together":** Parini, *John Steinbeck: A Biography,* 100.

71   **Financial breakthrough:** Benson, *True Adventures of John Steinbeck,* 317, 323; Loftis, *Witnesses to the Struggle,* 53.

72   **A steady flow:** Benson, *True Adventures of John Steinbeck,* 349, 356; Parini, *John Steinbeck: A Biography,* 182–183, 186, 195, 218.

72   **$10,000:** Parini, *John Steinbeck: A Biography,* 206. Other details on the Biddle Ranch are from the Center for Steinbeck Studies, San Jose State University.

72   **Swimming pool:** Benson, *True Adventures of John Steinbeck,* 385.

72   **Correct the galleys:** DeMott, *Working Days,* 14.

72   **"Lot of money":** April 17, 1939, letter from JS to EO, cited in Steinbeck and Wallsten, *Steinbeck: A Life in Letters,* 182; DeMott, *Working Days,* 97.

72   **Proletarian literature:** See Pells, *Radical Visions and American Dreams,* 202–219; and Peeler, *Hope Among Us Yet,* 165–174, 185–189.

72   **430,000 copies:** French, *Companion to The Grapes of Wrath,* 106; Parini, *John Steinbeck: A Biography,* 226.

72   **Film rights:** A copy of JS's contract can be found in FOX. Also see Benson, *True Adventures of John Steinbeck,* 402. In putting the figure at $75,000 (instead of $70,000), Benson calls it "at that time one of the largest sums ever paid."

72   **"Can't make money":** March 7, 1938, letter from JS to EO, JSP. Also included in Steinbeck and Wallsten, *Steinbeck: A Life in Letters,* 161–162.

72   **Hatched a plan:** Lisca, *The Wide World of John Steinbeck,* 146; Schamberger, "Steinbeck and the Migrants," 12.

72   **Printed this ditty:** Included in *Pro America,* September 1939, RCMP.

73   **"Personal attack":** August 28, 1939, letter from JS to EO, JSP. Also included in Shasky and Riggs, *Letters to Elizabeth,* 19; and Benson, *True Adventures of John Steinbeck,* 419.

73   **"Rock salt":** See Benson, *True Adventures of John Steinbeck,* 407–408.

73   **"A rape case":** Fensch, *Steinbeck and Covici,* 21; Steinbeck and Wallsten, *Steinbeck: A Life in Letters,* 187, citing a 1957 letter from JS to his friend Chase Horton; Parini, *John Steinbeck: A Biography,* 230.

73   **"Drunk driving charge":** March 4, 1939, letter from JS to EO, JSP. Also quoted in Benson, *True Adventures of John Steinbeck,* 394.

74   **"Mr. Brooks":** Benson, *True Adventures of John Steinbeck,* 403.

74   **Mail drop:** Ibid., 402.

74   **Safety deposit boxes:** Fensch, *Steinbeck and Covici,* 21.

74 **"A nose dive"**: June 23, 1939, letter from JS to Carlton Sheffield, included in Steinbeck and Wallsten, *Steinbeck: A Life in Letters*, 186–188. Also cited in Loftis, *Witnesses to the Struggle*, 172.

75 **Inch-thick file**: See FBI files nos. 9–4583 and 100–106224, available under the Freedom of Information Act.

75 **"Dangerous subversive"**: March 4, 1939, letter from JS to EO, JSP. Quoted, as well, in Benson, *True Adventures of John Steinbeck*, 394. Also see Parini, *John Steinbeck: A Biography*, 219.

75 **Lying about them**: July 20, 1939, letter from JS to EO, reprinted in Steinbeck and Wallsten, *Steinbeck: A Life in Letters*, 188. Also see Parini, *John Steinbeck: A Biography*, 230.

75 **"Migrant John"**: Noted in Lisca, *Wide World of John Steinbeck*, 145.

75 **Started to socialize**: See Benson, *True Adventures of John Steinbeck*, 294. Also see Keith Windschuttle, "Steinbeck's Myth of the Okies," *New Criterion*, June 2002. The notion that Carol was the one who was "more radicalized" is also reflected in Benson's interview with James Harkins, a friend of the Steinbecks, from this period, JB. Also see DeMott, *Working Days*, xxv.

75 **John Reed Club**: Benson, *True Adventures of John Steinbeck*, 294. Also see Benson's interviews with Francis Whitaker and Ella Winter, JB.

75 **"Discussion of questions"**: This is an excerpt from the Constitution of the Workers (Communist) Party of America, American Section of the Communist International, as quoted in George Ewart, "The Role of the Communist Party in Organizing the Cannery and Agricultural Workers' Industrial Union" (1973), PST.

76 **"Human background"**: Francis Whitaker, 1976 interview by Jackson Benson, JB.

76 **Famous names**: Taped interview in 1977 with Ella Winter and notes from 1970 and 1974 interviews with Carol Steinbeck, all by Jackson Benson, JB.

76 **"Writing propaganda"**: Winter interview, JB.

76 **"Very naïve"**: Whitaker interview, JB.

76 **Workers' tent city**: See Winter, *And Not to Yield*, 194–199.

76 **"Nomad harvesters"**: From the poem "Camp Corcoran," found in de L. Welch, *This Is Our Own*, 57.

76 **Hiding in an attic**: Benson, *True Adventures of John Steinbeck*, 297–299.

76 **Typed up instructions**: Cecil McKiddy's October 29, 1933, "Instructions to Central Strike Committee Members and Local Presidents and Secretaries," which he signed "Comradely Yours," can be found in FWP. For more on McKiddy's role, see his testimony in SCT.

77 **Loved to read**: From author interview with Roy Hamett, McKiddy's cousin.

77 **These particulars**: Benson, *True Adventures of John Steinbeck*, 297–299.

77 **"A silent man"**: Ibid., 315.

77 **"Justice and oppression"**: Ibid., 304.

77 **"Correct narrative"**: Steffens, *The Letters of Lincoln Steffens*, 1015.

78 **Had been arguing**: Loftis, *Witnesses to the Struggle*, 144. Also see JS's essay "A Primer on the '30s," *Esquire*, June 1960, reprinted in Steinbeck, *America and Americans*, 17–31.

78   **"Communistic":** As quoted in the caption that accompanies photograph no. 405 in the Helen Gahagan Douglas Collection, Carl Albert Congressional Research & Studies Center, University of Oklahoma.

78   **"Powerful influences":** Loftis, *Witnesses to the Struggle,* 144.

78   **The RA:** See April 30, 1935, Presidential Executive Order "Establishment of the Resettlement Administration." Also see "Federal Rural Development Policy in the Twentieth Century," U.S. Department of Agriculture, Economic Research Service, 2002.

78   **At the urging:** Brian Q. Cannon, "'Keep on a-goin': Life and Social Interaction in a New Deal Farm Labor Camp," *Agricultural History* 70 (Winter 1996): 4–5.

78   **"National catastrophe":** Loftis, *Witnesses to the Struggle,* 128.

79   **Most polarizing:** Baldwin, *Poverty and Politics,* 4.

79   **"Lincoln's ghost":** HHOH.

79   **"Scared to death":** Ibid.

79   **"Pie wagon":** Benson, *True Adventures of John Steinbeck,* 332; Parini, *John Steinbeck: A Biography,* 174.

79   **Thomsen had started:** Biographical details are from Alice Barnard Thomsen, "Eric H. Thomsen and John Steinbeck," *The Steinbeck Newsletter,* San Jose State University (Summer 1990). Also see Loftis, *Witnesses to the Struggle,* 145–146.

80   **"Why not?":** Alice Barnard Thomsen article cited above.

80   **"Inexcusable":** Eric H. Thomsen, "Migratory Labor's Right to Bargain Called Imperative," *Labor Herald,* August 10, 1937.

80   **Rats and dogs:** Parini, *John Steinbeck: A Biography,* 175.

80   **Once owned:** WCOH.

80   **Arvin camp:** Background on the camp is covered extensively in Benson, *True Adventures of John Steinbeck*; Loftis, *Witnesses to the Struggle*; and Brian Q. Cannon, "'Keep on a-goin': Life and Social Interaction in a New Deal Farm Labor Camp," *Agricultural History* 70 (Winter 1996).

81   **Collins grew up:** Biographical details are from Benson, "'To Tom Who Lived It,'" 151–210.

81   **Collins compiled:** All quotes are directly from TC. Also see Ann M. Campbell, "Reports from Weedpatch, California: The Records of the Farm Security Administration," *Agricultural History* 48, no. 3 (1974).

82   **Exotic contrivance:** See TC for the weeks ending August 8 and August 15, 1936, and Steinbeck, *TGOW,* 385.

82   **Jim Rawley:** Loftis, *Witnesses to the Struggle,* 149.

82   **Sherm Eastom:** Benson, *True Adventures of John Steinbeck,* 341.

82   **Cecil McKiddy:** Ibid.

83   **During the period:** See TC for the weeks ending August 22 and August 29, 1936.

83   **"Ghostly dirge":** Also quoted, in part, in Loftis, *Witnesses to the Struggle,* 161.

84   **Almost idyllic:** Background on JS's childhood in Salinas and his attitude toward the town are from Benson, *True Adventures of John Steinbeck,* 9–18.

84   **Full of resentment:** Ibid., 29.

84 **On edge:** Details on the events leading up to the lettuce strike are from Lambert, "Fascism, Communism and Collective Bargaining," 14. Also see Starr, *Endangered Dreams*, 182.

84 **$11 million:** "Salinas Arms for Bloodshed as Citizens Defy Strikers," *LAT*, September 18, 1936.

85 **Eighteen and forty-five:** *LAT*, September 18, 1936. Also see LF, Part 74.

85 **Hickory clubs:** *LAT*, September 18, 1936; Ella Winter, "Salinas Strike Facts Disclosed by Writer," undated clip, apparently from *People's World*, found in CMcWP.

85 **About fifteen hundred:** "The War in the Salinas Valley," *Pacific Rural Press*, September 26, 1936.

85 **Uncomfortable relationship:** The Communists in the first half of the 1930s went so far as to set up a rival labor federation to the AFL, the Trade Union Unity League (Lipset and Marks, *It Didn't Happen Here*, 220). Also see Klehr, *Heyday of American Communism*, 226–227.

85 **"Non-democratic organization":** From a Fruit and Vegetable Workers' Union flier, "A Few Reasons Why," UCAPAWA. Also cited in Lambert, "Fascism, Communism and Collective Bargaining," 16.

85 **"Boring from within":** Jamieson, *Labor Unionism*, 134. Also see Daniel, *Bitter Harvest*, 273; and Lambert, "Fascism, Communism and Collective Bargaining," 4.

85 **"Real political education":** Noted by Lambert, "Fascism, Communism and Collective Bargaining," 17.

85 **Red flags:** Noted in the October 9, 1936, edition of *The Timber Worker*, Harry Bridges Center for Labor Studies, University of Washington; Starr, *Endangered Dreams*, 186; and Schamberger, "Steinbeck and the Migrants," 86.

86 **Sirens rang out:** Starr, *Endangered Dreams*, 186–187.

86 **"Rats! Rats!":** Lambert, "Fascism, Communism and Collective Bargaining," 14.

86 **"Kept firing":** Affidavit of Otto Ables, UCAPAWA.

86 **Tear-gas bombs:** Starr, *Endangered Dreams*, 185.

86 **At the head:** "In the Matter of Grower-Shipper Vegetable Association of Central California and Fruit and Vegetable Workers' Union of California, No. 18211," Case No. C-178, National Labor Relations Board, UCAPAWA.

86 **Slipped a rope:** *Pacific Rural Press*, September 26, 1936.

86 **Razor blades:** See Strobel's testimony from LF, Part 60.

87 **"Sadism":** "In the Matter of Grower-Shipper Vegetable Association of Central California and Fruit and Vegetable Workers' Union of California, No. 18211," Case No. C-178, National Labor Relations Board, UCAPAWA. Also cited in Lambert, "Fascism, Communism and Collective Bargaining," 94.

87 **Passed through:** Lambert, "Fascism, Communism and Collective Bargaining," 62.

87 **"Dear little town":** Undated letter, clearly written sometime in 1936, from JS to George Albee, included in Steinbeck and Wallsten, *Steinbeck: A Life in Letters*, 132. Also cited in Lambert, "Fascism, Communism and Collective Bargaining," 62. JS went so far as to say that the violence in Salinas had included "killings," but

this wasn't accurate. Also see "Steinbeck's Letter" from *Writers Take Sides: Letters about the War in Spain from 418 American Authors* (New York: League of American Writers, 1938), reprinted in Steinbeck, *America and Americans*, 88.

87 **"It did happen"**: "Poison Gas in America's Salad Bowl," *Literary Digest*, October 10, 1936.

87 **"Badgered, tormented"**: Steinbeck, "Dubious Battle in California," *Nation*, September 12, 1936. Also reprinted in Steinbeck, *America and American*, 71–77.

87 **Make a connection**: Benson, "'To Tom Who Lived It,'" 202.

87 **Came his journalism**: All direct quotations and paraphrasing are taken from Steinbeck, *Harvest Gypsies*.

89 **Undercurrent of racism**: Charles Wallenberg, in his introduction to *The Harvest Gypsies*, also touches on this point. See, as well, Charles Cunningham, "Rethinking the Politics of *The Grapes of Wrath*," *Cultural Logic* 5 (2002).

90 **"I have heard"**: Benson, "'To Tom Who Lived It,'" 181.

90 **"Kneed friends"**: Ibid., 181–182.

90 **"Down the country"**: Undated postcard, evidently from 1936, from JS to Louis Paul, included in Steinbeck and Wallsten, *Steinbeck: A Life in Letters*, 129–130.

90 **They stopped in**: The Steinbecks' European itinerary is noted in Benson, *True Adventures of John Steinbeck*, 357.

91 **"Scares me"**: January 27, 1937, letter from JS to EO, reprinted in Steinbeck and Wallsten, *Steinbeck: A Life in Letters*, 134–135. Also cited in, among others, Benson, *True Adventures of John Steinbeck*, 349.

91 **Upon his return**: Details from this period are from Benson, "'To Tom Who Lived It,'" 182–183.

91 **"The Oklahomans"**: DeMott, *Working Days*, xxxvi.

91 **"To Visalia"**: Quoted in Benson, *True Adventures of John Steinbeck*, 368.

91 **"My old feud"**: Cited in Benson, "'To Tom Who Lived It,'" 204.

92 **"Set out on foot"**: Benson, *True Adventures of John Steinbeck*, 369–370.

92 **"Tag of shame"**: March 7, 1938, letter from JS to EO, JSP. Also included in Steinbeck and Wallsten, *Steinbeck: A Life in Letters*, 161–162.

92 **Channeled his rage**: See Steinbeck, "Starvation Under the Orange Trees," *Monterey Trader*, April 15, 1938. Also reprinted in Steinbeck, *America and Americans*, 83–87. Also see Steinbeck, "'Okies'—New Word and New Hate in California," *People's World*, April 8, 1938; and Steinbeck, "The Squatters' Camp," *People's World*, May 6, 1939.

92 **"The audience"**: March 7, 1938, letter from JS to EO, JSP. Also quoted in Horace Bristol, "Faces of 'The Grapes of Wrath,'" *SFC*, October 25, 1987. Also cited in Benson, "'To Tom Who Lived It,'" 185.

92 **Horace Bristol**: Bristol's poignant photographs of Dust Bowl migrants appeared in the June 5, 1939, and February 19, 1940, issues of *Life*. Also see Horace Bristol, "Documenting The Grapes of Wrath," *The Californians* (January/February 1988): 40–47; and "On the Road with Steinbeck," *BC*, April 8, 1990.

92 **Too far left**: Benson, *True Adventures of John Steinbeck*, 371. Bristol offered a different account, as reported by Rick Heredia in the April 23, 1989, *BC*: JS

"thought the story was too great to waste on a photographic book . . . . He was perfectly right. His novel was so much more moving and influential and reached so many more people."

92   **"Pig Sticking"**: Benson, "'To Tom Who Lived It,'" 185.

92   **"L'Affaire"**: Ibid.; Benson, *True Adventures of John Steinbeck,* 375–376; DeMott, *Working Days,* xxxviii–xl; Lisca, *Wide World of John Steinbeck,* 147.

93   **"Vicious book"**: May 1938 letter from JS to Annie Laurie Williams, cited in De-Mott, *Working Days,* xxxix.

93   **Last day of May**: As reflected in DeMott, *Working Days,* 19.

93   **The red country**: Steinbeck, *TGOW,* 3.

93   **"Finished this day"**: DeMott, *Working Days,* 93.

93   **Helped inspire**: Benson, *True Adventures of John Steinbeck,* 399–400.

93   **"Revolutionary feeling"**: March 6, 1938, letter from JS to Pare Lorentz, cited in Lorentz, *FDR's Moviemaker,* 122–124.

94   **"My stomach"**: Quoted in Benson, *True Adventures of John Steinbeck,* 353.

94   **"Pain in the ass"**: Ibid., 318.

94   **Began selling**: As reflected in copies of *RO* from that period.

94   **"The cause"**: Helen Hosmer, undated interview by Jackson Benson, JB.

94   **"A dime"**: HHOH.

94   **"Weathered the thing"**: Steinbeck, *Harvest Gypsies,* 22.

94   **Purity of blood**: HHOH; Hosmer interview, JB.

95   **Was a member**: HHOH.

95   **"To get you"**: As Hosmer recalled it in HHOH.

95   **On her own**: HHOH; also see Stein, *California and the Dust Bowl Migration,* 244. Also see David A. Diepenbrock, "Florence Wycoff, Helen Hosmer, and San Francisco's Liberal Network in the 1930s," *Ex Post Facto: Journal of the History Students of San Francisco State University* 3 (1994).

95   **Simon Lubin**: Biographical details are from his obituary in the *LAT,* April 16, 1936. Also see CMcW, "A Man, a Place and a Time," *American West* 7, no. 3 (1970): 40.

95   **Falsely accused**: See "Lubin's Daughter Demands Dies Testimony Retraction," *LAT,* October 28, 1938.

95   **"Political evils"**: From Lubin's "Labor Sunday Sermon" delivered September 2, 1934, at Grace United Church in San Francisco, FWP.

95   **"Can the radicals"**: From paper presented March 23, 1934, to the Commonwealth Club of San Francisco, FWP.

96   **She excoriated**: See, especially, the September/October 1938 "Special Issue" of *RO,* "Who Are the Associated Farmers?"

96   **"Decent, debtless"**: *RO,* September 1939, 4.

96   **"Absolute lie"**: LF, Part 48.

96   **"Channel through"**: Listing of "organizations which are either directly formed, controlled, dominated or used by the Communist Party for their purposes," found in WBCP.

97   **"Neglected us"**: HHOH.

97 **Who's Who:** Names listed in *RO*, September 1939, 4.

97 **"This pamphlet":** *RO*, September 1939, 3.

97 **"Necessary support":** Organizational brochure found in CMcWP. Also see "Program of the John Steinbeck Committee to Aid Agricultural Organization on Housing, Health and Relief for Agricultural Workers," CMcWP, PST; Stein, *California and the Dust Bowl Migration*, 244–245; DeMott, *Working Days*, 149.

97 **Helen Gahagan Douglas:** See Douglas, *A Full Life*, 141–146.

97 **"Will You Join":** From brochure, CMcWP.

97 **Christmas Eve party:** Details on the event can be found in "Summary Report of 'Christmas for One-Third of the Nation' Project" and an FSA news release, CMcWP. Also see DeMott, *Working Days*, 149–150.

98 **"Candy and food":** Steinbeck, "The Stars Point to Shafter," *People's World*, December 24, 1938.

98 **She looked up:** Steinbeck, *TGOW*, 581.

98 **Convened a conference:** Details are from "Report of the Bakersfield Conference on Agricultural Labor—Health, Housing and Relief—Held October 29, 1938, Bakersfield, California," CMcWP.

99 **Three hundred workers:** All details on the cotton strike and the controversy over public relief that it triggered are, unless otherwise noted, from Johns, "Field Workers in California Cotton," 100–111.

99 **Three thousand pickers:** Jamieson, *Labor Unionism*, 171.

100 **Scab or starve:** See "Harold Pomeroy—He Looks at Hungry Faces—and Laughs," *People's World*, October 14, 1938. For Pomeroy's take on his actions, see transcript of Conference on Field Labor held in Sacramento, June 12, 1939, CMcWP. Also see Chambers, *California Farm Organizations*, 84–85.

100 **$4.41 worth:** This detail and the back-and-forth between WBC and Jonathan Garst are from a transcript of an October 21, 1938, meeting at the Californian Hotel in Fresno between government officials and area farm leaders, WBCP.

101 **"Been mixed up":** *BC*, October 29, 1938.

101 **His personal views:** *FB*, November 1, 1938.

102 **An aide typed:** August 22, 1939, letter to CMcW from David L. Foutz, CMcWP.

102 **"Hearing will avert":** Copy of the petition found in CMcWP.

102 **First such hearing:** Transcript of May 9, 1939, hearing available in CMcWP; LF, Part 52. Also see CMcW, "A Man, a Place and a Time," *American West* 7, no. 3 (1970): 39–40.

103 **"Fair wage":** See Johns, "Field Workers in California Cotton," 112–113; Chambers, *California Farm Organizations*, 89; Stein, *California and the Dust Bowl Migration*, 247; and Burke, *Olson's New Deal*, 86–87.

103 **Since 1926:** Arax and Wartzman, *King of California*, 148.

103 **"One-sidedness":** Johns, "Field Workers in California Cotton," 114.

103 **"Loaf of bread":** From hearing transcript found in CMcWP.

104 **"Subsistence wage":** Johns, "Field Workers in California Cotton," 115.

104   **"Two-bits worth"**: *Tow-Sack Tattler,* September 29, 1939.

104   **"Were afraid"**: August 30, 1939, letter from CMcW to Gov. Culbert Olson, CMcWP.

104   **"Roman holiday"**: Johns, "Field Workers in California Cotton," 120.

104   **"Socialism came"**: Quoted in Healey and Isserman, *Dorothy Healey Remembers,* 69. Also cited in Richardson, *American Prophet,* 95.

105   **The CIO embraced:** See Klehr, *Heyday of American Communism,* 223–51; Zieger, *American Workers, American Unions,* 51–58; and Lipset and Marks, *It Didn't Happen Here,* 226–228.

105   **Cockney accent:** This description of Harry Bridges is from a history provided by the International Longshore and Warehouse Union, Local 19, Seattle.

105   **"Take the stand"**: Denning, *Cultural Front,* 16–17.

105   **In the middle of:** See Starr, *Endangered Dreams,* 84–120; Larrowe, *Harry Bridges: The Rise and Fall of Radical Labor in the U.S.*; Nelson, *Workers on the Waterfront*; and Selvin, *A Terrible Danger.*

105   **"March inland"**: Daniel, *Bitter Harvest,* 276; Denning, *Cultural Front* 17.

106   **"It is difficult"**: From "The ILWU Story–Origins," International Longshore and Warehouse Union, Local 5, Portland, OR.

106   **A step further:** See Grubbs, *Cry from the Cotton,* 166; and Dyson, *Red Harvest,* 158. Opponents of organized labor also voiced their fears that a successful maritime union would lead to "an industry-wide Communist-controlled agricultural union" (Starr, *Endangered Dreams,* 99–100).

106   **Was born:** The union's constitution and by-laws can be found in UCAPAWA.

106   **Slogan:** See Renshaw, *The Wobblies,* 77.

106   **Had tried previously:** As noted in "CIO Farm Labor Chief Urges Aid to Farmers," *People's World,* December 9, 1938.

106   **Drinking beer:** Wechsler, *The Age of Suspicion,* 43.

106   **"He's cheating"**: London and Anderson, *So Shall Ye Reap,* 32.

106   **"Communistically controlled"**: See "Cannery Workers Blast AFL Leaders; Associated Farmers Attack Packing Union," *SFC,* December 15, 1938.

106   **"Calling us names"**: "Farm Workers Bury a 'Red Herring,'" *SFC,* December 16, 1938.

106   **Possible deportation:** See "Federal Attorney Attacks Points of Bridges Witness," *LAT,* August 23, 1939.

107   **Sufficient funding:** As reflected in "Conference Minutes, UCAPAWA Field Worker Locals of San Joaquin Valley, held at Fresno, Nov. 26, 1939," CMcWP.

107   **Internal fight:** See, especially, Grubbs, *Cry from the Cotton,* 179–190.

107   **125,000 members:** *SFC,* December 15, 1938; *Time* magazine, March 20, 1939.

107   **"First thing"**: 2004 author interview with Dorothy Healey.

108   **"Mostly drilling us"**: From "Into the Valley: The Beginning of Cotton Compress Unionism in California's Central Valley 1937–1938," an oral history project of the International Longshore and Warehouse Union.

108   **"Behead the giant"**: August 22, 1939, letter to CMcW from J. B. Ely, CMcWP.

CHAPTER FOUR: WEDNESDAY

109 "Knowed a fella": Steinbeck, *TGOW*, 493.

109 "Scarcely able": August 29, 1939, letter from GK to California State librarian Mabel Gillis, BML.

109 William Saroyan: See "Fresno Author Hits Ban on Steinbeck, Defends Dialog," *FB*, August 25, 1939.

109 Broadway production: Saroyan's *My Heart's in the Highlands* had a run of forty-four performances at the Guild Theatre during April and May 1939, according to the Internet Broadway Database.

110 "As champions": See "Liberties Group to Fight Ban on Steinbeck Novel," FB, August 23, 1939.

110 "Our industrial machine": *Kern County Union Labor Journal*, August 25, 1939.

111 Born in 1881: Biographical details on RH are from a variety of sources, including RHP; California death records, state Department of Health Services; the Boalt Hall Law School Archives at the University of California at Berkeley; and court and military records.

111 "Country lawyer": December 2, 1939, letter from RH to Jacobus tenBroek, RHP.

111 A twang: 2006 author interview with Kingsley Price, who as a young advocate for the blind worked with RH in the 1940s.

111 "Summer moon": May 31, 1939, letter from RH to Jacobus tenBroek, RHP.

112 "Pitch hay": This and the other details of how Henderson survived during this period are from a March 24, 1941, letter from RH to state senator Robert Kenny, RHP; and a March 26, 1941, letter to Rep. Jerry Voorhis, RHP.

112 Debating championships: As noted in an October 2, 1942, letter from RH to Wayne Dickens, RHP.

112 "Would not hire": This and all other direct quotations in this paragraph are from an October 2, 1942, letter from RH to Karsten Ohnstad, RHP.

112 "Sincere respect": The union official was Samuel S. White, manager of the San Francisco Joint Board, International Ladies' Garment Workers' Union. This quotation can be found in "Union-Smashing in Sacramento: The Truth about The Criminal Syndicalism Trial," National Sacramento Appeal Committee, August 1935.

113 "Savage repression": June 22, 1935, letter to CMcW from RH, CMcWP. Also see "Farm Workers Turned Fighters," a typescript in CMcWP by Herbert Klein and CMcW in which RH is cited.

113 Went into partnership: As reflected in letters found in RHP; and *Polk's Bakersfield City Directory.*

113 Cry upon command: See "Wiley Left His Mark," BC, September 11, 1974.

113 "Reds and pinks": June 4, 1927, letter from RH to Herbert White, RHP.

113 Pork chops: This remark, similar to others found in RH's correspondence, is from a January 3, 1929, letter to Herbert White, RHP.

113 Would marry: Details on this part of RH's life are from a 2006 author interview and correspondence with Kipp Dawson, a granddaughter of RH's wife.

113 **Wide-ranging:** As reflected in various letters found in RHP.

113 **"From snoring":** June 24, 1928, letter from RH to LT, RHP.

113 **"Drabness":** June 4, 1927, letter from RH to Herbert White, RHP.

113 **Famous coda:** Steinbeck, *TGOW*, 537.

114 **Work stoppage:** See "Wobbling," *Time* magazine, December 5, 1927; September 22, 1927, letter from LT to RH, RHP.

114 **Artistic outpouring:** Guthrie's "Ballads of Sacco & Vanzetti" were recorded in 1946 and '47. Kent's engraving "August Twenty-Third" was produced in 1927. Shahn's series "The Passion of Sacco and Vanzetti" was painted in 1931–32. Millay's "Justice Denied in Massachusetts" was published in 1927. And Sinclair's novel *Boston* came out in 1928.

114 **"Two innocent men":** Dos Passos, *The Big Money*, 362. Also quoted, in part, in Ybarra, *Washington Gone Crazy*, 147.

114 **Ten thousand coal diggers:** November 2, 1927, "Dear Friend" letter from the IWW's General Defense Committee, RHP; Renshaw, *Wobblies*, 213.

114 **Had done legal work:** As reflected in the Industrial Workers of the World Collection, Walter P. Reuther Library, Wayne State University.

114 **"Mussolini":** November 16, 1927, letter from RH to LT, RHP.

114 **"Starve the strikers":** November 17, 1927, letter from RH to LT, RHP.

115 **Columbine:** Details on this episode are from *Time* magazine, December 5, 1927; letters found in RHP; and information from the Colorado Historical Society.

115 **"Death trap":** Thanksgiving Day, 1927, letter from RH to LT, RHP.

115 **"Cursing and beating":** Ibid.

115 **About to raid:** This and the other particulars in this paragraph are from a January 15, 1928, letter from RH to LT, RHP.

115 **Keys to the city:** February 5, 1928, letter from RH to LT, RHP.

116 **"Battling Kid":** See February 4, 1930, letter from LT to RH, RHP.

116 **"Threatened with arrest":** December 10, 1927, letter from RH to LT, RHP.

116 **"Abuse these cattle":** January 15, 1928, letter from RH to LT, RHP.

117 **"The emancipation":** Renshaw, *Wobblies*, 46; Dubofsky, *We Shall Be All*, 46.

117 **McKees Rock:** Renshaw, *Wobblies*, 81–83; Dubofsky, *We Shall Be All*, 114–121.

117 **Lawrence:** Dubofsky, *We Shall Be All*, 132–150; Renshaw, *Wobblies*, 97–111.

117 **A presence:** Renshaw, *Wobblies*, 221–238.

117 **"Free speech fights":** Ibid., 87–95; Dubofsky, *We Shall Be All*, 89–113; Auerbach, *Labor and Liberty*, 16–17.

117 **Fresno:** Details are from Renshaw, *Wobblies*, 88–89.

118 **"The Comrades":** January 5, 1931, letter from RH to LT, RHP.

118 **"Capitalist institution":** September 25, 1928, letter from RH to LT, RHP.

118 **"Human brain":** May 10, 1929, letter from RH to LT, RHP.

118 **Dollar-a-day:** Renshaw, *Wobblies*, 213.

118 **Quickly faded:** Ibid., 213–214.

118 **Fought with those:** Ibid., 56.

118 **Centrally controlled:** Ibid., 210–211; Dubofsky, *We Shall Be All*, 260–266.

118 **Ten thousand:** Renshaw, *Wobblies*, 214.

118   One hundred thousand: Ibid., 137.

118   Out to damage: Ibid., 174.

119   Beaten, shot: Ibid., 187.

119   166 IWW leaders: Dubofsky, *We Shall Be All*, 244. In *The Wobblies*, 174, Renshaw says 165 were indicted.

119   Found guilty: Dubofsky, *We Shall Be All*, 249–50; Renshaw, *Wobblies*, 186.

119   Twenty-one states passed: Excerpt from an article on the history of criminal syndicalism by Lewis L. Lorwen in the *Encyclopedia of Social Sciences*, vol. 4, typescript in FWP.

119   Taken their cue: Renshaw, *Wobblies*, 39–40, 127–128.

119   "The real purpose": March 13, 1929, letter from RH to Denver lawyer Floyd Miles, RHP.

119   Most aggressive: The California figures are provided in the Lorwen article in the *Encyclopedia of Social Sciences*, FWP.

119   Construction worker: This and his other occupations are noted in Ahmed A. White, "The Crime of Economic Radicalism: Criminal Syndicalism Laws and the Industrial Workers of the World, 1917–1927," *Oregon Law Review* 85, no. 3 (2006): 747-749.

119   "Fomenting trouble": Superintendent's Report for November 1924, Yosemite National Park.

119   Preamble: That the preamble was printed on his membership card is noted in *Burns v. United States*, 274 U.S. 328 (1927). The preamble wording itself is from the front matter in Renshaw, *Wobblies*.

120   "Slow down": November 15, 1924, letter from RH to Herbert White, RHP.

120   "Like 'em": February 12, 1928, letter from RH to LT, RHP.

120   Fifteen months: Superintendent's Report for November 1924, Yosemite National Park.

120   Clarence Darrow: Walter Pollak's role is noted in Richard M. Cornelius, "World's Most Famous Court Trial," reprinted from History of Rhea County, Tennessee, Rhea County Historical & Genealogical Society, 1991.

120   *Gitlow*: For a discussion of this case and Pollak's "spirited and eloquent" plea for freedom of speech, see *Great American Court Cases, Vol. 2* from Law Library—American Law and Legal Information, http://law.jrank.org/collection/28/Great-American-Court-Cases.html.

120   Scottsboro Nine: Pollak argued the appeal to the U.S. Supreme Court in October 1931, according to "A Scottsboro Chronology," Modern American Poetry, http://www.english.uiuc.edu/maps/poets/a_f/boyle/boyle.htm.

120   "Amazes Court": *LAT*, November 25, 1926.

120   A rarity: Information from the Braille Institute, Los Angeles.

121   "By association": *LAT*, November 25, 1926.

121   The court ruled: See *Burns v. United States*, 274 U.S. 328 (1927).

121   "'California Justice'": May 29, 1927, letter from RH to LT, RHP.

121   Shoveling paperwork: As indicated by Warren's daily calendar, California State Archives.

264   *Notes to pages 121–126*

121   **Formal request:** Copy in SCTM.

121   **Playing out:** All details related to the Sacramento Conspiracy Trial and the background of the defendants were taken directly from SCT, unless otherwise noted. All quotations, unless otherwise indicated, are straight from the trial transcript or other official court documents. Some of the courtroom testimony, however, has been judiciously trimmed to avoid repetition and to otherwise speed along the narrative. Any edits within a quotation are marked by ellipses. In addition, a handful of words from the transcript have been changed slightly (to make verb tenses consistent, for instance) so as to improve a passage's readability.

122   **Cause celebre:** See, for example, "The Battle of Sacramento," *New Republic*, February 13, 1935; "Trial by Vigilantes," *New Masses*, February 19, 1935; and "Red-Baiters' Holiday in Sacramento," *Nation*, March 13, 1935.

122   **Bill Hamett:** Arax and Wartzman, *King of California*, 155; Benson, *True Adventures of John Steinbeck*, 342.

122   **"Most chilling":** Starr, *Endangered Dreams*, 116.

122   **Still patrolling:** Starr, *California: A History*, 208.

122   **Arresting twenty-four:** Starr, *Endangered Dreams*, 167.

122   **Fourteen:** They were NM, Pat Chambers, Harry J. Collentz, Nora Conklin, Jack Crane, Caroline Decker, Albert Hougardy, W. H. Huffine, Lee Hung, Fred Kirkwood, Lorene Norman, Mike Plesh, Jack Warnick, and Martin Wilson.

123   **"Right to a living":** This was from Martin Wilson. Also see NM, "That California Dictatorship," *Nation*, February 20, 1935.

123   **"A thorn":** Defendant Jack Crane said that.

123   **Telegraph operator:** The jurors' occupations are listed in the March 30, 1935, SB.

123   **"Class battles":** Worley, *In Search of Revolution*, 1–2. Also see 203–219. See, as well, Klehr, *Heyday of American Communism*, 153–166; Ybarra, *Washington Gone Crazy*, 176; and Diggins, *Rise and Fall of the American Left*, 173.

124   **Communist sympathizers:** SB, January 15, 1935.

125   **Guard colonel:** Starr, *Endangered Dreams*, 170.

125   **Five hundred businessmen:** Ibid.

125   **Twenty-seven days:** SB, January 3, 1935.

125   **Named a special:** This created something of a controversy because McAllister had just been rejected by voters in his bid for re-election as district attorney of Sacramento County. See Starr, *Endangered Dreams*, 169.

125   **260 prospective:** SB, January 1, 1935.

125   **Half-inch holes:** SB, April 2, 1935; SB, April 3, 1935.

125   **Longest-running:** Starr, *Endangered Dreams*, 172; Watkins, *Hungry Years*, 419.

125   **Red flag:** SB, January 26, 1935.

126   **Remarkable patience:** Some critics of Judge Lemmon, including Kevin Starr, have painted him as biased in favor of the prosecution. At the time of the trial, those on the left undoubtedly viewed him that way. (See, for example, "Union-Smashing in Sacramento: The Truth About The Criminal Syndicalism Trial," National Sacramento Appeal Committee, August 1935.) But my own reading of a huge part of the trial transcript has led me to conclude that Lemmon was open-minded and, all

in all, quite evenhanded. It is worth noting, in that regard, that the state Court of Appeal called Lemmon "very patient and liberal in allowing [the defendants] great latitude in cross-examination of witnesses" in the case. Certainly, Lemmon was no right-wing flamethrower. In fact, the well-respected jurist was elevated to the federal bench in 1947 by President Harry Truman, a Democrat.

126 **Nobody's dummy:** Details on Gallagher's personal history can be found in Starr, *Endangered Dreams,* 168. Also see Gallagher's files at the Southern California Library for Social Studies and Research, Los Angeles.

126 **"Jurors' ears":** See "Court Flays Red Lawyer," *LAT,* February 2, 1935.

126 **"Stool pigeons":** From "The C. S. Case Against Labor: The Story of the Sacramento Criminal Syndicalism Railroading," International Labor Defense, CMcWP.

126 **Tall, flabby:** As described in "The C. S. Case Against Labor: The Story of the Sacramento Criminal Syndicalism Railroading," International Labor Defense, CMcWP.

128 **Hadn't made up:** Even the conservative *LAT* gave Gallagher credit, running a headline on March 14, 1935, that read: "Defendants Score Points . . . Communist Trial Evidence Refutes Kidnap Story of State Witness."

128 **Gilbert Parker:** Starr, *Endangered Dreams,* 170.

128 **William Hynes:** Loftis, *Witnesses to the Struggle,* 92; Daniel, *Bitter Harvest,* 253.

128 **Guernsey Frazer:** Daniel, *Bitter Harvest,* 253. Also see LF, Part 62, which includes an AF memo from September 1934, which spells out the organization's close cooperation with the prosecution.

129 **Only child:** Biographical details on NM are drawn from, in addition to SCT, the author's 2005 interview with his widow, Kleo Mini; Schwartz, *From West to East,* 221; and "Personal Record of the Said Defendant Norman Mini," SCTM.

129 **West Point:** NM's record as a cadet was assembled from various memoranda, court martial orders, correspondence, and other material provided by the U.S. Military Academy.

129 **Even confiscated:** Author interview with Kleo Mini.

130 **"In the ranks":** In late 1934, after his indictment, Mini had a falling out with the other defendants in the criminal syndicalism case, who accused him of being a snitch for the state. In actuality, Mini was nothing of the sort. He had, though, begun associating with a group of Trotskyists who were on the outs with Sam Darcy, the head of the Communist Party in California. Mini himself had some nasty words to say about Darcy, and Darcy tried to smear Mini. For more on this, see Schwartz, *From West to East,* 260–261; Loftis, *Witnesses to the Struggle,* 91; "The C. S. Case Against Labor: The Story of the Sacramento Criminal Syndicalism Railroading," International Labor Defense, CMcWP; and a November 23, 1934, letter from NM to the editors of *Western Worker,* CMcWP. Sam Darcy's papers can be found at the Tamiment Library/Robert F. Wagner Labor Archives at New York University.

132 **Charles M. Schwab:** Information on Schwab is drawn from Hendrick, *The Age of Big Business,* 73.

134 **Most exciting:** Tanenhaus, *Whittaker Chambers*, 92–93; Ybarra, *Washington Gone Crazy*, 152; Schlesinger, *The Coming of the New Deal*, 45–46; Culver and Hyde, *American Dreamer*, 123.

134 **Part of the AAA:** The factions are described in Culver and Hyde, *American Dreamer*, 122; Tanenhaus, *Whittaker Chambers*, 93; Scott and Shoalmire, *The Public Career of Cully A. Cobb*, 222; CCOH; and WCOH.

135 **Difference between:** See Schlesinger, *Coming of the New Deal*, 51; Ybarra, *Washington Gone Crazy*, 153.

135 **"Completely contrary":** CCOH.

135 **"Hair ablaze":** Schlesinger, *Coming of the New Deal*, 46; Culver and Hyde, *American Dreamer*, 122.

135 **"Foolish stuff":** Nelson, *King Cotton's Advocate*, 83.

135 **"Detailed plan":** This entire episode—and WBC's reaction to it—was recounted by agricultural consultant Stanley F. Morse in a March 14, 1939, letter to WBC, WBCP.

135 **"Monkey business":** CCOH. Note that WBC was present for Cobb's oral history interview and also spoke for the record about events at the AAA.

136 **Alger Hiss:** Biographical details can be found on "The Alger Hiss Story" website at http://homepages.nyu.edu/~th15/home.html.

136 **"Cotton Ed":** This scene is from Irons, *The New Deal Lawyers*, 160. For a slightly different account, see Kennedy, *Freedom from Fear*, 212. Other details on Smith are from "Curtains for Cotton Ed," *Time* magazine, August 7, 1944.

136 **With loopholes:** Grubbs, *Cry from the Cotton*, 42; Culver and Hyde, *American Dreamer*, 154; Irons, *New Deal Lawyers*, 160–161.

136 **"Luscious fruits":** Quoted in Grubbs, *Cry from the Cotton*, 41.

136 **"Just isn't true":** From an October 8, 1936, speech by WBC to a "Conference of Negro Leaders at Spartanburg, South Carolina," WBCP.

137 **Thorough study:** Duke University's Calvin B. Hoover undertook the study. For details see Irons, *New Deal Lawyers*, 161; and Grubbs, *Cry from the Cotton*, 34–35. Also see Schlesinger, *Coming of the New Deal*, 77.

137 **A delegation:** See Mitchell, *Mean Things Happening in This Land*, 56–57; and Grubbs, *Cry from the Cotton*, 47.

137 **Internal investigation:** Mary Connor Myers led the inquiry. See Grubbs, *Cry from the Cotton*, 48–52; and Irons, *New Deal Lawyers*, 171–172.

137 **Aligned himself:** Culver and Hyde, *American Dreamer*, 154.

137 **Hirman Norcross:** Irons, *New Deal Lawyers*, 166–173; Grubbs, *Cry from the Cotton*, 43–45; Nelson, *King Cotton's Advocate*, 79–80; Mitchell, *Mean Things Happening*, 46–47.

137 **Needed it most:** These examples of how growers could get around this stipulation are found in Grubbs, *Cry from the Cotton*, 45–46.

137 **"Simply and solely":** Cited in Irons, *New Deal Lawyers*, 173.

137 **Out of town:** Culver and Hyde, *American Dreamer*, 155; Schlesinger, *Coming of the New Deal*, 78.

138 **Arkansas congressman:** Irons, *New Deal Lawyers*, 174; Culver and Hyde, *American Dreamer*, 155; Nelson, *King Cotton's Advocate*, 86.

138 **Able to mollify:** Nelson, *King Cotton's Advocate*, 86.

138 **An ultimatum:** Grubbs, *Cry from the Cotton*, 55; Culver and Hyde, *American Dreamer*, 155; Schlesinger, *Coming of the New Deal*, 79.

138 **Just being loyal:** Irons, *New Deal Lawyers*, 176.

138 **Alternative version:** Recounted in various pieces of correspondence in WBCP; CCOH; Scott and Shoalmire, *Public Career of Cully A. Cobb*, 230–231; and Briggs and Cauthen, *Cotton Man*, 133–134.

139 **"Action is taken":** CCOH.

139 **Convene a meeting:** Scott and Shoalmire, *Public Career of Cully A. Cobb*, 230–231.

139 **"Cling Peaches":** Ybarra, *Washington Gone Crazy*, 166.

139 **Groom recruits:** Schlesinger, *Coming of the New Deal*, 54; Tanenhaus, *Whittaker Chambers*, 96.

139 **Music shop:** Tanenhaus, *Whittaker Chambers*, 96; Schlesinger, *Coming of the New Deal*, 53; Ybarra, *Washington Gone Crazy*, 166.

139 **Passed along reports:** Ybarra, *Washington Gone Crazy*, 166–167.

139 **Anti-Communist:** Schlesinger, *Coming of the New Deal*, 53.

140 **Watershed:** See "The Alger Hiss Story," http://homepages.nyu.edu/~th15/home.html.

140 **"Abiding faith":** January 4, 1949, letter from Cully Cobb to WBC, WBCP.

140 **"Those skunks":** January 12, 1949, letter from WBC to Cully Cobb, WBCP.

141 **At age sixteen:** Biographical details are from CDOH.

142 **Inconsistencies:** Noted in Starr, *Endangered Dreams*, 171.

142 **"Dare you":** See *LAT*, March 28, 1935.

142 **Such theatrics:** A copy of Neil McAllister's closing, in addition to SCT, can be found in CMcWP.

144 **Sixty-six hours:** *Sacramento Union*, April 2, 1935; Daniel, *Bitter Harvest*, 254.

144 **118 ballots:** *SB*, April 1, 1935.

144 **Stood watch:** Ibid.

144 **"Step backwards":** Ibid.

144 **"Long struggle":** Ibid.

145 **Three years:** Kushner, *Long Road to Delano*, 69–70.

146 **Prisoner no. 57606:** Noted in brief item, "Write to Comrades in Prison," *Western Worker*, May 23, 1935; Schwartz, *From West to East*, 261.

146 **Five years:** California Board of Prison Terms and Paroles records, SCTM.

147 **Lost several years:** Actually, NM had been released on parole after a year (Schwartz, *From West to East*, 261; "Ex-Red Discloses Plots to State Senate Group," *LAT*, December 16, 1950). Decker was released after about two years, her sentence shortened because she taught piano to her fellow inmates and took part in other public-service activities (Loftis, *Witnesses to the Struggle*, 94). Some of the others, however, were still incarcerated at the time of the Court of Appeal decision.

147   **Found their way:** See George Ewart, "The Role of the Communist Party in Organizing the Cannery and Agricultural Workers' Industrial Union," 1973, PST.

147   **"By the summer":** Klehr, *Heyday of American Communism,* 386.

147   **"Hangman's rope":** See NM, "The Struggle in California," *New International,* March 1939.

147   **"Different turn":** CDOH.

147   **"Went pow":** CDOH. Also see Watkins, *Hungry Years,* 419, where Decker discusses how her time in prison affected her.

148   **Verbal gymnastics:** Klehr, *Heyday of American Communism,* 387–399.

148   **Never regain:** Ibid., 400–409; Crossman, *The God That Failed,* xvii. For a particularly passionate account of the betrayal that one person felt from the pact, see Spivak, *A Man in His Time,* 464–465. Also see "Honorable in All Things," an interview with CMcW by the Oral History Program, Department of Special Collections, UCLA Research Library. In it, CMcW says: "We went through that disastrous period in August 1939 [with] the Nazi-Soviet Pact. This had a tremendous impact; it ruptured friendships. People weren't speaking to other people, the Left was in the doghouse, and [it was a] very bad time, very, very bad time. I think the foundations were laid then for the subsequent witch-hunting that came along later. It was a very, very bleak period."

148   **"Shocked and surprised":** August 27, 1939, radio address by RH, transcript in BML.

CHAPTER FIVE: THURSDAY

149   **The boxcars:** Steinbeck, *TGOW,* 524.

149   **L. E. Plymale:** Biographical details from *Who's Who in Kern County, 1941.*

149   **"Damnable book":** WCOH.

149   **Into anonymity:** The August 24, 1939, *BC* gives no photo credit. *Look* magazine also doesn't cite the photographer. And neither library at the *BC* nor the KCM has any record of who the photographer was.

150   **Grace the pages:** *Look* magazine, October 24, 1939.

150   **Then recounted:** The entire dialogue is from Thelma Miller's *KH* column of August 24, 1939.

151   **"Absurd":** *Selma Irrigator,* August 24, 1939.

151   **"Terrible stew":** *Dinuba Sentinel,* August 24, 1939.

152   **"Didn't blame them":** WCOH.

152   **Swashbuckling:** For a wonderful portrait of Philip Bancroft, see Starr, *Endangered Dreams,* 207–208.

152   **"A libel against":** From a March 29, 1940, address before the Commonwealth Club of San Francisco, "Is 'Grapes of Wrath' Justified by California Farm Condition?" PB. See also Bancroft's comments in "The Okies," *Time* magazine, April 1, 1940.

152   **"Humorous and wise":** From undated letter, JHJP. Also cited in Schamberger, "Steinbeck and the Migrants," 13.

152 **Ambivalent:** See Gregory, *American Exodus,* 111; and Loftis, *Witnesses to the Struggle,* 189.

152 **James Lackey:** From COP.

152 **Lula Martin:** Ibid.

152 **Frank Manies:** Ibid.

152 **Vera Criswell:** Ibid.

152 **Clara Davis:** Ibid.

153 **Preeminent icons:** See Meltzer, *Dorothea Lange,* 132–136.

153 **"Wish she hadn't":** "'Migrant Mother' Feels Exploited," Associated Press dispatch in the *LAT,* November 17, 1978. Also see Martha Rosler, "In, Around, and Afterthoughts (on Documentary Photography)," in Wells, *The Photography Reader,* 267–268.

153 **"Under the bridge":** Quoted in "Return to the Dust Bowl," *Historic Preservation* 36, no. 5 (October 1984): 32–37.

153 **Evidence would emerge:** Author interviews with and information provided by Sally Stein, University of California at Irvine historian of photography. Also see Geoffrey Dunn, "Photographic License," *Metro,* San Jose, CA, January 19–25, 1995.

153 **"All the suffering":** Stryker and Wood, *In This Proud Land,* 19.

153 **Active in the union:** 2004 author interview with Florence Thompson's daughter, Katherine McIntosh; Geoffrey Dunn, "Photographic License."

153 **"Very strong woman":** Quoted in Dunn, "Photographic License."

154 **In his corner:** See Gregory, *American Exodus,* 100–101.

154 **"Today they tell us":** *OP,* August 31, 1939. Also cited in Lingo, "Forbidden Fruit," 363–364; and Dunn and Durham, "The Grapes of Wrath in Kern County," 29.

155 **Closely allied:** Stein, *California and the Dust Bowl Migration,* 97, 100.

155 **"Back to Oklahoma?":** Ibid., 99.

155 **"Wayfarers go for relief":** Cited in Stein, *California and the Dust Bowl Migration,* 101–102. Also see "California's Adult Children," *Country Gentleman,* February 1940, DBMA.

155 **Friend of Bill Camp's:** As reflected in WBCP.

155 **"The poor white":** From "What is the Solution to California's Transient Labor Problem," June 22, 1938, typescript found in WBCP.

155 **"Outraging his daughter":** The farming organization official is Frank Palomares, head of the Agricultural Labor Bureau of the San Joaquin Valley, as quoted in "The Dust Bowl Moves to California," *California,* August 1938, DBMA.

156 **"To hell with":** CMcW interview, "California's Olson-Warren Era: Migrants and Social Welfare," Earl Warren Oral History Project, 1976, University of California. A somewhat different account (cited in Loftis, *Witnesses to the Struggle,* 165) can be found in "Footloose Army," *Country Gentleman,* February 1940. That article says Lee Stone could be found sitting in a booth at the Madera County Fair with a sign reading: "Madera County Health Unit boasts 2,600 Cabins in

Grower Labor Camps. TO HELL with 'The Grapes of Wrath' and 'Factories in the Field.'"

156 **A survey:** Lillian Creisler, "Little Oklahoma" (master's thesis, University of California, 1935), 68, DBMA. Creisler's work is also cited in Stein, *California and the Dust Bowl Migration*, 62; and Gregory, *American Exodus*, 84.

156 **Steady drumbeat:** Creisler thesis, 90–94.

156 **"Will deny it":** All direct quotations from Al Meadors and his story are based on 2005 author interviews with him and Jess Campbell's daughter, Lacie Coffman. Also see Meadors's reminiscences in the *Arvin Tiller*, October 14, 1998. For more on Jess Campbell, see "Labor on Wheels," *Country Gentleman*, July 1938.

158 **"You jes' waltz":** Steinbeck, *TGOW*, 405.

158 **Eual Stone:** Dunn and Durham, "The Grapes of Wrath in Kern County," 9–10. Also see Samuel E. Wood, "Administrative and Social Problems of Agricultural Migrants," 1939 typescript, Farm Security Administration Region IX Materials, Bancroft Library, University of California at Berkeley, 2.

159 **"Dirty dish rag":** Lillian Creisler, "Little Oklahoma" (master's thesis, University of California, 1935), 52, DBMA. The poem was written by Myrle Dansby in December 1938. A similar notion was captured in a labor camp song popular with migrants: *Rather drink muddy water/An' sleep in a hollow log/Rather drink muddy water/An' sleep in a hollow log/Than to be in California/Treated like a dirty dog.*

159 **"Means you're scum":** Steinbeck, *TGOW*, 264–65. The dialogue has been abridged for pacing and readability. Also cited in Judith Anne Gilbert, "Migrations of the Oklahoma Farm Population" (thesis, University of Oklahoma Graduate College, 1965), 4, DBMA.

160 **"Apprehensive and alarmed":** "What Shall We Do With Them," address before the Commonwealth Club of San Francisco, April 15, 1938, PST.

160 **Indispensable book:** Starr, *Endangered Dreams*, 264–265. Also see Loftis, *Witnesses to the Struggle*, 178–181.

160 **More than forty-five thousand:** "Migrants: A National Problem and Its Impact on California," California State Chamber of Commerce, May 1940, 13.

160 **Property taxes:** Ibid., 12.

160 **"Goose that lays":** *San Francisco Examiner*, February 27, 1939.

160 **$43 a month:** Stein, *California and the Dust Bowl Migration*, 17.

160 **Vast overstatement:** See Stein, *California and the Dust Bowl Migration*, 16–24.

161 **Would croon:** From "California Cottonfields," sung by Merle Haggard and written by Dallas Frazier and Earl Montgomery.

161 **Federal Emergency Relief Administration:** See Cross and Cross, *Newcomers and Nomads in California*, 59–75.

161 **"No legal settlement":** Cited in Stein, *California and the Dust Bowl Migration*, 142.

161 **$250,000 or more:** Ibid.

161 **Seventy thousand people:** Gregory, *American Exodus*, 80.

161 **FERA was abandoned:** Stein, *California and the Dust Bowl Migration*, 143.

161 **Rehabilitation loans:** Samuel E. Wood, "Administrative and Social Problems of Agricultural Migrants," 1939 typescript, Farm Security Administration Region IX Materials, Bancroft Library, University of California at Berkeley, 21.

161 **Migrant camps:** Wood, p. 31, notes that by 1939, the FSA was running twelve camps in California with a total population of about ten thousand.

161 **Grant-in-aid:** Stein, *California and the Dust Bowl Migration,* 85.

162 **Works Progress Administration:** Ibid.

162 **To get Washington:** See, for example, "Interstate Migration and Its Effect on California," a 1935 statement by Jerry Voorhis, http://www.learncalifornia.org/doc.asp?id=1700.

162 **Harold Pomeroy:** See Stein, *California and the Dust Bowl Migration,* 82; and Burke, *Olson's New Deal,* 79.

163 **"Becoming Voters":** Article can be found in DBMA. Also see Sue Sanders, "The Real Causes of Our Migrant Problems," DW.

163 **Unflinching supporters:** Stein, *California and the Dust Bowl Migration,* 92.

163 **$30 every Thursday:** This was to have been dispensed through special scrip.

163 **Ham and Eggs:** See Starr, *Endangered Dreams,* 197–222; and Gregory, *American Exodus,* 153–154.

163 **Upton Sinclair:** Burke, *Olson's New Deal,* 111.

163 **Culbert Olson:** Ibid.

163 **Carey McWilliams:** See CMcW, "Ham and Eggs," *Nation,* October 25, 1939.

163 **In 1938:** The vote was 1,143,670 in favor and 1,398,999 against (Starr, *Endangered Dreams,* 211).

163 **In '39:** The vote was 993,204 in favor and 1,933,557 against (Starr, *Endangered Dreams,* 215). There were some important differences between the 1938 and '39 measures, as noted by Burke, *Olson's New Deal,* 109.

163 **"Feeling kinda blue":** *Covered Wagon News,* November 11, 1939.

164 **Sense of shame:** See Walter J. Stein, "The 'Okie' as Farm Laborer," *Agricultural History* 49, no. 1 (January 1975): 202–215.

164 **"In the face":** Don Jackson's words are captured in "Social Attitudes Expressed by Migrants," April 1941 typescript found in CMcWP.

164 **"I'd rather not":** Hunter's lyrics can be found online through the American Memory Project, Library of Congress, http://memory.loc.gov/cgi-bin/query/r?ammem/todd:@field(DOCID+st045).

164 **On the doorstep:** Burke, *Olson's New Deal,* 80.

164 **Less than a third:** Ibid., 81.

165 **Friend of the governor's:** For background on Dewey Anderson, see Florence Richardson Wyckoff oral history, McHenry Library, University of California at Santa Cruz.

165 **"New philosophy":** Burke, *Olson's New Deal,* 83.

165 **Slowly and carefully:** Ibid., 79.

165 **"Eye to eye":** Ibid., 84.

165 **Accusations flew:** Ibid., 85.

165 **"An oathbound kind"**: Ibid.

165 **"Plunkertism"**: Ibid.

165 **"Loss of nerve"**: Ibid.

165 **"Communist infiltration"**: Ibid., 134.

166 **Redirected from the state**: Chambers, *California Farm Organizations*, 92–93. Also see a January 3, 1940, memo by CMcW on "the question of why administration of relief should not be returned to the counties," CMcWP.

166 **Whittled down**: Burke, *Olson's New Deal*, 88–91.

166 **"Not the desire"**: Ibid., 91.

166 **Nepotism**: Ibid., 91–92.

166 **Quit**: Ibid., 93.

166 **One year to three**: Ibid., 133; Luck and Cummings, *Standards of Relief in California, 1940*, 16–17.

166 **"Start popping"**: "McWilliams Warns on State Relief: Tells U.S. Officials That Disaster May Follow Cuts," *SFN*, March 5, 1940.

166 **136 cops**: "Indigents Barred at Arizona Line," *Los Angeles Herald-Express*, February 4, 1936. Also see Stein, *California and the Dust Bowl Migration*, 73–75; and Gregory, *American Exodus*, 80.

166 **"Determined effort"**: *The Literary Digest*, February 15, 1936, DBMA.

167 **Woody Guthrie**: See Haslam, *Workin' Man Blues*, 72. Also noted in Klein, *Woody Guthrie*, 84, 98. Also see Bryant Simon and William Deverell, "Come Back, Tom Joad: Thoughts on a California Dreamer," *California History* 4 (Winter 2000/01): 185–186.

167 **"Kind of an outrage"**: *LAT*, February 5, 1936. Also cited in *The Literary Digest*, February 15, 1936, DBMA.

167 **Lasted about two months**: Mitchell, *Pensions, Politics, and the Elderly*, 76–77. Also see "Chief Davis's 'Foreign Legion,'" *Open Forum*, February 15, 1936; and "Border Patrol Ruled Illegal, Webb Reveals," *San Francisco Examiner*, March 8, 1936.

168 **Their own budgets**: See Luck and Cummings, *Standards of Relief*, 3, 68, 82, 151.

168 **Enough gasoline**: Samuel E. Wood, "Administrative and Social Problems of Agricultural Migrants," 1939 typescript, Farm Security Administration Region IX Materials, Bancroft Library, University of California at Berkeley, 7.

168 **License plates**: Ibid.

168 **Knocked six hundred families**: Alan Rudy, "Environmental Conditions, Negotiations and Crises: The Political Economy of Agriculture in the Imperial Valley of California, 1850–1993," (thesis, University of California at Santa Cruz, 1995), 203.

169 **Class, not race**: For an interesting take on *TGOW*, race, and class, see Charles Cunningham, "Rethinking the Politics of *The Grapes of Wrath*," *Cultural Logic* 5 (2002).

169 **"Anti-Okie law"**: Roske, *Everyman's Eden*, p. 504, is among those who use this term.

169 **Hadn't been trotted out**: Gregory, *American Exodus*, 98–99.

169 **Civil libertarians:** See "Liberties Group Protests Valley 'Deportations,'" *FB*, January 4, 1940.

169 **Raymond Henderson:** He handled the appeal of a Tulare County man named Richard Ochoa, who was charged with bringing his indigent mother-in-law and father-in-law into California from Arizona (*Open Forum*, May 25, 1940; *LAT*, March 26, 1940).

169 **Fred Edwards:** Details on Edwards and his case, including all quotations from the opinions of the justices, are taken directly from *Edwards v. California*, 314 U.S. 160 (1941). Additional interpretation can be found in Stein, *California and the Dust Bowl Migration*, 130–133; Ellis, *A Nation in Torment*, 475; Gregory, *American Exodus*, 99; and Loftis, *Witnesses to the Struggle*, 175–176.

170 **Important precedent:** Attorney John Caragozian, an adjunct professor at Loyola Law School in Los Angeles, graciously provided the author with important information in this area. He pointed out, for instance, that *Edwards* was crucial in *United States v. Guest*, 383 U.S. 745 (1966), in which the high court "established a constitutional right to interstate travel and upheld Congress' right to enact a statute . . . which punished persons who interfere with that right." Caragozian noted that *Edwards* has also been cited in other Supreme Court cases "invalidating state poll taxes, invalidating state residency requirements for welfare eligibility, invalidating long residency requirements for state voter registration" and more.

170 **Clell Pruett:** All quotations by him and information on him, unless otherwise noted, are from author interviews conducted in 2004 with Clell and his younger brother Farrell.

172 **Hundred million acres:** Egan, *The Worst Hard Time*, 9.

173 **Playing Marc Antony:** Details from the Internet Movie Database at imdb.com.

173 **Scattering of oaks:** The area around Sherwood Lake is described this way in Gillis, *California: A Guide to the Golden State*, 396.

174 **Ira and Ortha Taylor:** All quotations by her and information on the Taylors, unless otherwise noted, are from author interviews conducted in 2004 with Ortha.

176 **Clell would sneak:** Author interview with Ortha Taylor.

177 **"Back in the Saddle":** This and "San Antonio Rose" were two of the most popular country songs in the United States in 1939.

177 **"Oranges to be dumped":** Steinbeck, *TGOW*, 301.

180 **Dorothy Rose:** Rose's poem "Salinas 1939" can be found in her book *Dustbowl Okie Exodus*.

CHAPTER SIX: FRIDAY, SATURDAY, SUNDAY

181 **Tom stepped clear:** Steinbeck, *TGOW*, 382.

181 **Solid six-footer:** All personal and biographical details are from an author interview with his grandson, Charles Wimmer; and *BC* obituary, November 15, 1948.

181 **Peter Wimmer:** Peter and Elizabeth's connection to the Gold Rush is from an article by Anne Dismukes Amerson for Gold Rush Gallery Inc.; and a 1998 news

release by the University of California at Berkeley, which had "the Wimmer nugget" on display.

182 **Vigilante attack:** Author interview with grandson Charles Wimmer.

182 **Called Gretchen Knief:** August 29, 1939, letter from GK to California State librarian Mabel Gillis, BML.

182 **"Board's business":** *BC*, August 25, 1939; *FB*, August 26, 1939.

183 **The two had tried:** *FB*, April 10, 1939.

183 **Health care:** See the controversy over the ouster of the superintendent of Kern County Hospital, *FB*, November 11, 1941.

183 **Welfare policy:** Specifically, Wimmer and Lavin would oppose the transfer of the administration of relief programs to the counties from the state, *FB*, February 21, 1941.

183 **Solid bloc:** As reflected in newspaper coverage of the board's actions.

183 **Sweet science:** Author interview with Roy's son, James Woollomes.

183 **Elected to the board:** Biographical details from "Woollomes Not Only Knows Area But Helped Make Kern What It Is," *McFarland Press*, November 29, 1957; "Woollomes to Close Distinguished Supervisorial Career January 1," *BC*, December 29, 1948; and *BC* obituary, May 12, 1964.

184 **"Easily understandable":** August 29, 1939, letter from GK to California State librarian Mabel Gillis, BML.

184 *North of the River News:* Copy of the article can found in BML.

184 **Radio station KERN:** A transcript of RH's remarks is in BML. Also reprinted in *Kern County Union Labor Journal,* September 8, 1939. Note that the transcript misstates the day RH delivered his address, putting it at August 27. But references in the *BC*, as well as correspondence from GK, make clear that this radio speech was in fact made on Friday, August 25.

186 **M.V. or Uncle Marsh:** Biographical details and information on Marshall Hartranft's business ventures were primarily gleaned from material found at the Bolton Hall Museum in Tujunga, CA. This includes listings of Hartranft's extensive corporate holdings; Hartranft for Congress paraphernalia from his 1934 campaign; "The Western Empire Land Banking and Home Securing Plan"; California Home Extension Association periodicals; and other fact sheets and tributes.

188 **Wasco:** Hartranft's effort to settle Wasco was done under the name of the Fourth Home Extension Colony. Information provided by the city of Wasco.

188 **Bringing water:** Hundley, *The Great Thirst,* 114–115.

188 **"New crusade":** Smythe, *The Conquest of Arid America,* 266–267.

188 **Flowed a second:** See the introduction by Lawrence B. Lee to the 1969 edition of Smythe's book, xl–xli. Also see Smythe, *City Homes on Country Lanes.* And see Lawrence B. Lee, "The Little Landers Colony of San Ysidro," *Journal of San Diego History* 21, no. 1 (Winter 1975): 26–48.

188 **Six lots:** This and other details on Tujunga's evolution are from Henry Chu, "Paradise Lost," *LAT*, January 7, 1996. Also see Hitt, *Sunland and Tujunga,* 32–39.

189 **"We are authorized":** Hartranft, *Grapes of Gladness,* 12–13.

189 **"Suckered":** Ibid., 30.

189 "Land of Sunshine": Ibid., 33.

190 "Thoreau's philosophy": Ibid., 70.

190 "Under the desk": Ibid., 74.

190 "Profanity-belching": Ibid., 48.

190 "Disease of unemployment": From Preliminary Declaration, Social Adjustments Inc., "A non-profit league for orderly Population diffusion," February 12, 1940, CMcWP. Hartranft sent CMcW this plan to "alleviate some of the migrant trouble," adding in a cover letter dated August 15, 1940: "While you have plenty of faith in the political action of the mass of people in curing matters of this kind, and I have not, I imagine that we both have the same desirable ends in view." Also see November 19, 1938, United Press dispatch, "Colonies in California for 'dust bowlers' planned," CMcWP.

191 "The growers' side": Miron, *The Truth about John Steinbeck and the Migrants,* preface.

191 "Over-simplification": Ibid., 4.

191 "Gone berserk": Ibid., 5.

191 "Struggling writer": 2006 author interview with Bill Miron.

191 Born in 1906: All biographical details are culled from Miron, *A Love Affair with the Angels.*

192 Still to arrive: In 1900, L.A.'s population stood at barely more than 100,000; by 1930, it topped 1.2 million. For a look at the industries that drove the city's boom during the 1920s, see Starr, *Material Dreams,* 94.

192 "Generation of protest": Miron, *Love Affair with the Angels,* 85.

192 "First-hand study": Miron, *Truth about John Steinbeck,* 19.

192 "More money per day": Ibid., 21.

192 "Gorging fresh fruits": Ibid., 20.

192 "No other novel": Ibid., 7.

193 Twenty-seven books: As noted by the University of Virginia on its website "Uncle Tom's Cabin & American Culture" at http://www.iath.virginia.edu/utc/sitemap.html.

193 "Nurtured in violence": The full text of Eastman's book can be found on the University of Virginia website at http://www.iath.virginia.edu/utc/sitemap.html.

193 "Total revolution": The full text of *Ellen; or, The Fanatic's Daughter* by Mrs. V. G. Cowdin can also be found at http://www.iath.virginia.edu/utc/sitemap.html.

194 "You are very happy": The full text of *Antifanaticism: A Tale of the South* by Miss Martha Haines Butt can also be found at http://www.iath.virginia.edu/utc/sitemap.html.

194 The *Forum*: This piece can be found in, among other places, FTP and DBMA. It was also reprinted in Donohue, *Casebook on The Grapes of Wrath,* 8–19. Also see CMcW's letter to the editor, rebutting Taylor's article, in the *Forum,* January 1940.

194 "Strike menace": Loftis, *Witnesses to the Struggle,* 158, quoting from a piece called "The Right to Harvest," which Taylor wrote for the October 1937 issue of *Country Gentleman.*

194 **"Greatest agricultural empire"**: Loftis, *Witnesses to the Struggle*, 158, quoting from a piece called "The World's Greatest Empire," which Taylor wrote for the January 8, 1951, issue of *Fortnight*.

194 **"Terrorists"**: Loftis, *Witnesses to the Struggle*, 159, quoting from a piece called "The Merritt System" in the February 1919 issue of *Reader's Digest*.

194 **"Little question"**: Undated Q&A with JS, probably from 1939, JHJP.

195 **"Good intentions"**: "California's Grapes of Wrath," *Forum*, November 1939.

195 **"Better than anything"**: Undated Q&A with JS, JHJP.

195 **"Human interest items"**: All facts and direct quotations from Taylor's time as a United Press correspondent in Europe are taken, unless otherwise noted, from a manuscript shared with the author by Taylor's grandson Curt. Curt's uncle, Paul, and brother, Jim, were also extremely generous in sharing information about Frank Taylor.

198 **"Seen the future"**: Steffens made this remark—the perfected form of at least a couple of variations of the catchphrase that he had tried out—on more than a few occasions when he arrived in Paris from Russia in 1919. See Kaplan, *Lincoln Steffens: A Biography*, 250–251. These same words can also be found in Steffens, *Letters of Lincoln Steffens*, 463, in his April 3, 1919, letter to Marie Howe.

199 **United Airlines**: Taylor's book on the carrier was called *High Horizons*, FTP.

199 **Union Oil**: See *The Black Bonanza* and *The 76 Bonanza*, both by Earl M. Welty and Frank Taylor, FTP.

199 **Southern Pacific**: See *Southern Pacific: The Roaring Story of a Fighting Railroad* by Neill C. Wilson and Frank Taylor, FTP.

199 **Force to be venerated**: Actually, it was a mutual admiration society. FTP is full of letters of thanks from publication-relations people and other executives from companies that Taylor wrote about.

199 **"Propaganda front"**: JS to EO, undated letter, probably from November 1939, JSP. Also cited in Loftis, *Witnesses to the Struggle*, 158.

199 **Gladly reprint**: A copy of the article, issued by the AF of Ventura County, can be found in WBCP.

199 **"Born to the hoe"**: From editor's note in *Country Gentleman*, February 1941, FTP.

199 **"Something from seeds"**: Benson, *Looking for Steinbeck's Ghost*, 57–58.

200 **"Lord knows"**: NJOH.

200 **Fake name**: Shindo, *Dust Bowl Migrants in the American Imagination*, 159; McBride, *Searching for John Ford*, 309; Stempel, *Screenwriter: The Life and Times of Nunnally Johnson*, 84; Bluestone, *Novels into Film*, 159; French, *Companion to The Grapes of Wrath*, 163; Frank Condon, "The Grapes of Raps," *Collier's*, January 27, 1940.

200 **"Usual custom"**: Behlmer, *Memo from Darryl F. Zanuck*, 34. Also noted in Gussow, *Don't Say Yes Until I Finish Talking*, 90; Shindo, *Dust Bowl Migrants*, 233; and Behlmer, *America's Favorite Movies*, 123.

201 **"A monster"**: See Steinbeck, *TGOW*, 41–42.

201 **Popular tastes**: Shindo, *Dust Bowl Migrants*, 158.

201 **"Raise hell"**: Behlmer, *Memo from Darryl F. Zanuck*, 35; McBride, *Searching for John Ford*, 311. Also recounted in NJOH.

201 **A boycott**: Behlmer, *America's Favorite Movies*, 121.

201 **Bury it**: See, for instance, "'Grapes' Film Suppression Rumors Hit," *Hollywood Citizen-News*, August 28, 1939.

201 **A special clause**: As reflected in a copy of the contract and supporting documents, FOX. Also noted in Behlmer, *America's Favorite Movies*, 119.

201 **"Highly suspicious"**: Behlmer, *Memo from Darryl F. Zanuck*, 35.

201 **Private eyes**: Benson, *True Adventures of John Steinbeck*, 409; Charles Wallenberg, in his introduction to JS's *The Harvest Gypsies*, xiv; Behlmer, *America's Favorite Movies*, 121; McBride, *Searching for John Ford*, 310; Dunn and Durham, "The Grapes of Wrath in Kern County," 30.

202 **"Stirring indictment"**: Cited in Rebecca Pulliam, "The Grapes of Wrath," *Velvet Light Trap* (August 1971): 3; and Robert E. Morsberger, "Steinbeck and Censorship," *Cal Poly Pomona Journal of Interdisciplinary Studies* 16 (Fall 2003): 31.

202 **Fifteen thousand letters**: Stempel, *Screenwriter*, 84; Bluestone, *Novels into Film*, 159; Frank Condon, "The Grapes of Raps," *Collier's*, January 27, 1940.

202 **Getting squeezed**: A headline in the September 1, 1939, *Hollywood Reporter* read, "Organized Groups Fighting Make of 'Grapes of Wrath': Pressure Exerted in Every Direction."

202 **"Too Hot"**: *Look* magazine, October 24, 1939.

202 **"Paying no attention"**: Ibid.

202 **"Spirits rise"**: Stempel, *Screenwriter*, 84–85.

202 **Critics have cited**: See, for instance, Bluestone, *Novels into Film*, 159–160.

203 **"Cop-out analysis"**: Shindo, *Dust Bowl Migrants*, 231, citing Michael Dempsey, "John Ford: A Reassessment," *Film Quarterly* 28, no. 4 (Summer 1975).

203 **"From 'I' to 'we'"**: Steinbeck, *TGOW*, 194.

204 **"Simple people"**: Bogdanovich, *John Ford*, 76. The Bogdanovich interview is also cited in Behlmer, *America's Favorite Movies*, 119.

204 **"Famine in Ireland"**: Bogdanovich, *John Ford*, 76.

204 **"As characters"**: Bowser, *Film Notes*, 106.

204 **"Love America"**: Shindo, *Dust Bowl Migrants*, 160.

204 **"Always had been"**: NJOH.

204 **"In Socialism appeal"**: Behlmer, *Memo from Darryl F. Zanuck*, 156–157.

204 **The sequencing**: Bluestone, *Novels into Film*, 165–166; McBride, *Searching for John Ford*, 311; Stempel, *Screenwriter*, 81.

205 **Two-thirds of the way**: Noted in McBride, *Searching for John Ford*, 313.

205 **"Only real change"**: Behlmer, *America's Favorite Movies*, 123.

205 **"Nine-tenths"**: Quoted in Shindo, *Dust Bowl Migrants*, 159.

205 **Goodwill**: See Frank Condon, "The Grapes of Raps," *Collier's*, January 27, 1940.

205 **"Expensive odors"**: As quoted in Joe Morgenstern, "Vintage Hollywood—50 Years Ago: The Grapes of Wrath Shines on the Screen," *Memories* (December 1989/January 1990): 47.

205 **Makeup was prohibited**: Noted in publicity material, *TGOW*-F.

205   **No fake tears:** Noted in publicity material, *TGOW-F.*

205   **"Some hoax":** Behlmer, *America's Favorite Movies,* 128.

205   **Documentary films:** McBride, *Searching for John Ford,* 314.

206   **"Howl his head":** June 22, 1939, letter from JS to EO, reprinted in Steinbeck and Wallsten, *Steinbeck: A Life in Letters,* 185–186. Also cited in Behlmer, *America's Favorite Movies,* 128–129.

206   **Sex scandals:** Black, *Hollywood Censored,* 30–31.

206   **"Do's and don'ts":** Hiebert and Gibbons, *Exploring Mass Media for a Changing World,* 193.

206   **Postmaster general:** Background on Will Hays can be found in Black, *Hollywood Censored,* 31.

206   **A priest:** Black, *Hollywood Censored,* 6.

206   **$25,000 fine:** King, Tichenor, and Watkins, *The Motion Picture in Its Economic and Social Aspects,* 153.

206   **"Window dressing":** Hiebert and Gibbons, *Exploring Mass Media,* 193.

206   **Fewer than 10 percent:** Black, *Hollywood Censored,* 287.

206   **Moralistic:** For background on Joseph Breen, see Black, *Hollywood Censored,* 38–39. Also see Leff and Simmons, *The Dame in the Kimono,* 34–35.

207   **"Incites to revolution":** August 30, 1939, letter to Hays from Di Giorgio, WBCP.

207   **Tulare County:** Reflected in correspondence found in *TGOW-F.* A December 27, 1939, letter from Breen to his associate Francis Harmon says: "I am now pleased to advise you that we have been informed . . . that Mr. Zanuck has removed from the film all references to 'Tulare County.' The several speeches, in which such references were made, have been painted out of the sound track and new lines inserted. We are now about to issue to the studio our formal certificate of approval on this film." The congressman they were trying to appease was Alfred Elliott. Presumably, he was happy about the changes to the movie. He didn't have much good to say about the novel, though, calling *TGOW* "the most damnable book ever written or permitted to be put out" (*LAT,* March 12, 1940).

207   **Dozen or so changes:** As spelled out in a September 29, 1939, letter from Breen to Twentieth Century-Fox executive Jason Joy, *TGOW-F.*

207   **"The association":** September 29, 1939, letter from Breen to Twentieth-Century Fox executive Jason Joy, *TGOW-F.*

207   **Flagged by Breen:** December 7, 1939, letter from Breen to Will Hays, *TGOW-F.*

207   **Innocuous:** Noted by, among others, Bluestone, *Novels into Film,* 160–161. In the original script, Tom asks, "What is these reds anyway?" A friend, working alongside him on the ditch bank, answers that he once heard it's anybody who "wants 30 cents an hour when I'm payin' 25." In the final print, however, the farmer they're working for delivers a much more evasive answer: "I ain't talkin' about that one way 'r another."

207   **Who'd joined Fox:** Leff and Simmons, *Dame in the Kimono,* 23.

207   **"The handbills":** Typed notes from July 19, 1939, conference with Zanuck, FOX. Also cited in Behlmer, *America's Favorite Movies,* 125.

207   **"Question of policy":** September 29, 1939, letter from Breen to Hays, *TGOW-F.*

207 **"Legitimate drama"**: December 7, 1939, letter from Breen to Will Hays, *TGOW*-F.

208 **"Inescapable"**: Ibid.

208 **"Fascists will say"**: Behlmer, *America's Favorite Movies,* 124.

208 **More than $1 million**: McBride, *Searching for John Ford,* 315.

209 **"Motherlove"**: December 7, 1939, letter from Breen to Will Hays, *TGOW*-F.

209 **"Contradictions and inequities"**: Bluestone, *Novels into Film,* 168. Bluestone's chapter on *TGOW* is also reprinted in French, *Companion to The Grapes of Wrath,* 165–189. McBride, in *Searching for John Ford,* makes a similar point on page 313: "While *The Grapes of Wrath* can be appraised in terms of how much has been lost from Steinbeck's book, it also can be looked at in terms of how much the filmmakers have retained from the novel. What remains is powerful enough to make the film Hollywood's strongest indictment of depression era socio-economic conditions."

209 **Glowing reviews**: See, for instance, the roundup in *Motion Picture Daily,* January 26, 1940, *TGOW*-F. Among the most oft-cited reviews is Frank Nugent's from the *New York Times,* which said: "In the vast library where the celluloid literature of the screen is stored there is one small, uncrowded shelf devoted to the cinema's masterworks . . . . To that shelf of screen classics 20th Century-Fox has added its version of John Steinbeck's 'The Grapes of Wrath.'"

209 **Seven Academy Awards**: See http://www.filmsite.org/aa40.html.

209 **"Kept his word"**: December 15, 1939, letter from JS to EO, reprinted in Steinbeck and Wallsten, *Steinbeck: A Life in Letters,* 195–197. This letter is also cited in Benson, *True Adventures of John Steinbeck,* 410–411; Behlmer, *America's Favorite Movies,* 132; and McBride, *Searching for John Ford,* 314.

209 **"I am grateful"**: *OP,* August 31, 1939; *KH,* September 5, 1939.

CHAPTER SEVEN: SOME DAY

211 **"Don't you fret"**: Steinbeck, *TGOW,* 360.

211 **'39 cotton harvest**: *BC,* August 26, 1939.

211 ***The Wizard of Oz***: Ibid.

211 **Possible break**: *BC,* August 24, 1939. The murder would never be solved, as noted by Newton, *Justice for All,* 94.

211 **"Union of the unemployed"**: Gregory, *American Exodus,* 154–155.

212 **Packed the chamber**: This rendering of the meeting is derived from a combination of sources: KCBS; *BC,* August 28 and August 29, 1939; *KH,* August 31, 1939; *OP,* August 31, 1939; August 29, 1939, letter from GK to California State librarian Mabel Gillis, BML. All direct quotations, unless otherwise noted, are found in the newspaper articles just cited. Because no transcript of the meeting exists, the exact sequencing of who said what, and when, is unclear. Different newspapers also quote certain speakers slightly differently. But this reconstruction is as faithful to the facts as possible, given the sources available.

212 **"Hellfire and damnation"**: 2007 author interview with Bakersfield resident Helen Smith.

213   **She had . . . married:** Bertha's husband, Edward Rankin, was the son of Walker Rankin, who had come west from his family's farm in Pennsylvania right after the start of the Civil War. He mined for gold and did a little dairy ranching before he became a cattleman, importing the first purebred Herefords into the area. In 1868, Walker wed Lavinia Lightner, the daughter of a Missouri wagon train captain who'd landed in California even earlier, in 1850. (Biographical details on Bertha and her family are from *Who's Who in Kern County, 1941*; *Memorial and Biographical History of the Counties of Fresno, Tulare and Kern California*, 385–387; and information from the Rankin Ranch.)

213   **"Beginnings of Communism":** 2004 author interview with Alice Beard.

215   **On an apple:** Author interview with Hallie Killebrew.

216   **Fifty-four-year-old grandmother:** California death records, state Department of Health Services.

220   **The following week:** "Grapes Fails to Create Any Commotion at Board Meet," *BC*, September 5, 1939; KCBS.

220   **Letters of protest:** KCBS.

220   **"Loaning county property":** *KH*, June 16, 1940.

220   **Dust Bowl Days:** For more, go to http://www.weedpatchcamp.com/Festival/festival.htm.

221   **Belt buckles:** See Gregory, *American Exodus*, 245.

221   **Converted railcar:** See the liner notes to the CD collection *Merle Haggard: Down Every Road.*

221   **Mega-hits:** "Okie from Muskogee" reached no. 1 while "I Take a Lot of Pride in What I Am" hit no. 3 among Billboard's Hot Country Songs.

222   **"Shocking degree":** Cited in Benson, *True Adventures of John Steinbeck*, 422.

222   **Convinced the senator:** Auerbach, *Labor and Liberty*, 180. Also see *Time* magazine, August 21, 1939, which notes: "Senator La Follette's show will be cast along the lines of Author John Steinbeck's best-selling novel . . . ."

222   **500-plus subpoenas:** These statistics are from Starr, *Endangered Dreams*, 267.

222   **"Local fascism":** Cited in Auerbach, *Labor and Liberty*, 187.

222   **Great eagerness:** In his letter to Ralph Lavin, for example, JS noted that the AF's "preoccupation with morals" was "a colossal stupidity" given that the La Follette Committee was on its way to California.

222   **"Infiltrated by Communists":** "Commies Dominated La Follette Committee," *Associated Farmer* (July/August 1953), WBCP.

222   **Top ten best seller:** W. J. Weatherby, "Mighty Words of Wrath," *Guardian*, April 17, 1989; French, *Companion to The Grapes of Wrath*, 106.

222   **Generate news:** See, for example, "Mrs. Roosevelt Tours Mecca of Migrants: Inspects California Camps and Says Steinbeck Told Truth," *New York Times*, April 3, 1940. Also see "California Replies to Steinbeck," *BusinessWeek*, May 11, 1940.

222   **Town Meeting of the Air:** Much material on this event can be found in CMcWP.

222   **"Rapes of Graft":** Klein, *Woody Guthrie*, 146–147.

222   **Credit his performance:** "There had been other folk music recitals," Klein writes in *Woody Guthrie*, "but this would be remembered as the first really important

one . . ." This is, in part, because in the audience that night was Alan Lomax, the famed folk archivist from the Library of Congress who did much to popularize the genre. This was the first time he'd ever heard Guthrie play. The significance of this show is also noted in the curriculum guide for an audio play version of *TGOW*, part of a program called Alive & Aloud by L.A. Theatre Works, 2002. Guthrie's appearance is mentioned, as well, in Bryant Simon and William Deverell, "Come Back, Tom Joad: Thoughts on a California Dreamer," *California History* 4 (Winter 2000/01): 183.

223   **"So You've Seen":** The flier is found in CMcWP.

223   **"Forgot them":** See Charles Wallenberg's introduction to *The Harvest Gypsies*, xvi.

223   **Blue-collar jobs:** For a discussion of and statistics on the migrants' economic rise, see Gregory, *American Exodus*, 182–190.

223   **Didn't hang around:** Author interview with Pruett.

224   **Seconded a motion:** *BC*, January 27, 1941; *FB*, January 27, 1941; *KH*, January 28, 1941.

224   **"Fifteen minutes":** January 27, 1941, letter from GK to A. W. Noon, BML.

224   **State librarian:** Knief's career in Washington State is recounted in Reynolds, *The Dynamics of Change*, 28–35.

224   **She married:** *Tehachapi News*, June 26, 1942.

224   **Pushed to desegregate:** See Kayla Barrett and Barbara A. Bishop, "Integration and the Alabama Library Association: Not So Black and White," *Libraries & Culture* 33, no. 2 (Spring 1998): 141–161.

224   **"Need to be shielded":** Schenk, *County and Regional Library Development*, 200.

224   **Died in 1989:** *Foley (Ala.) Onlooker*, May 25, 1989.

224   **Redevelopment official:** *Who's Who in the West, 1963–64*. Also see Stanely Abel's *BC* obituary, November 12, 1975.

224   **Union leader:** Author interview with Ralph Abel's niece, Barbara Brown.

224   **Charles Wimmer:** *BC* obituary, November 15, 1948.

224   **C. W. Harty:** KCBS.

224   **Roy Woollomes:** *BC* obituary, May 12, 1964.

224   **Was campaigning:** *BC*, May 10, 1946.

225   **"Little monuments":** From Lavin's friend, Judge Ardis Walker, BML.

225   **"Had lost all":** "Ex-Red Discloses Plots to State Senate Group," *LAT*, December 16, 1950.

225   **Began to mentor:** Author interview with Norman Mini's widow, Kleo Mini. Also noted in Schwartz, *From West to East*, 497–498.

225   **"Best first novel":** Miller, *Big Sur and the Oranges of Hieronymus Bosch*, 12.

225   **Emory Gay Hoffman:** See "Kern's Past," *BC*, September 24, 1990.

225   **Continued to write:** RCMP.

225   **Heart failure:** Conaway, *Los Gatos*, 98.

226   **"Would have desired it":** March 29, 1945, obituary, Bolton Hall Museum in Tujunga, CA.

226   **Red Skelton:** Author interview with Bill Miron, Thomas Miron's nephew.

226   **Take his own life:** *SFC* obituary, October 24, 1972; 2005 author interview with Taylor's grandson Curt.

226   **Backing a succession:** As reflected in WBCP.

226   **Religious Heritage:** The event is described in Briggs and Cauthen, *Cotton Man,* 328.

226   **"Under God":** As noted by the University of Maryland, which holds the papers of Harold Dudley, founder of the Washington Pilgrimage, which later became known as Religious Heritage of America.

226   **Right to Work Committee:** Briggs and Cauthen, *Cotton Man,* 332.

226   **Stubbornly traditional:** Gregory's book, *American Exodus,* looks in-depth at this "plain-folk Americanism."

226   **Difficult to unionize:** Stein, *California and the Dust Bowl Migration,* 243–278.

226   **Realigned themselves:** Morgan, *Rising in the West,* 234. He writes: "In 1964, Johnson swamped Goldwater in all six southernmost valley counties. But two years later, Ronald Reagan, in defeating the liberal Democrat Edmund G. 'Pat' Brown for governor, won all six. Then, in 1968, a fundamental realignment began. Hubert Humphrey, running for President against Richard Nixon, won Merced County, barely edged out Nixon in Fresno, Madera, and Kings, but lost Kern and was badly beaten in Tulare. The deeper one went into Okie strongholds, the weaker Humphrey became . . . . In the next few years, Kern County voted more conservatively than the rest of California on a series of key state measures, including the death penalty, marijuana legislation, homosexual rights, and school busing." In recent years, Bakersfield has been ranked as the most conservative city in California and one of the ten most conservative in the country.

226   **Fired McWilliams:** Newton, *Justice for All,* 174; Richardson, *American Prophet,* 111.

226   **Mainly a symbol:** Starr, *Endangered Dreams,* 268, makes this point most insightfully.

226   **West Coast correspondent:** Richardson, *American Prophet,* 137.

227   **Wrote about the dramas:** Richardson, *American Prophet,* includes a bibliography of CMcW's magazine pieces.

227   **Died in 1980:** Richardson, *American Prophet,* 286.

227   **"World is sick":** November 13, 1939, letter from JS to Carlton Sheffield, reprinted in Steinbeck and Wallsten, *Steinbeck: A Life in Letters,* 193–194.

227   **Nobel Prize:** JS won in 1962.

227   **As a traitor:** Benson, *True Adventures of John Steinbeck,* 718–720.

227   **"Middle class":** Ibid., 796.

227   **"Joads in the Jag":** Ibid., 747.

227   **Anti-Marxist:** Ibid., 956, 967.

227   **Hawkish stance:** Ibid., 1000.

227   **"Will fight for":** From JS's essay "I Am a Revolutionary," first published in *Le Figaro*'s magazine, and reprinted in Steinbeck, *America and Americans,* 90.

227   **"Filled naturally":** Voice of America interview, February 11, 1952, transcript in BML.

228   **Ashes were scattered:** Benson, *True Adventures of John Steinbeck,* 1038.

228   **Declaring October:** KCBS.

228   **An apology:** See *BC,* July 22, 2002. Kern County wasn't the only place that once reviled JS and embraced him in the end. His hometown of Salinas did as well. And Sallisaw, Okla., launched a "Grapes of Wrath Festival" in 1990.

229   **Others would invoke:** Official minutes, Board of Trustees meeting, Kern High School District, February 2, 2004. The controversy raged for months in late 2003 and early '04, until the school board voted four to one on a compromise that allowed teachers of Advanced Placement English students in the higher grades to continue to assign *The Bluest Eye,* while also giving parents the option of having their children read a different book.

229   **Two thousand or so:** The American Library Association's Office for Intellectual Freedom tracked between 400 and 650 challenges to books each year in the United States between 2000 and 2005. But it estimates that for each challenge reported, as many as four or five go unreported.

229   **Hundred thousand copies:** The figure is from the National Steinbeck Center in Salinas, Calif.

229   **Bruce Springsteen:** See Bryant Simon and William Deverell, "Come Back, Tom Joad: Thoughts on a California Dreamer," *California History* 4 (Winter 2000/01): 187-191.

229   **Enough food:** "Hunger in America 2006," a study from America's Second Harvest. It says 13.5 million households, with an estimated 38 million people, are "food insecure," which it defines as a "lack of access, at all times, to enough food for an active, healthy life for all household members; limited or uncertain availability of nutritionally adequate foods."

229   **Third of the population:** See Jared Bernstein, "Work, Work Supports, and Safety Nets: Reducing the Burden of Low-Incomes in America," Economic Policy Institute briefing paper, October 2, 2007. Those in this group, Bernstein notes, bring in about twice as much income as those who fall below the government's official poverty threshold (which stands today at about $20,000 for a family of four with two children).

229   **Income inequality:** See http://www.demos.org/inequality/.

229   **"Our people":** Steinbeck, *TGOW,* 307–308.

Bibliography

BOOKS

The books listed are those used by the author, not necessarily the original editions, so that the page numbers cited in the endnotes will correspond.

Arax, Mark, and Rick Wartzman. *The King of California: J. G. Boswell and the Making of a Secret American Empire*. New York: PublicAffairs, 2003.

Arthur, Anthony. *Radical Innocent: Upton Sinclair*. New York: Random House, 2006.

Auerbach, Jerold S. *Labor and Liberty: The La Follette Committee and the New Deal*. Indianapolis: Bobbs-Merrill Company, 1966.

Austin, Mary. *The Land of Little Rain*. Albuquerque: University of New Mexico Press, 1974.

Bald, Margaret. *Banned Books: Literature Suppressed on Religious Grounds*. New York: Facts on File, 1998.

Baldwin, Sidney. *Poverty and Politics: The Rise and Decline of the Farm Security Administration*. Chapel Hill: University of North Carolina Press, 1968.

Behlmer, Rudy. *America's Favorite Movies: Behind the Scenes*. New York: Frederick Ungar Publishing Company, 1982.

———. *Memo from Darryl F. Zanuck: The Golden Years at Twentieth Century-Fox*. New York: Grove Press, 1993.

Benson, Jackson J. *Looking for Steinbeck's Ghost*. Reno: University of Nevada Press, 2002.

———. *The True Adventures of John Steinbeck, Writer*. New York: Viking Press, 1984.

Bentley, Eric, ed. *Thirty Years of Treason: Excerpts from Hearings Before the House Committee on Un-American Activities, 1938–1968*. New York: Thunder's Mouth Press/Nation Books, 2002.

Berg, Norman. *A History of Kern County Land Company*. Bakersfield, CA: Kern County Historical Society, 1971.

Bierce, Ambrose. *The Devil's Dictionary*. Mineola, NY: Courier Dover Publications, 1993.

Black, Gregory D. *Hollywood Censored: Morality Codes, Catholics, and the Movies*. Cambridge: Cambridge University Press, 1996.

Blodget, Rush Maxwell. *Little Dramas of Old Bakersfield*. Los Angeles: Carl A. Bundy Quill & Press, 1931.

Bluestone, George. *Novels into Film: The Metamorphosis of Fiction into Cinema.* Berkeley: University of California Press, 1966.

Bogdanovich, Peter. *John Ford.* Berkeley: University of California Press, 1978.

Bowser, Eileen. *Film Notes.* New York: Museum of Modern Art, 1969.

Boyd, W. Harland, John Ludeke, and Marjorie Rump. *Inside Historic Kern.* Bakersfield, CA: Kern County Historical Society, 1982.

Boyer, Paul S. *Purity in Print: The Vice-Society Movement and Book Censorship in America.* New York: Charles Scribner's Sons, 1968.

Brewer, William H. *Up and Down California in 1860–1864: The Journal of William H. Brewer.* Berkeley, University of California Press, 2003.

Briggs, William J. and Henry Cauthen. *The Cotton Man: Notes on the Life and Times of Wofford B. ("Bill") Camp.* Columbia: University of South Carolina Press, 1983.

Burke, Robert E. *Olson's New Deal for California.* Berkeley: University of California Press, 1953.

Chambers, Clarke A. *California Farm Organizations.* Berkeley: University of California Press, 1952.

Chase, Stuart. *A New Deal.* New York: Macmillan Company, 1932.

Conaway, Peggy. *Los Gatos.* Charleston, SC: Arcadia Publishing, 2004.

Coodley, Lauren, ed. *The Land of Orange Groves and Jails: Upton Sinclair's California.* Berkeley, CA: Heyday Books, 2004.

Cross, William T., and Dorothy E. Cross. *Newcomers and Nomads in California.* Stanford, CA: Stanford University Press, 1937.

Crossman, Richard H., ed. *The God That Failed.* New York: Columbia University Press, 2001.

Culver, John C., and Henry Hyde. *American Dreamer: A Life of Henry A. Wallace.* New York: W. W. Norton & Company, 2000.

Daniel, Cletus. *Bitter Harvest: A History of California Farmworkers, 1870–1941.* Berkeley: University of California Press, 1982.

De L. Welch, Marie. *This is Our Own.* New York: Macmillan Company, 1940.

DeMott, Robert, ed. *Working Days: The Journals of The Grapes of Wrath.* New York: Viking Penguin, 1989.

Denning, Michael. *The Cultural Front: The Laboring of American Culture in the Twentieth Century.* London: Verso, 2000.

Diggins, John Patrick. *The Rise and Fall of the American Left.* New York: W. W. Norton, 1992.

Ditsky, John, ed. *Critical Essays on Steinbeck's The Grapes of Wrath.* Boston: G. K. Hall, 1989.

Donohue, Agnes McNeill, ed. *A Casebook on The Grapes of Wrath.* New York: Thomas Y. Crowell, 1968.

Dos Passos, John. *The Big Money.* New York: Mariner Books, 2000.

Douglas, Helen Gahagan. *A Full Life.* Garden City, NY: Doubleday, 1982.

Dubofsky, Melvyn. *We Shall Be All: A History of the Industrial Workers of the World.* Urbana: University of Illinois Press, 2000.

Dyson, Lowell K. *Red Harvest: The Communist Party and American Farmers.* Lincoln: University of Nebraska Press, 1982.

Egan, Timothy. *The Worst Hard Time: The Untold Story of Those Who Survived the Great American Dust Bowl.* New York: Houghton Mifflin, 2006.

Ellis, Edward Robb. *A Nation in Torment: The Great American Depression, 1929–1939.* New York: Kodansha International, 1995.

Ernst, Morris L., and Alexander Lindey. *The Censor Marches On: Recent Milestones in the Administration of the Obscenity Law in the United States.* New York: Doubleday, Doran & Company, 1940.

Fensch, Thomas, ed. *Conversations with John Steinbeck.* Jackson: University Press of Mississippi, 1988.

_____. *Steinbeck and Covici: The Story of a Friendship.* Middlebury, VT: Paul S. Eriksson, 1979.

Folsom, Franklin. *Days of Anger, Days of Hope: A Memoir of the League of American Writers, 1937–1942.* Niwot: University Press of Colorado, 1994.

French, Warren, ed. *A Companion to The Grapes of Wrath.* New York: Penguin Books, 1989.

Gentry, Curt. *Frame-Up: The Incredible Case of Tom Mooney and Warren Billings.* New York: W. W. Norton, 1967.

Gillis, Mabel R., ed. *California: A Guide to the Golden State.* New York: Hastings House, 1939.

Green, Jonathon, and Nicholas J. Karolides. *Encyclopedia of Censorship.* New York: Facts on File, 2005.

Gregory, James N. *American Exodus: The Dust Bowl Migration and Okie Culture in California.* New York: Oxford University Press, 1989.

Grubbs, Donald H. *Cry from the Cotton: The Southern Tenant Farmers' Union and the New Deal.* Chapel Hill: University of North Carolina Press, 1971.

Gussow, Mel. *Don't Say Yes Until I Finish Talking: A Biography of Darryl F. Zanuck.* Garden City, NY: Doubleday, 1971.

Harmon, Robert B. *John Steinbeck: An Annotated Guide to Biographical Sources.* Lanham, MD: Scarecrow Press, 1996.

Hartranft, M. V. *Grapes of Gladness.* Los Angeles: DeVorss, 1939.

Haslam, Gerald W. *Coming of Age in California.* Walnut Creek, CA: Devil Mountain Books, 2000.

_____. *The Other California: The Great Central Valley in Life and Letters.* Reno: University of Nevada Press, 1994.

_____. *Workin' Man Blues: Country Music in California.* Berkeley: University of California Press, 1999.

Hayashi, Tetsumaro, ed. *John Steinbeck: The Years of Greatness, 1936–1939.* Tuscaloosa: University of Alabama Press, 1993.

Healey, Dorothy, and Maurice Isserman. *Dorothy Healey Remembers: A Life in the American Communist Party.* New York: Oxford University Press, 1990.

Hendrick, Burton J. *The Age of Big Business.* New York: Cosimo, 2005.

Hiebert, Ray Eldon, and Sheila Jean Gibbons. *Exploring Mass Media for a Changing World.* Mahwah, NJ: Lawrence Erlbaum Associates, 2000.

Hitt, Marlene A. *Sunland and Tujunga: From Village to City.* Charleston, SC: Arcadia Publishing, 2003.

Humes, Edward. *Mean Justice.* New York: Simon & Schuster, 1999.

Hundley, Norris, Jr. *The Great Thirst: Californians and Water: 1770s-1990s.* Berkeley: University of California Press, 1992.

Igler, David. *Industrial Cowboys: Miller & Lux and the Transformation of the Far West, 1850–1920.* Berkeley: University of California Press, 2001.

Irons, Peter H. *The New Deal Lawyers.* Princeton, NJ: Princeton University Press, 1982.

Jamieson, Stuart. *Labor Unionism in American Agriculture.* New York: Arno Press, 1976.

Johnson, Stephen, Gerald Haslam, and Robert Dawson. *The Great Central Valley: California's Heartland.* Berkeley: University of California Press, 1993.

Kaplan, Justin. *Lincoln Steffens: A Biography.* New York: Simon & Schuster, 2004.

Karolides, Nicholas J. *Banned Books: Literature Suppressed on Political Grounds.* New York: Facts on File, 2006.

Karolides, Nicholas J., Lee Burress, and John M. Kean. *Censored Books: Critical Viewpoints.* Metuchen, NJ: Scarecrow Press, 1993.

Kennedy, David M. *Freedom from Fear: The American People in Depression and War, 1929–1945.* New York: Oxford University Press, 2005.

King, Clyde Lyndon, Frank A. Tichenor, and Gordon S. Watkins, eds. *The Motion Picture in Its Economic and Social Aspects.* Manchester, NH: Ayer Publishing, 1970.

Klehr, Harvey. *The Heyday of American Communism: The Depression Decade.* New York: Basic Books, 1984.

Klein, Joe. *Woody Guthrie: A Life.* New York: Delta, 1999.

Kushner, Sam. *Long Road to Delano.* New York: International Publishers Company, 1975.

Larrowe, Charles P. *Harry Bridges: The Rise and Fall of Radical Labor in the U.S.* Westport, CT: Lawrence Hill, 1977.

Latta, F. F. *Black Gold in the San Joaquin.* Caldwell, ID: Caxton Printers, 1949.

Leff, Leonard J., and Jerold L. Simmons. *The Dame in the Kimono: Hollywood, Censorship, and the Production Code.* Lexington: University of Kentucky Press, 2001.

Lipset, Seymour Martin, and Gary Marks. *It Didn't Happen Here: Why Socialism Failed in the United States.* New York: W. W. Norton, 2001.

Lisca, Peter. *The Wide World of John Steinbeck.* New Brunswick, NJ: Rutgers University Press, 1958.

Loftis, Anne. *Witnesses to the Struggle: Imaging the 1930s California Labor Movement.* Reno: University of Nevada Press, 1998.

London, Joan, and Henry Anderson. *So Shall Ye Reap.* New York: Thomas Y. Crowell, 1971.

Lorentz, Pare. *FDR's Moviemaker: Memoirs and Scripts.* Reno: University of Nevada Press, 1992.

Lowitt, Richard, and Maurine Beasley, eds. *One Third of a Nation: Lorena Hickok Reports on the Great Depression.* Urbana: University of Illinois Press, 2000.

Luck, Mary Gorringe, and Agnes B. Cummings. *Standards of Relief in California, 1940.* Berkeley: University of California Press, 1945.

Mattson, Kevin. *Upton Sinclair and the Other American Century.* Hoboken, NJ: John Wiley & Sons, 2006.

McBride, Joseph. *Searching for John Ford.* New York: St. Martin's Press, 2001.

McDevitt, Ray, ed. *Courthouses of California: An Illustrated History.* San Francisco: California Historical Society; Berkeley, CA: Heyday Books, 2001.

McWilliams, Carey. *The Education of Carey McWilliams.* New York: Simon & Schuster, 1979.

———. *Factories in the Field.* Boston: Little, Brown, 1939.

Meister, Dick, and Anne Loftis. *A Long Time Coming: The Struggle to Unionize America's Farm Workers.* New York: Macmillan, 1977.

Meltzer, Milton. *Dorothea Lange: A Photographer's Life.* Syracuse, NY: Syracuse University Press, 2000.

Memorial and Biographical History of the Counties of Fresno, Tulare and Kern California. Chicago: Lewis Publishing Company, 1892.

Miller, Henry. *Big Sur and the Oranges of Hieronymus Bosch.* New York: New Directions Publishing, 1957.

Miron, George Thomas. *A Love Affair with the Angels: Vignettes of Old L.A.* Long Beach, CA: University Print, 1979.

———. *The Truth about John Steinbeck and the Migrants.* Los Angeles: Haynes Corporation, 1939.

Mitchell, Daniel J. B. *Pensions, Politics, and the Elderly.* Armonk, NY: M. E. Sharpe, 2000.

Mitchell, Greg. *The Campaign of the Century: Upton Sinclair's Race for Governor of California and the Birth of Media Politics.* New York: Random House, 1992.

Mitchell, H. L. *Mean Things Happening in This Land: The Life and Times of H. L. Mitchell, Co-Founder of the Southern Tenant Farmers Union.* Montclair, NJ: Allanheld, Osmun, 1979.

Mitchell, Ruth Comfort. *Of Human Kindness.* New York: D. Appleton-Century, 1940.

Mooney, Patrick H., and Theo J. Majka. *Farmers' and Farm Workers' Movements: Social Protest in American Agriculture.* New York: Twayne Publishers, 1995.

Moore, Harry Thornton. *The Novels of John Steinbeck: A First Critical Study.* Chicago: Normandie House, 1939.

Morgan, Dan. *Rising in the West: The True Story of an "Okie" Family from the Great Depression Through the Reagan Years.* New York: Alfred A. Knopf, 1992.

Nelson, Bruce. *Workers on the Waterfront: Seamen, Longshoremen, and Unionism in the 1930s.* Urbana: University of Illinois Press, 1990.

Nelson, Lawrence J. *King Cotton's Advocate: Oscar G. Johnston and the New Deal.* Knoxville: University of Tennessee Press, 1999.

Newton, Jim. *Justice for All: Earl Warren and the Nation He Made.* New York: Riverhead Books, 2006.

Parini, Jay. *John Steinbeck: A Biography.* New York: Henry Holt, 1995.

Peeler, David P. *Hope Among Us Yet: Social Criticism and Social Solace in Depression America.* Athens: University of Georgia Press, 1987.

Pells, Richard H. *Radical Visions and American Dreams: Culture and Social Thought in the Depression Years.* Urbana: University of Illinois Press, 1998.

Peters, Charles. *Five Days in Philadelphia: The Amazing "We Want Willkie!" Convention of 1940 and How It Freed FDR to Save the Western World.* New York: PublicAffairs, 2005.

Renshaw, Patrick. *The Wobblies: The Story of the IWW and Syndicalism in the United States.* Chicago: Ivan R. Dee, 1999.

Reynolds, Maryan E. *The Dynamics of Change.* Pullman: Washington State University Press, 2001.

Richardson, Peter. *American Prophet: The Life and Work of Carey McWilliams.* Ann Arbor: University of Michigan Press, 2005.

Rintoul, William. *Oildorado: Boom Times on the West Side.* Fresno, CA: Valley Publishers, 1978.

Robinson, W. W. *The Story of Kern County.* Los Angeles: Title Insurance and Trust Company, 1961.

Roosevelt, Eleanor. *My Day: The Best of Eleanor Roosevelt's Acclaimed Newspaper Columns, 1936–1962.* New York: Da Capo Press, 2001.

Rose, Dorothy. *Dustbowl Okie Exodus.* Big Timber, MT: Seven Buffaloes Press, 1987.

Roske, Ralph Joseph. *Everyman's Eden: A History of California.* New York: Macmillan, 1968.

Schenk, Gretchen Knief. *County and Regional Library Development.* Chicago: American Library Association, 1954.

Schlesinger, Arthur M., Jr. *The Coming of the New Deal: 1933–1935.* Vol. 2 of *The Age of Roosevelt.* Boston: Mariner Books, 2003.

_____. *The Politics of Upheaval: 1935–1936.* Vol. 3 of *The Age of Roosevelt.* Boston: Mariner Books, 2003.

Schwartz, Stephen. *From West to East: California and the Making of the American Mind.* New York: Free Press, 1998.

Scott, Roy V., and J. G. Shoalmire. *The Public Career of Cully A. Cobb: A Study in Agricultural Leadership.* Jackson: University and College Press of Mississippi, 1973.

Selvin, David F. *A Terrible Anger: The 1934 Waterfront and General Strikes in San Francisco.* Detroit: Wayne State University Press, 1996.

Shasky, Florian J., and Susan F. Riggs, eds. *Letters to Elizabeth: A Selection of Letters from John Steinbeck to Elizabeth Otis.* San Francisco: The Book Club of California, 1978.

Shindo, Charles J. *Dust Bowl Migrants in the American Imagination.* Lawrence: University Press of Kansas, 1997.

Sinclair, Upton. *Oil!* Berkeley: University of California Press, 1997.

Smythe, William E. *The Conquest of Arid America.* Seattle: University of Washington Press, 1970.

_____. *City Homes on Country Lanes.* New York: Macmillan Company, 1921.

Soule, George. *The Coming American Revolution.* New York: Macmillan, 1934.

Sova, Dawn B. *Banned Books: Literature Suppressed on Sexual Grounds.* New York: Facts on File, 2006.

_____. *Banned Books: Literature Suppressed on Social Grounds.* New York: Facts on File, 2006.

Spivak, John L. *A Man in His Time.* New York: Horizon Press, 1967.

St. Pierre, Brian. *John Steinbeck: The California Years.* San Francisco: Chronicle Books, 1983.

Starr, Kevin. *California: A History.* New York: Modern Library, 2005.

———. *Endangered Dreams: The Great Depression in California.* New York: Oxford University Press, 1996.

———. *Material Dreams: Southern California through the 1920s.* New York: Oxford University Press, 1996.

Steffens, Lincoln. *The Letters of Lincoln Steffens.* New York: Harcourt, Brace, 1938.

Stein, Walter J. *California and the Dust Bowl Migration.* Westport, CT: Greenwood Press, 1973.

Steinbeck, Elaine, and Robert Wallsten, eds. *Steinbeck: A Life in Letters.* New York: Penguin, 1989.

Steinbeck, John. *America and Americans and Selected Nonfiction.* New York: Penguin, 2002.

———. *The Grapes of Wrath.* New York: Penguin, 1976.

———. *The Harvest Gypsies.* Berkeley, CA: Heyday Books, 1988.

Stempel, Tom. *Screenwriter: The Life and Times of Nunnally Johnson.* San Diego: A. S. Barnes, 1980.

Street, Richard Steven. *Beasts of the Field: A Narrative History of California Farmworkers, 1769–1913.* Stanford, CA: Stanford University Press, 2004.

———. *A Kern County Diary: The Forgotten Photographs of Carleton E. Watkins, 1881–1888.* Bakersfield, CA: Kern County Museum, 1983.

Stryker, Roy Emerson, and Nancy Wood. *In This Proud Land: America 1935–1943 As Seen in the FSA Photographs.* Boston: New York Graphic Society, 1975.

Tanenhaus, Sam. *Whittaker Chambers: A Biography.* New York: Modern Library, 1998.

Taylor, Paul S. *On the Ground in the Thirties.* Salt Lake City: Gibbs M. Smith, 1983.

Terkel, Studs. *Hard Times: An Oral History of the Great Depression.* New York: New Press, 1986.

Treadwell, Edward F. *The Cattle King.* Sana Cruz, CA: Western Tanager Press, 1981.

Turner, John. *White Gold Comes to California.* Fresno, CA: Book Publishers Inc., 1981.

Watkins, T. H. *The Hungry Years: A Narrative History of the Great Depression in America.* New York: Henry Holt, 1999.

Weber, Devra. *Dark Sweat, White Gold: California Farm Workers, Cotton, and the New Deal.* Berkeley: University of California Press, 1996.

Wechsler, James A. *The Age of Suspicion.* New York: Donald I. Fine, 1981.

Wells, Liz, ed. *The Photography Reader.* London: Routledge, 2003.

Winter, Ella. *And Not to Yield.* New York: Harcourt, Brace & World, 1963.

Worley, Matthew. *In Search of Revolution: International Communist Parties in the Third Period.* London: I. B. Tauris, 2004.

Worster, Donald. *Rivers of Empire: Water, Aridity, and the Growth of the American West.* New York: Oxford University Press, 1992.

Ybarra, Michael J. *Washington Gone Crazy: Senator Pat McCarran and the Great American Communist Hunt.* Hanover, NH: Steerforth Press, 2004.

Zieger, Robert H. *American Workers, American Unions.* Baltimore: Johns Hopkins University Press, 1994.

SELECTED SCHOLARLY WORKS

Benson, Jackson J. "'To Tom Who Lived It': John Steinbeck and the Man from Weed-patch," *Journal of Modern Literature* 5, no. 2 (April 1976): 151–210.

Dunn, Larry, and Kathi Durham, eds. "The Grapes of Wrath in Kern County," Bakersfield College, 1982.

Johns, Bryan Theodore. "Field Workers in California Cotton." Master's thesis, UCLA, 1947.

Lambert, Melissa. "Fascism, Communism and Collective Bargaining: The Salinas Lettuce Strike of 1936." Senior honors thesis, Stanford University, 2002.

Lingo, Marci. "Forbidden Fruit: The Banning of *The Grapes of Wrath* in the Kern County Free Library." *Libraries & Culture* 38, no. 4 (Fall 2003): 351–377.

Schamberger, John Edward. "Steinbeck and the Migrants: A Study of The Grapes of Wrath." Master's thesis, University of Colorado, 1960.

Index

Rick Wartzman is director of the Drucker Institute at Claremont Graduate University, an Irvine senior fellow at the New America Foundation, and a columnist for *BusinessWeek* magazine. Previously, he spent two decades as a reporter and editor at the *Wall Street Journal* and the *Los Angeles Times*. He is the coauthor, with Mark Arax, of *The King of California: J. G. Boswell and the Making of a Secret American Empire*. A best seller, it was named one of the ten best nonfiction books of 2003 by the *Los Angeles Times* and one of the ten best books of the year by the *San Francisco Chronicle*. It also won, among other honors, a California Book Award and the William Saroyan International Prize for Writing. (Photo by Emma Wartzman)

PublicAffairs is a publishing house founded in 1997. It is a tribute to the standards, values, and flair of three persons who have served as mentors to countless reporters, writers, editors, and book people of all kinds, including me.

I.F. STONE, proprietor of *I. F. Stone's Weekly*, combined a commitment to the First Amendment with entrepreneurial zeal and reporting skill and became one of the great independent journalists in American history. At the age of eighty, Izzy published *The Trial of Socrates*, which was a national bestseller. He wrote the book after he taught himself ancient Greek.

BENJAMIN C. BRADLEE was for nearly thirty years the charismatic editorial leader of *The Washington Post*. It was Ben who gave the *Post* the range and courage to pursue such historic issues as Watergate. He supported his reporters with a tenacity that made them fearless and it is no accident that so many became authors of influential, best-selling books.

ROBERT L. BERNSTEIN, the chief executive of Random House for more than a quarter century, guided one of the nation's premier publishing houses. Bob was personally responsible for many books of political dissent and argument that challenged tyranny around the globe. He is also the founder and longtime chair of Human Rights Watch, one of the most respected human rights organizations in the world.

•   •   •

For fifty years, the banner of Public Affairs Press was carried by its owner Morris B. Schnapper, who published Gandhi, Nasser, Toynbee, Truman, and about 1,500 other authors. In 1983, Schnapper was described by *The Washington Post* as "a redoubtable gadfly." His legacy will endure in the books to come.

Peter Osnos, *Founder and Editor-at-Large*